Mastering
BEADWORK

A Comprehensive Guide to Off•loom Techniques

CAROL HUBER CYPHER

INTERWEAVE
interweavebooks.com

Photography, Joe Coca
Illustrations, Bonnie Brooks

 Interweave Press LLC
201 East Fourth Street
Loveland, Colorado 80537 USA
interweavebooks.com

Printed in Malaysia by TWP Sdn. Bhd.

Library of Congress Cataloging-in-Publication Data

Cypher, Carol Huber.
Mastering beadwork : a comprehensive guide to off-loom techniques / Carol
Huber Cypher.
    p. cm.
 Includes index.
 ISBN 978-1-59668-013-5
 1. Beadwork--Patterns. I. Title.
 TT860.H83 2007
 745.58'2--dc22

                          2006024461

10 9 8 7 6 5

In loving and joyful remembrance of Randy Ligotino, DRSFPMG

Acknowledgments

I've been blessed with an abundance of ambitious, inspired, and talented students who propel me ever-forward. Thank you, Annette, Beatrice, Britt, Cookie, Cindy, Gladys, Helen, Karen, Janet, Judy, Louise, Pamela, Mary, Mary Ellen, Marianne, Robin, Susan, Sylvia, Terry, and Valerie. Thanks to Amy Raff, Elaine Tate, Elizabeth Buchtman, Ellen Mahnken, Fran X. Hancock, Irma Sherman, Jane Booth, Jill Van Etten (aka Jilly Beads), Kaja Dedijer, Kitty Moynihan, Kristine Flones, Louann Joyce, Martha Arginsky, and Myrna Jargowsky for loaning beadwork for photographs here.

I also wish to thank:
Susan Vazquez, for hosting my first teaching gig; Phyllis Dintenfass, for always being at the other end of the phone to share bead adventures; Amy Raff, librarian and super-hero, for her sage counsel, infinite patience, wisdom, strength, and sweetness; Morty (Jay) Cypher, my beloved husband and best buddy, for keeping my battery charged, and heart full, my spirit light; Rebecca Campbell, Anne Merrow, Betsy Armstrong, and Jean Campbell for bringing this book to print; Joe Coca for his brilliant photography; and Bonnie Brooks for her precise and beautiful illustrations; Alysse Adularia for her scalloped lacy necklace that has influenced the way I finish the Oglala stitch bracelet.

Contents

Introduction

What is it about beads that speaks to us? Their sparkle and brilliance, array of colors and finishes? Their origins? Imagine what it takes to refine a stone to two millimeters of round perfection and then drill a hole through its center! Or the ubiquitous seed bead, born of a breath captured in molten glass, drawn thin, cut, and polished. It's no wonder that beadwork is associated with power, status, and the supernatural the world over. As mindful meditation, a spiritual practice, beadwork provides those inherent healthful benefits of meditation with the reward of beautiful jewelry. The sharp detail of each bead becomes just an element in a composition of hundreds.

In my daydreams, I teach the world to bead, and peace and harmony prevail. Toward that end, I offer these test-driven beadwork recipes, rich in information, peppered with tips and "best practices," infused with knowledge and experience gleaned by working with and teaching hundreds of beaders, and sweetened with stunning photographs.

Each stitch is reduced to its bare bones and compared to other stitches. This eases you into a deeper and more intimate understanding of the technique. For most stitches, I suggest a mantra to propel you smoothly through the beadwork.

You're spared the mistakes—over the years I've made them all, so you don't have to! You'll be alerted to possible pitfalls. Unapologetically, I've glossed over or completely ignored history and origins in favor of technique.

How to Use This Book

Mastering Beadwork will be many things to many people, but I suggest carefully reading through the first two chapters, "What You Need" and "What You Need to Know." These chapters illustrate all the things you need for setting up your own beadworking studio, have helpful materials and tools lists, are full of great tips, and give you a base about the lingo and general beady know-how I'll assume you know as you travel through the book.

Once you've taken in those first two chapters, use this book as it suits your needs. It may be helpful as a guide to supplement what you've learned in beading classes; as a bead "cookbook," as a reference book; or to simply inspire and inform your work.

If you're looking for classes to master beadwork:
Make each of the projects in succession. They've been arranged to introduce a stitch and then explore

its structure while progressively sharpening your skills. In many projects, I've included a mantra to repeat as you work; this makes the technique easier to follow and memorize. Each subsequent project builds on that foundation, expanding your repertoire and providing a sound and comprehensive beadwork education that closely parallels that of ongoing studio students.

If you're in need of bead "recipes":

Select one of the five dozen gorgeous projects and simply whip it up. The easy-to-follow directions will help you learn the technique, and a "Try this" section at the end of many projects offers the opportunity to create stunning and unique variations.

If you long for a beading encyclopedia:

Mastering Beadwork includes sixteen different stitches, finishing techniques, designs, and tips. Select a project for the stitch, design, style, or closure you seek. New beaders will learn through the many stitches and techniques. Intermediate beaders will acquire new skills while refining and building on current ones. Serious beaders will expand their range, acquire a keen understanding of beadwork composition, and learn to manifest their wildest bead imaginings.

Finally, if you're just looking for inspiration and information:

Flip through these colorful, instructive pages, savoring the gorgeous photographs and scouring the sidebars for tips, hints, and tricks. You'll be on your way to creating your own beautiful beadwork designs in no time.

What You Need, or The Beadworker's Studio

All you need to start mastering off-loom beading techniques are some beads, a needle and thread that will fit through the beads, and the ability to see the hole in the bead. Therefore, anywhere you arrange your beading materials (*mise en place*) becomes your beadworking studio.

I begin all my beadwork borrowing from a practice that professional chefs use: *mise en place*, French for "put in place." It requires that at the onset of each project, my work area is arranged so that necessities are at hand and ready to use, rather than interrupting the process to retrieve them one by one. To chefs, it means never burning the chocolate while fetching eggs from the cooler. Though beadwork doesn't entail these particular dangers, adapting this practice makes you more efficient and simplifies your work.

The *mise en place* for nearly all my beadweaving is:
- piles of beads on the beading mat
- scissors and other necessary tools and findings within reach
- adequate lighting and/or magnification
- an appropriate needle centered on a length of thread that has a masking-tape bead stop (see page 10) attached

I really encourage you to embrace the *mise en place* concept. It's a great place to start, and once you do, you can then go on to finesse the rest of your studio. When you get to that point, begin with this list of must-haves.

Work Station
You'll sometimes find yourself spending hours at your beadwork station so make sure it's pleasant, comfortable, and, especially, ergonomic.

Seating
I prefer beading while seated tableside. Select a comfortable chair you could spend hours in at a table of appropriate height. Avoid sitting before a fan or in a breeze, as the blowing thread will tangle, knot, annoy, and sully an otherwise pleasant pastime.

Light
Any lamp that provides ample lighting will do, but simulated daylight lamps provide true color while reducing eyestrain and glare. Daylight simulation replacement bulbs that fit standard screw-in fixtures also offer energy efficiency over incandescent bulbs.

Magnifier
If needed, you can purchase magnifying lenses of 3½" (9 cm) or larger. The type many beadworkers like are on a gooseneck with a clamp or stand so you can have hands-free magnification, and many have lamps included. Wearable magnifiers are also useful. Head-mounted magnifiers are available

with interchangeable magnifying lenses in a range of strengths, with or without battery-operated spotlights. Eyeglasses in an array of strengths of magnification are sold in drug and craft stores. Clip-on style magnifiers are handy for eyeglasses.

Tools

Other than needles and scissors, there are only a handful of tools necessary to get your beading studio up and running. Here are the few I feel are most important.

Bead Board

Available in smooth or flocked, single or multistrand, a bead board is useful for stringing jewelry. Its channels are meant for layout, design, and measuring. The curve helps prevent the finished piece from being too linear to drape beautifully.

Bead Mat

Many surfaces can serve as the palette from which to bead: sectioned ceramic watercolor dishes, gently sloping soapstone saucers, suede, velvet, or terry cloth. My hands-down preference is a Vellux bead mat. Vellux is a nonwoven synthetic fabric composed of a nylon flocked face of even and straight pile on a base of polyurethane foam, commonly available hemmed and sold as blankets. Bead stores sell placemat-size pieces in assorted colors. I have light-colored ones for general use and dark-colored ones for working with light-colored beads or pearls. Rather than rolling around, beads placed on a bead

Two Bead Mat Ideas

Two of my favorite beaders have designed a couple of great beadwork surfaces that you can easily make for yourself. One is a picture frame with a bead mat replacing the glass. Glue a small magnet (a place to park needles) and a length of measuring tape to the side, clip on a book light, and you're good to go.

Another design requires both a piece of fabric and a bead mat sized to 1" (2.5 cm) larger on all edges than a notebook or pad of paper. Fold and sew the edges of the bead mat under, producing a hem. Thread a long shoelace through the hem on all four sides. Fold the edges of the fabric under. With wrong sides together, sew the fabric to the mat on 3 sides, producing a pocket. A notepad slipped into this pocket produces a flat and firm bottom. Pull the shoelace to gather the sides and bring them up perpendicular to the bottom and tie it into a bow. This is a bead tray with paper at hand for making notes or drawing designs, which can be rolled up when the notepad is removed.

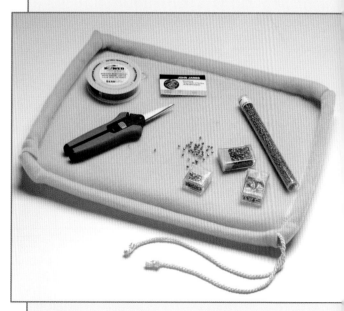

mat just sit there, making it easy to sort, separate, and arrange piles of beads on the surface. With no warp/weft threads or loops, a needle is less apt to snag the fabric when you pick up a bead.

It may be easy to keep track of which is which when using recipes calling for just a few bead types. But when using recipes of multiple bead types, simplify and expedite the work by labeling the little piles of beads on the bead blanket. Write the letters on pieces of masking tape placed near the appropriate pile. Remove the tape as soon as the work is over to prevent gummy residue.

If I need to put a project aside, rather than sort and replace the beads in their vials or bags, I place another mat on top of the abandoned one and stroke the top mat, causing the two to stick together. This creates a short stack of unfinished works, instantly accessible whenever I have a few moments.

Slide the mat onto a tray or box top to move the work to another location. For beading on-the-go, roll the beadwork up in its blanket and place it inside a ziplock bag. For portable small-scale beading projects, line small tins or CD cases with cut-to-size bead mats.

Beading Awl

When stringing or knotting, I often use an awl for positioning the knots or picking open unintended or misplaced knots. A T-pin is a useful substitute.

Caliper

This sliding gauge measures bead sizes, answering those pesky questions like, "Is this pearl 5 mm or 6 mm?"

Glue

Though originally used by watchmakers for gluing watch crystals, Hypo-Tube Cement is also useful for the beadworker. Its thin hypodermic needle-type

applicator produces and delivers pinpoint drops of glue with precision. Use it to seal knots when stringing.

Gorilla Glue is very strong and suitable for metal and stone. It requires the presence of moisture, which causes it to foam up and expand.

E6000 industrial strength glue is one of my favorites because it dries clear and it is very strong. But it's carcinogenic and must be used cautiously and with ventilation.

Journal

Don't be surprised when, even though you may be completely engaged in your current beadwork project, visions of future beadwork dance into your head. To make sure you never lose an idea, keep a blank journal at hand to record your inspirations.

Masking Tape

Masking tape can be useful as a bead stop. Traditional stop beads are beads that are added at the beginning of a project, meant to be taken out later. But I've been teaching beadwork several days a week for years, and I've yet to see anyone accidentally incorporate a piece of masking tape into their work! To make this kind of bead stop, fold a small, thin piece of masking tape over the thread, sticky sides together at least 8" (20.5 cm) from the end of the thread to create the tail. Pinch the tape to slide it along or off the thread. Another handy quality of this method is that the tape also serves as a handle when grasped between the thumb and forefinger, allowing the beadwork to sit at the thumbnail ready for the next stitch.

Measuring Tape or Ruler

Use these for measuring beadwork and for sizing jewelry.

Needles

There are so many choices of beading needles. The only rule is to choose a needle that will accommodate your thread choice and pass easily through the beads of the project. Length varies from ⅞" (2.2 cm) quilting needles to 4½" (11.5 cm) big eye needles. Needles labeled as beading needles have narrow eyes and are offered in sizes 10, 12, 13, 15, and 16, in short and long versions. Size 10, being the "beefiest," is easiest to thread and will work with Japanese cylinder beads, seed beads as small as size 11°, and even most pearls (which are notorious for their tiny holes). For smaller beads, use size 12 or 13. Minute and rare seed beads in sizes 16° to 24° require needles in sizes 15 and 16. Only Monocord size 000 and possibly Kevlar thread will fit in their eyes.

Twisted wire needles are made of a length of wire folded in half and plied together. The fold becomes a collapsible eye. They come in many sizes and are flexible, large-eyed for ease in threading and very useful for stringing.

Big eye needles are made of two parallel wires soldered at the ends, creating a needle with an eye that runs its length. They are available in 2⅛" (5.4 cm) and 4½" (11.5 cm). Meant for stringing, they can be used for beadweaving beads size 8° and larger and even some Japanese size 11°. Avoid snagging the thread in the soldered ends or corners of the eye, which causes it to fray. Keep the thread passing freely through the center of the eye. Quality varies between needle brands. Economy needles are generally softer and tend to curl and bend. Some brands of economy needles have damaged or ill-formed eyes. John James brand is annealed, producing a harder metal that stays straighter. The downside of a stiff needle is that it is brittle and might snap off in situations when soft needles would bend.

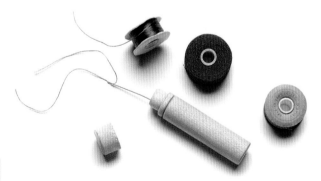

Needle Case

There are several choices, from wooden vials (many beaders cover theirs in peyote-stitched beads) to thin magnetic-lined boxes. You could even use an empty bead vial. If you promise to know the whereabouts of your needles, I'll spare you the myriad horror stories I've heard about the hapless loved one or pet that has "come across" an errant needle.

Don't Get Caught Strong-Arming Your Needle

The strong-arm tactic of yanking a needle through a bead is risky business. If several previous thread passes prevent the needle from passing through the bead, it's tempting to see if the needle will squeeze through if pulled with pliers. You run the risk of breaking the bead, breaking the needle, or splitting open its eye.

Permanent Markers

Multipurpose, colorful, and fun, use them to label tools, color thread, and color wooden bead bases of beaded beads.

Pliers

Chain-Nose Pliers

These finely tapered needle-nose pliers have half-rounded jaws. In beadwork, they are primarily used for making sharp bends in metal wire, for opening and closing loops and jump rings, for pulling a reluctant needle through a bead, or for removing a bead from the beadwork. These are the most important pliers for a beadworker.

Crimping Pliers

These special pliers produce consistent, professional, and enduring crimping for securing crimp beads to flexible beading wire. There are three different sizes—one that accommodates the most common-size (2 x 2mm) crimp beads, one that fits small (1 x 1mm) crimp beads, and another that fits large (3 x 3mm) crimp beads. While squeezing the tool shut, notice that it has two openings. The inner one resembles the silhouette of lips, the outer one the silhouette of an eye. See page 26 to learn how to use this type of pliers.

Round-Nose Pliers

Both jaws of these pliers are cone-shaped to form wire loops for eye pins or head pins.

Bent-Nose Pliers

The jaws of these chain-nose-style pliers curve, allowing access in tight areas and small places.

Scissors

Choose very sharp scissors with fine points for getting into tight places. Tiny European embroidery scissors are wonderful if reserved for cutting only thread and perhaps delicate silk beading cord.

Fiskars Softouch is an excellent line of all-purpose scissors. The rubber-handled 6" (15 cm) style can be found in both the metal and thread/yarn departments of craft stores. They have sharp, fine points that can be resharpened with a Fiskars hone sold for the purpose.

The new synthetic beading threads, favored for their abrasion resistance, are difficult to cut with even the best scissors. Astonishingly, the plastic-handled Fiskars children's scissors (available wherever crayons are sold and commonly displayed for a buck or two in supermarket aisles) work great on these tough threads.

Sorting Triangle

This is the best buck you'll ever spend. Most bead stores sell these 4½" (11.5 cm) metal triangles. Slide an edge along the surface of the bead mat to pick up a huge amount of beads at once, then pour the contents neatly from one of the three points into a vial or ziplock bag. Or sort a pile of beads by spilling them on a bead mat and using one of the three points to separate one or more beads from the rest. The long, thin brass-colored crumber that waiters carry in their pockets or the clip-less variation sold in bead stores are handy but still not as useful as the triangle.

Thread Burner

This battery-operated tool cuts and cauterizes synthetic threads while producing a tiny melted blob and preventing the thread from fraying. Be mindful, and steady-handed when using one. I have both witnessed and experienced firsthand the trauma of unintentionally melting nearby threads. That said, it is less scary than using a match or lighter to do the same.

Wire Cutters

Wire cutters are made up of sharp pointed blades, one side that cuts the wire in a V, the other side flat. Use your best set to cut metal wire; a more dull set for cutting flexible beading wire (the stainless steel will eventually dull your blades).

The Stash

Ahhh, the beads! And the threads, wire, strings, ribbons, findings, and whatever is necessary to assemble the rascals into beadwork. Bead booty varies in size and assortment. I've seen a few packages of seed beads and thread stuffed in a cosmetics case; a shoebox of recycled costume jewelry and glass pearls; a cookie tin of jelly jars of jet beads, hematite, and rocailles; a scrapbooker's tote full of labeled bobbin cases of neatly organized seed beads; a mechanic's tool chest replete with a full complement of seed beads, gemstones, pearls, crystals, vintage, and lampworked beads.

You can never have too many beads. They won't spoil, rot, deteriorate, or go off. They'll be there whenever you get around to them. They are wonderful to have around, lovely to look at, relaxing to sort through, and a delight to ponder. Just having them at hand will kick-start your creativity. When you see beads that hum at you, buy them if you can—don't take for granted that any bead will be available again.

Seed Beads

Seed beads are tiny glass beads that come in a seemingly infinite variety.

Sizes and Shapes

Seed beads are manufactured in sizes that range from tiny 15° (0.062", or 1.57 mm) to large 3° (0.220", or 5.5 mm). Antique beads as small as 24° (0.036", or 0.091 mm) are still available.

Traditional French, Italian, or Czech seed beads, those marketed on hanks, are plump donuts. Japanese seed beads are more squared, as tall as they are wide, and sold loose in bags or vials. Other Asian (Indian, Chinese, Korean) seed beads vary in size and quality. Charlottes, prized for their sparkle, result by grinding one spot on the seed bead to make a single, crisp facet.

Where Did They Come From?

Antique seed beads that date from before 1880, some as small as 0.036" (0.091 mm) (sizes 16° to 24°), are still around. Of course I have some, along with the requisite size 000 monocord and size 15 needle to use them. Precious and dainty, they are nothing short of awe-inspiring. They were created by Italian and French glassblowers, who filled a gather (glob of hot glass) with their breath. A coworker placed a punty or pontil (a rod used to handle molten glass) on the other end. The workers quickly and smoothly moved apart, stretching and pulling (drawing) the hollow glass into a long tube (cane). The cane was broken into manageable lengths. Over a small flame, perhaps intensified by bellows, another worker pulled the canes into finer tubes, which yet another worker cut into beads. The beads were reheated to soften and smooth their sharp edges.

Historically, seed beads were made from drawn glass, but the more modern beads manufactured in Japan are made by extruding the glass. These cylinder beads, favored for their large holes and uniformity, are particularly suited to loomwork, peyote stitch, and brick stitch. They are available in three sizes: one similar to a size 12° seed bead, one 3.3mm size similar to a size 8° seed bead, and a new line similar to a size 10° seed bead. Each of the three Japanese manufacturers of seed beads uses a different name for their cylinder beads: Miyuki calls their cylinder beads Delicas, Matsuno calls theirs Dynamites, and Toho calls their line Treasures. Toho also has a new line of precision cylinder beads that boast a tolerance less than 0.01mm. These Aiko beads are hugely popular for loomwork, producing a sleek and uniform surface.

Shaped seed beads are also available, including triangles in sizes 11°, 10°, 8°, 5°, and cubes in 4mm, 3mm, and 1.5mm sizes. Miyuki and Matsuno brands have round holes, while the hole in Toho brand cubes is diamond-shaped and large enough to accommodate many yarns and sizes of crochet hooks.

This offers a few ways to easily incorporate them into knitting and crochet. Do expect to sort out, or "cull," the misshapen beads from the rest. Throw out any beads with chipped holes—a chip may cut the thread.

Japanese drop beads fit among other beads like a size 8° but have the high profile of a tiny egg protruding from the beadwork. Having been fire-polished, their holes are less abrasive and less likely to cut the thread, so these are a good choice for off-loom work.

Magatamas, another high-profile Japanese seed bead, look like a splot of glass with an off-center hole.

Czech drop beads are actually not a seed bead but a pressed bead (see page 16). Their holes can be abrasive, so I reserve them for fringe where they are less likely to damage the thread.

Bugle Beads

Bugle beads are longer segments of drawn (or extruded) glass that has not been fire-polished. Students tease me about my stutter-and-wince response to their inquiries about "bbbugle" beads. A traumatic experience with them in my youth still haunts me. Like shards of glass, they are raw and sharp, unlike seed beads, which are rounded and smoothed by heat. Even the new abrasion-resistant beading threads cannot withstand the insidious bugle bead. But if you must use them, be sure to place a seed bead at each end to soften the angle of the thread over the sharp edge. Use hex seed beads, 2- and 3-cut seed beads, and satin-finish seed beads with the same caution.

Bead Color Considerations

When observing seed beads in a tube, in a bag, or strung on hanks (12 strands tied together), the color is rich and dense. Taken individually, a single bead may take on a very different appearance; place that single bead in a composition with other beads and once again its appearance is altered. If your work is monochromatic (one color), then what you see is what you get. Otherwise, each bead's color can be affected by the neighboring beads. This is one of the most exciting and compelling features of composing work from hundreds of such tiny units. While a hank of fuchsia beads and a hank of orange beads may look garish, the individual beads may work very well together. And their pairing looks one way used among black and white beads and quite differently used among various green beads. The bead is defined by the company it keeps.

The color of the bead is also tempered by the thread used. When using transparent or translucent beads, the thread color may alter the appearance of the beads considerably. To see this for yourself, use permanent markers to color a length of white thread, changing color every inch or so. String several transparent beads and see how their look changes along with the thread.

Consider the value. Imagine a black-and-white photocopy of your bead palette. Is it simply gray, or is it a mix of black and white and shades of gray? There's no right or wrong answer—it's just something to consider.

Each bead's color is affected by its neighbor.

Cheap, Irregular Yet Irresistible Seed Beads

It's okay—go ahead and buy imperfect seed beads, even though they are technically inferior. Some are tall and some are short; some are smaller than the others, and there is the odd big one. When culling your beads, remove the misshapen ones, but cherish the odd-size ones and save them for your off-loom work increases and decreases.

Seed Bead Color

The glass used for making seed beads varies from transparent to opaque with translucent greasy, opal, and satin types in between. They come in an exhaustive array of colors, and color isn't just a factor of the glass itself—the beads can also have a colored or metallic lining such as silver, copper, or gold, making them highly reflective. Seed beads can also be dyed or painted to create even more variety.

Finishes

A number of finishes can be applied to the beads to change their appearance. One popular finish gives the appearance of oil on water and is known by several names: rainbow, iris, iridescent, and Aurora Borealis, or AB for short. Luster is a shiny

A variety of finishes.

finish that makes opaque beads look like pearls, and when applied to translucent beads it's called Ceylon. Sometimes beads take on a fumed appearance, which is an extreme-heat vaporization process that imparts a tiny amount of gold, silver, or platinum to the bead's surface. The results range from a subtle tint to a shiny metallic surface, depending on the amount of condensation. Frosted beads, also called matte, are the velvety result of etching the glass. There are even semigloss beads whose satiny finish is between polished and matte. Galvanized beads have a metal or metal-like coating, which can chip or flake. Metallic beads that have been treated with nickel and then electroplated won't have that problem, but the plating may wear off over time.

The Rest of the Beads

"Hoo-hahs" are what I call all the bigger-than-seed beads, which I love to incorporate into beadwork.

Glass

Unlike the drawn and extruded glass that produces seed beads, other glass beads are made from wound or molded glass.

Lampworked Beads

Glass rods are melted in a torch flame and wound on a mandrel by lampworkers, the artists responsible for these brilliant baubles. Ranging from pea- to golf ball–size, these beads beg to be collected. M&M size and smaller are great for embellishment, fringe, in ropes, and strung. Larger ones serve as focal elements. They are found in vibrant colors and clean geometric shapes, minute sculptures, elaborate seascapes encased in clear glass, floral motifs, implosions and, of course those ubiquitous dots that beaders love. These dots may have been layered, built up or melted down, encased, or surround a bubble. Because lampworkers coat the mandrel in bead release before adding the hot glass, the center of a lampworked bead can become very gritty and abrasive—an enemy to thread. See page 19 for a technique on avoiding the heartache of broken thread.

Crystals

Machine-faceted leaded glass beads come in many sizes, colors, finishes, styles, facet designs, and shapes (bicone, round, oval, square).

Swarovski Crystal

The blingiest of all Austrian crystal, Swarovski crystals are known for their clarity, brilliant color, and precise facets, but there's a trade-off for all their bling, beauty, sparkle, and shine: There's a high risk that their holes will cut the thread. Some beaders deal with this dilemma by weaving with the most abrasion-resistant thread and using a seed bead at each end of the crystal.

Minimize the risk by taking a moment to test each crystal before weaving with it. String the crystal on a separate foot (30 cm) of thread. Holding the thread taut, pinch the crystal and work it up and down the thread while pulling it. If the thread is not frayed or cut, use it. Set aside those that cut or abrade the thread and use them to string on beading wire. A diamond dust bead reamer can also be helpful to smooth a sharp bead hole.

Czech Fire-Polished "Crystals"

Fire-polishing, or smoothing the beads' sharp edges by reheating them, reduces their potential for cutting thread but also, regrettably, the amount of reflection off each facet.

Pressed Glass

Molds and pressing machines produce simple

round beads, called druks, and other shapes that include bells, cylinders, drops, ovals, polygons, rondelles, daggers, commas, lentils, cupped flowers, flat blossoms, tulips, hearts, leaves, and petals, which can be flat or curved and drilled with holes lengthwise, widthwise, or crosswise. Variously shaped vintage glass beads, generally of German and French origin, are available in wonderful and sometimes rare colors.

Pearls

Freshwater pearls and Akoya, a kind of cultured saltwater pearl, come in white and a few natural colors. Dyeing and irradiation produce additional colors. Shapes were once confined to those that occurred naturally, like round, tear, oval, and rice. Today, pearls can be found in many shapes that include coin, stick, square, diamond, even heart. To create these shapes, a shaped piece of shell is inserted in the mollusk, where layers of nacre build up. Pearls have tiny holes, but most accept three passes of beading thread on a size 12 needle.

Gemstones, Rocks, and Minerals

These mined, shaped, and drilled stones vary in source, shape, and value. Some are simply tumbled chips, while others are sculpted, shaped, and faceted. Gemstones can have very abrasive holes, so choose carefully. Consider smoothing the holes with a bead reamer.

Polymer Clay, Metal Clay, Clay, Ceramic, Porcelain

These hand-formed beads vary from irregularly shaped and primitive-looking to elaborately designed and refined. Earth clay can be sculpted, cane-constructed, painted, or glazed. Polymer clay, a moldable PVC, available in an array of blendable colors, can produce convincing faux ivory and gemstones. A moldable colloid of finely powdered silver or gold in a binder, when shaped and fired (to burn off the binder), is used to make metal beads as well as finished jewelry and findings.

Bakelite, Resin, Plastic

These dense polymerized synthetic or chemically modified natural resin (including polyvinyl, polystyrene, and polyethylene) beads may be cheap playground plastic at worst or beautifully colored or shaped at best. A few exceptional ones will make their way to your stash.

Metal

Examine metal beads with a lens or magnifier to see if they are intact and free of cracks. Liquid silver beads, for example, are little rectangles of metal rolled into a

tube. They are wonderful but must be used with care, as thread may snag or slip through a crack.

Beads masquerading as metal may actually be made of plastic that has been coated with metal or metal-looking paint. These will chip and peel.

Wood

Beads with exotic wood, interesting grain, and unusual shapes are beautiful. Pedestrian natural, painted, or dyed beads also have a place—they are wonderful for covering with beadwork.

Shell, Horn, Bone

Entire tropical mollusk shells (cowrie), the pearly interior of other mollusks (mother-of-pearl), and bits of mollusk shell formed into small cylinder-shaped beads have over the years served as ornament and even currency. Non-marine shell can also be used as bead material—ostrich egg shells are used for flat heishi beads. Horn makes beautiful beads with subtle luster and enticing translucence. Bone beads appear on every continent in simple shapes or complexly carved.

Other Organic Beads

Amber beads are made from fossilized tree resin. Jet, a form of fossilized wood, is a dense, hard coal that takes a high polish. Jet beads were hugely popular in Victorian times.

Coral beads are made from the calcareous skeletal secretions of colonized marine organisms. Some seeds and nuts are used as beads in their natural form. Others, like the dense white seeds of tagua trees, are used as a vegetable substitute for ivory.

Threads

Nylon beading thread comes in wonderful colors and several different types.

Silamide is a plied version and comes in one size, A. Many beaders use it at the exclusion of anything else. I avoid it; the plying introduces an energy and kinkiness that I find ineffably at odds with my beadweaving. There's no reason to follow my lead here; decide for yourself. Nymo, Nylux, and C-lon are flat nylon threads avail-

Bead Soup

When you are finished beading, scoop all the remaining beads together into a small ziplock bag or prescription bottle. That little package of bead soup will serve you in ways that putting them all back into their proper containers cannot. It might inspire the next project or colorway, be made into earrings to match the piece just finished, be combined with additional beads.

Much of my beadwork starts as bead soup. After gathering the vials and hanks for a project, I spill little piles of them onto the bead blanket and see how these beads react to each other in community. Which beads tend to draw back and which pop forward? Which appear muddy because of their proximity to another? What beads should be added to this soup before beading begins? Undulating Peyote Tube (on page 60), Tangy Credit Card Case (on page 79), and Bead Happy Bracelet (on page 177) all depend on these considerations.

able in many colors and sizes and easy to thread onto a beading needle.

Kevlar is a very strong thread, the material that bullet-proof vests are made of. It frays easily in chapped hands, on ragged nails, or in abrasive beads, and then each independent fiber breaks easily. Use accordingly.

Fireline, a particular type of fishing line, has become such a favorite among beaders that it is commonly available in bead stores. Use clear or gray, carefully avoiding the neon colors (unless you really mean to use a neon one). The gray line marks your fingers, but it washes right off. It is strong and fairly abrasion resistant. It has a wiriness that makes it unsuitable for some stringing; lightweight beads, like pearls, do not hang in a supple drape as they would on silk. Instead they are suspended in a kinky, almost scraggly curve. Most of the time I use the 10-pound size, but for use with size 15° seed beads, I drop to the 4-pound size for its ability to fit through the beads a few times. Fireline is also available in 6- and 8-pound sizes. It's easiest to thread Fireline through the slender eye of a beading needle if you first flatten the tip between your front teeth.

Power Pro is another line that captures the fancy of beaders. This polyethylene braid is the most abrasion resistant beadweaving thread there is, though I've seen it cut by a chipped bead hole or an occasional Swarovski crystal. It is available in white and moss green. I color the white kind near the beadwork

with permanent markers as I work. It doesn't accept the color densely, but it takes up enough color to blend in. The all-purpose 10-pound size will fit within the eye of a size 12 beading needle and even through most pearls, known for their very thin holes, for three passes. Flatten the tip between your teeth, a flat-nosed pliers, or a thumbnail and finger before attempting to thread it. Even though it knots beautifully and securely, most knots can be picked open with an awl without fraying the thread. Use a finer weight if you want more supple results. Keep some on hand for beadweaving with abrasive beads. (Dandyline and Tough Thread are similar products.)

With longevity and endurance a priority, I never use cotton thread, elastic, or monofilament fishing line for beadweaving.

Waxes and Thread Conditioners
If you're using thread, you should have at least one of these products in hand. I have each but generally only wax the thread when I want stiffer beadwork or, if the thread has frayed, to bond it together.

Beeswax
Beeswax is a natural material that coats and protects thread from abrasion, prevents it from fraying, and is useful for its stickiness or tackiness. An extremely light application will make bead crocheting with slick thread a joy instead of a struggle, while a thick application will stiffen the end of yarn or heavy thread to string without a needle.

Microcrystalline Wax
This synthetic wax produces a sleek, nongummy coating on the thread.

Thread Heaven
Thread Heaven is to thread what conditioner after a

shampoo is to hair: a means to prevent tangling. It doesn't alter the body of the thread in the way that waxes do. It affects static charge so that the two ends of the thread repel each other. It produces a slippery surface on the thread so the beads slide easily.

Stringing Materials

Beading wire has come a long way in the past four decades. Back in olden times, necklaces were often strung on plastic-coated wire so stiff that the beads were held in a ring around the wearer's neck, rather than draping. They were frequently closed with a barrel clasp, which would unwind during wear even when firmly screwed together. This millennium ushered in a new generation of beading wire, incredibly thin metal wire cabled in bunches of seven and coated in nylon in a range of colors. The cables are in turn cabled together, providing a range from seven strands to forty-nine. The finest-quality wire, composed of seven cables of seven strands each, boasts a drape and hand similar to that of thread. It comes in many finishes and diameters. Some brands can even be knotted, though you will likely want to use crimp beads to secure your beading wire.

Bead cord has been used for years in jewelry-making. Silk bead cord is the traditional choice for knotting pearls, favored for its fluid drape under the nearly weightless pearls. A synthetic version made of polyamide is popular for its longevity. Both are offered in many colors and sizes. Griffin sells a two-meter length with a needle attached to one end wound on a card.

To use a carded bead cord like Griffin's, first unwind the entire two meters from the card. Pull and stretch it before use so it won't stretch and slacken when the piece is completed.

Figure 1

Soldering

The more proficient you become at beadwork, the more apt you'll be to create your own findings and closures from beads. That said, for those instances when you use jump rings, I can almost guarantee that you'll lose the piece unless the jump rings are soldered closed. Avoid the temptation to use a split ring as an alternative.

You could get a torch. You could get a high tech jump ring soldering machine for under $600. Instead, I use this accessible and doable approach to soldering. It works. It ain't pretty. It might not even be orthodox. But it works for me. In a well-ventilated studio, I plug in a hardware store soldering iron. I touch the jump ring with Stay-Clean Flux. I touch the iron to Stay-Brite Solder and then the jump ring. The flow temperature is a low 430º F (221º C) and works just fine for this purpose. Warning: soldering jump rings that are attached to beadwork will melt the beading thread. Solder and cool several jump rings to have on hand. Rather than open these you will weave, sew, or crimp them into place.

Next, place a knot at the opposite end from the needle. String a bead tip from the inside out so that the knot settles within the tip and the loop extends outward (Figure 1).

String your beads (with or without knots between) and finish by adding another bead tip, strung from the bottom this time. Now face the challenge of placing a knot as close as possible to the bead tip.

Elastic and invisible lines are too short-lived for use in fine jewelry.

Wire mesh, rattail (satin cord), leather, synthetic leather, ribbons, and rubber cords are versatile stringing materials.

Memory wire, treated to remain coiled, is popular for the instantaneous results it provides. Purchase the nipper meant for memory wire rather than ruin other wire cutters.

Findings

These are all the little metal bits that might be used for closures and connectors.

Crimp beads, bead tips, and knot covers are used to attach flexible beading wire to clasps or other findings.

Opening Jump Rings

Use a jump ring tool or two pliers to torque the ends of the jump ring open, rather than pulling them apart. This prevents metal fatigue and makes it easier for the ends to meet upon reclosing. There is a clever little tool for this purpose. Place it on the first half of an index finger, as though wearing a ring. Use the slot or screw head area to torque the jump ring open and then reclose it. Jump rings need only to open a slight amount to allow the thread to slip out. Use soldered jump rings to prevent losing beadwork.

Clasps come in a variety of forms including lobster claw, figure eight, ball and socket, hook and eye, toggle, and magnetic.

Earring wires, posts, hoops, nuts, clip-ons, and screw-backs make the beadwork ear-wearable.

Pin backs and bails transform beadwork into brooches and pendants.

Crimp ends offer a distinctive metal finish to beadwork, ribbon, rubber cord or band, wire mesh, leather, and satin cord, while providing a place to attach a clasp.

Head and eye pins are used for connecting pieces of beadwork and for making dangles.

Jump rings are used to link jewelry components. Decorative findings include end cones, bead caps, end caps, and spacers.

What You Need To Know:
Beadwork Glossary

On your way to mastering beadwork you will encounter these commonly used terms. Read through these words now. Later, when you see them used in context, they will be familiar.

Beadwork Lingo

High bead: The highest-profile bead of the previous row, the bead that sits above the adjacent beads just waiting for your needle. In peyote stitch, it is the bead added in the previous row. In netting, it is the center bead of each set of beads.

Pass back through: Make a U-turn and re-enter the end of the bead that the threaded needle exited.

Pass through: Enter the same end of the bead (in the same direction) as when it was picked up. (You may also see this written as "pass through again," which means the same thing.) The distinction between "pass through again" and "pass back through" is meant to clarify which end of the bead is to be entered. Sadly, sometimes it is misunderstood because of the dual meaning of back as both turning around and repeating. It is common when told to "pass through" a bead for a student to reply to me, "back through this bead?" I reiterate to "pass through this bead again, in the same direction as before" (Figure 1). The student used "back" to mean "once again," but I reserve the word back to indicate reversing the direction of the thread and needle path (Figure 2).

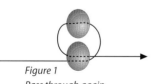

Figure 1
Pass through again

Figure 2
Pass back through

Pick up: Put a bead on your threaded needle. Because beadweaving is gen-erally accomplished with one, two, or three beads at a time, I prefer the term pick up to string.

Shank: The stem or stalk on the underside of a button by which it is attached. A shank permits the loop of a button-and-loop jewelry closure to slip not just over, but also beneath the bead or button. A bead or two serve as a shank for making most any bead or button a suitable closure.

Toggle

Shank

Side view of braclet

Step-up: Pass through the first bead of this round to bring you up to the level of the new round.

Tail: The far end of the thread where the beads stop. (To learn about making a masking-tape bead stop, see page 10.)

Turning bead: A bead added before passing back through a bead or beads just added, to prevent the bead(s) just added from falling off. For example, when making fringe, the instructions might say, "Pick up beads W, X, Y, Z, and a turning bead. Pass back through beads Z, Y, X, W." If no turning bead were present, beads Z, Y, X, and W would fall from the thread.

Wingspan of thread: This is the distance between your outstretched arms when your hands are held as far from each other as possible. Fold it nearly in half, allowing one half to be a tail's length longer than the other. Doubled thread complicates things, so use it singly. Because it is your own wingspan, the entire thread can be pulled through the beads by simply extending your arm. *Note:* Some beaders use thread several yards long. Thread longer than your wingspan requires reeling in with every stitch, affording greater opportunity for the thread to tangle, knot, snag, fray, and weaken—and by the time you've pulled all the thread through, you've forgotten what to do.

General Beading Know-How

Now that you're familiar with the lingo, read on so you'll know everything necessary to navigate your way through the beads and the stitches.

Establishing Beadweaving

More often than not, step 1 establishes the width of the piece, step 2 establishes a foundation for step 3, which is repeated until the desired size is achieved.

Threading a Needle

Some beaders wet the thread in their mouths, while others say it helps to wet the eye instead. After wet-

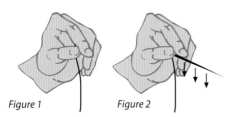

Figure 1   Figure 2

ting, flatten the thread tip by a pulling it through your clenched front teeth or pinched thumbnail and index finger. Align the flattened thread with the needle's eye. Push the thread into the eye. Or hold the thread in the nondominant hand and slide the needle onto the thread. My favorite technique is to pinch the thread between the thumb and index finger of the nondominant hand so that just the hint of the top is visible (Figure 1). Place the eye of the needle over the area of the thread tip. Maintaining the pressure of the pinch, slide the needle down between the pinched thumb and index finger (Figure 2), and voilà, this usually works.

Holding the Beadwork

New beaders tend to keep their beadwork on the table while they work. This is fine, but at some point, most beaders prefer to hold the work in their non-dominant hand, generally between their thumb and index fingers. Some beaders go through incredible gyrations and ergonomic feats rather than simply situate the beadwork differently. Feel free to rotate the beadwork or flip it over to execute a stitch. Having said that, when a recipe refers to left or right, top or bottom, let's agree that the tail will come out the bottom of the work, just the way a tail should, and to the left, as we read from left to right.

Establishing Orientation

Occasionally you'll be called away from the beadwork, be distracted, or even decide to accept a better offer. (If Antonio Banderas or Johnny Depp shows up at your door and asks if you want to lunch, go ahead—the beads will wait.) Have no fear that you can resume right where you left off, without skipping a beat(d). Hold or lay down the work so that the tail is on the bottom left. Let's agree to default to this orientation when working from the recipes, so that directional information like left or right, up or down are meaningful. Referring back to the pattern, it is easier to locate the last worked row of the recipe and go on your merry way.

Adding a New Thread

When only 8" (20.5 cm) of thread remains in your needle, you'll need to abandon it. Simply remove the needle and fold the thread back alongside the work. Cut a new wingspan of thread, thread the needle, and mark the tail with tape.

Many beaders secure a new thread in the beadwork and while attempting to emerge from the single correct bead, experience an "oops." Tidy beaders, deciding to weave the abandoned thread into the work before adding a new thread—another oops—might not know where to resume the beadwork. Oops-proof your new thread additions by simply passing the newly threaded needle through the bead that has the abandoned thread dangling from it. Be certain that the abandoned thread and the new thread are extending from the same place. Firmly hold both the abandoned thread and the new tail aside and resume weaving. The beadwork will slacken if tension is not maintained on the abandoned thread.

It's both symmetric and poetic to weave the old into the new and the new into the old. Practically, it also makes a stronger join. So, after holding the abandoned thread aside while weaving a couple rows/rounds with the new thread, weave the old (abandoned) thread into the new beadwork. Then slide the tape from the new tail and weave it into the old beadwork section.

Adding Thread in the 2-needle Method

To add thread when working with two needles in odd-count peyote stitch (see page 47), place a needle on each end of a new wingspan of beading thread. Pass through all of the beads of the last two rows (Figure 3). Center the thread and continue.

To add thread when working with two needles in cross-needle weaving, place a needle on each end of a new wingspan of beading thread. Plass through the last bead crossed through and center the thread.

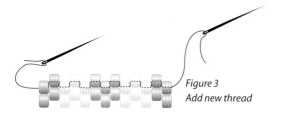

Figure 3
Add new thread

Weaving in the Thread or Tail (Knotting or Securing the Thread)

Recently I read an article that asked, if you aren't willing to spend the time to finish off the work securely,

where will you find the time to repair or replace the piece? It sure hit home. Now I cheerfully give the same time and attention to finishing the piece that I employed in its design and construction. Confident that it will endure, I'm free to move on to new pieces.

Secure the thread and tail by making no fewer than four half hitches in four locations (see below). Make a half hitch on another thread coming out of the bead that the needle and thread just exited. Pass through an adjacent bead, following the thread path, and make a half hitch here. Repeat, placing no fewer than four knots total. Continue to travel through a few beads before cutting the thread. (If the thread is cut directly after a half hitch, it will simply come undone, leaving only three half hitches.)

Always use this method unless the beadwork is too tight to slide a half hitch between the beads, as when doing peyote stitch with Japanese cylinder beads. In this case, skittle (see page 25) instead of making knots.

Making Knots

You'll need to know how to make knots when tying off and beginning new threads. Here are several of the knots you'll use.

Half Hitch

Pass under the thread that links the bead just exited to another bead. Do not pull the thread all the way through, but allow a small loop to remain. Pass back through that loop (Figure 4).

Figure 4
Half hitch

Now pull the thread, making certain that the knot formed settles in exactly the intended place. Sometimes it jumps over a bead or two, leaving thread showing on the outside of beads, and we hate it when the thread is on the outside of the beads.

Lark's Head

Fold the thread (or yarn, ribbon, rope, or chain) in half. Place the fold behind or beneath the place where the knot will be secured. Place both ends through the loop and pull (Figure 5).

Figure 5

Square Knot

When making this handy knot, just remember "right over left, left over right."

Figure 6

Cross the right end over the left end. Drop it down behind and bring it up (Figure 6).

Cross it over the other end. Drop it down, behind, and bring it up through the middle (Figure 7).

Figure 7

Surgeon's Knot

This is a square knot with an additional wrap in the second of the two steps (Figure 8).

Figure 8

Placing Knots

If the beadwork is fringed, weave the threads into the fringe, rather than clogging the other beads with thread. If given a choice of threads to tie the half hitch onto, choose a lateral one (Figure 9). This way a tug will not drag the half hitch up through the thread path.

Maintain even tension throughout the weaving in so the piece does not warp.

Figure 9

Skittling Thread

Skittling is an alternative to knotting for tightly woven peyote stitch beadwork. To skittle, either change direction

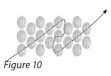

Figure 10

Change direction several times

by making a U-turn into an adjacent bead (one that is side by side rather than end-to-end with the bead you're exiting); or by passing the needle diagonally through one or two beads at a time and making another turn. Attempting to pass through more than a couple beads of the beadwork at a time may break them. Stay within the beads so that the thread does not show on the surface. Change direction several times in order to secure the thread (Figure 10). It takes several turns in the thread path to prevent the thread from being pulled through the beads. Continue through the beads diagonally until ready to change direction again. Zigzag the thread back and forth down the center of the beadwork by repeatedly changing direction (Figure 11). Passing across the entire width of the work may cause it to wave and distort.

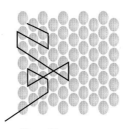

Figure 11

Crimping on Wire

Crimping is a method for securing flexible beading wire to findings. While squeezing the crimping pliers shut, notice that it has two openings. The inner one resembles the silhouette of lips, the outer one the silhouette of an eye.

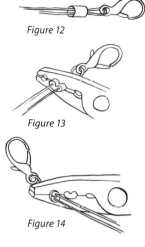

Figure 12

Figure 13

Figure 14

To crimp, string a crimp bead on the beading wire, an optional seed bead or two, and your finding. Pass the beading wire back through the seed beads and the crimp bead (Figure 12). Open the crimping pliers. Lay the crimp bead in the lower lip adjust the two beading wires to lie parallel within the crimp bead (Figure 13). Squeeze the crimping pliers—but not so hard the veins pop in your neck; a white-knuckle squeeze will tear the beading wire's nylon coating, exposing the wire to oxidation. The hanging-down center of the upper lip depresses or crimps the crimp bead, securing the wires. Loosen your grip. Having been crimped, the round crimp bead is flattened and elongated. Turn the bead on its side and nestle it in the lower front notch. Squeeze the pliers, folding the crimped bead in half, minimizing its size and producing professional-looking beadwork (Figure 14).

Supporting Tubular Beadwork

Put a stick in it! When performing the first several rounds of any tubular stitch it may be easier to work with it placed on a stick. Once the ladder or first row is formed into a ring, slip it onto a piece of skewer, straw, tubing, or knitting needle about 4" (10 cm) long. Hold the stick so that the tail comes out the bottom. Hold the stick just beneath the beadwork and continue weaving on the top of the ring.

Many beaders make the mistake of holding the work flat for the first few rounds, as it can be awkward to grasp. While this is fine for making a doily or other circular piece, where each concentric circle exceeds the previous one, tubular weaving depends on each round stacking up directly on top of the previous one.

Incorporating Lampworked Beads

Lampworked beads naturally have a gritty interior because of the way they're made. Unfortunately the holes are so abrasive that they can wear and break thread. Creating a finding with flexible beading wire, attaching it to the lampworked bead, and then using the finding to make the bead-to-thread connection is a great way to avoid this problem.

To make a finding for lampworked beads, cut a piece of medium beading wire 2" (5 cm) longer than the measurement of the bead from hole to hole. Place a crimp bead and a size 6° seed bead (or any size too big to slip into the bead hole) on the beading wire (Figure 15). Fold the tip of the wire and pass back through the seed bead and crimp bead, creating a loop no bigger than the size of the seed bead. Place a safety pin or paper clip in the loop so the bead stays put. Crimp. Pass the other end of the beading wire through the lampworked bead until it's stopped by the seed bead. Mark the beading wire where it exits the lampworked bead. Remove the beading wire from the bead. String a crimp bead and a size 8° seed bead (or one small enough to fit within the lampworked bead hole, yet large enough to accommodate both passes of the beading wire) on the beading wire. Fold the tip of the beading wire back and through the seed bead and crimp bead. At the mark, create a loop no bigger than the size of the seed bead.

Check the size again before finalizing it by crimping the second crimp bead. (Always check the work before crimping the second crimp bead in any project—words to live by and as essential as "look both ways before crossing the street.") Crimp (Figure 16). Thread this new beading-wire finding into the lampworked bead, securing this end with a safety pin or paper clip in the loop.

Figure 15

Figure 16

Adding Basket-weave Crimp End Findings

In this book, basket-weave crimp-end findings are used for finishing bands of Japanese cylinder beadwork from ⅜–1½" (1–3.8 cm) (Figure 17). Use flat-nose pliers to squeeze the finding to the perfect fit, one that permits the beadwork to slide into place from the side but cannot be freed with a tug. If you "over-squoze," open it up just a tad with a screwdriver.

Figure 17

Slide the beadwork out. Apply glue along the edge. Slide the beadwork back into the finding and permit it to dry.

Troubleshooting

I like to think that, because I've made all the mistakes, my forewarning will spare you. Regardless, there are instances when you might run into trouble.

Remove an Extra Bead Without Undoing the Beadwork

Figure 18, Wrong

Figure 19, Correct

Isolate the errant bead. Use a flat-nosed pliers to break the bead, but don't give into the impulse to squeeze the bead so the hole collapses (Figure 18). This will cut the thread. Instead, squeeze just the edge of the bead, as though taking a bite out of it (Figure 19). Cover it or move your hands under the table to prevent the shattered glass from getting into your eyes. Glass cannot be seen in an X-ray!

Removing Knots

Knots happen. Don't let them dampen your bead bliss. Pause for a moment. Use a couple pins or needles to tease the knot open. What appears to be a knot is sometimes just a kinked thread. Power Pro always unknots. Fireline almost always unknots. If it doesn't, and the alternative is to cut the thread, try this first: squeeze the knot gently with flat-nosed pliers and try again to tease the knot open. Sometimes flat beading thread will fray, but it is worth a try. Silamide and plied threads are generally more difficult to unknot, but I have teased some open.

Undoing or Ripping the Beadwork

Most beaders regard an error in their beadwork as unacceptable and are willing to take out the beadwork to correct it. I highly agree! When this becomes necessary, first remove the needle. Even if you think it's pesky to rethread the needle, do not take the risk of trying to "unbead" your way back to the error. This is potential disaster. Please, do yourself a favor and remove the needle, pull the beads off, a few at a time, rethread the needle, and be on your way.

One

Peyote Stitch

Peyote stitch produces beautiful, yet deceptively easy-to-do beadwork. Peyote stitch's rhythmic, bead-by-bead repetition exemplifies beadwork as mindful meditation (with the added reward of beautiful jewelry). Many beaders credit peyote stitch as the stitch that introduced, if not seduced, them to off-loom beadweaving. Each added bead is "sewn" into place, producing a fabric of tightly integrated beads and leaving no evidence of the thread that connects them.

The first step is to string beads to the desired width. The second step is to weave new beads into the first, displacing every other bead by half a step. (To see what I mean, pick up 8 beads. Slide an unthreaded needle through beads 1, 3, 5, 7, every odd-numbered bead.) The beads that sit 50% higher than the others are referred to as "high beads." In the third step and each subsequent row you weave into the high beads of the previous row. Each additional row adds only half the number of beads of Row 1, adding a bead to every other bead of the beadwork.

As in most beadweaving projects, the first step establishes the size, the second step sets up the foundation, and the third step is repeated until finished.

1 *Pick up an even number of beads to establish desired width.*

2 *Offset every other bead of Step 1 by one-half step, producing high beads.* Pick up a bead, skip the last bead, and pass through the next bead. Pick up a bead, skip the next bead and pass through the following bead. Repeat across the row.

3 *Pick up a bead and pass back through the last bead of the previous row.* Pick up another bead and pass through the next high bead of the previous row, working toward the opposite edge. Expect the 2 side-by-side high beads from Steps 1 and 2 to do-si-do, causing confusion about which bead of the two is the high bead. (If one is green and one is lavender, and

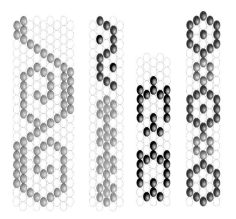

Figure 1

Figure 2

the pattern calls for a green bead, pass through the green bead. Otherwise, either one is OK.)

Repeat Step 3 until desired length is reached.

The stacks of side-by-side (as opposed to end-to-end) beads produce linear vertical rows of beads (Figure 1). This composition permits a broad range of charted or planned designs and borders that include geometric, Celtic, stripes, zigzag, floral, and pictorial shapes (Figure 2).

To count rows of peyote-stitched beadwork, count the number of beads on each edge and add them together (Figure 3), or start at a low bead of Row 1 and count diagonally up the length of the work (Figure 4).

Each bead type produces a different result. Peyote stitch with cube, cylinder, triangle, or any seed beads; weave two beads at a time (and finish in nearly half the time); combine several bead sizes and styles in sequence, pattern or free-form.

Japanese cylinder beads weave together precisely, and each added bead nearly clicks into place. Weaving them is so satisfying that the luscious and supple result is nearly incidental. This is true the first time and forty-thousandth time!

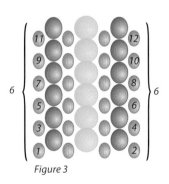

Figure 3

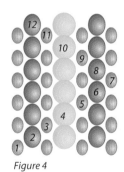

Figure 4

What's In a Name?

Over the years I have heard beaders get their knickers in a knot over the names of stitches. Peyote stitch is one of them. The arguments center on whether the name is a respectful and dignified acknowledgment of the source of the stitch or an opportunistic and crass appropriation. Attempting to sidestep the issue, some beaders call "peyote stitch" (referring to the sacred beadwork for ceremony) by an alternate name, "gourd stitch." By any name, this stitch belongs to no single source and is found in several disparate cultures around the globe. My intention is to convey reverence and gratitude for both the beadwork and the beaders who developed styles and techniques that have endured over generations and will continue to speak to beaders in the years to come.

Band of Triangles Bracelet

· · · · · · · · · · · · ·

This elegant band of Japanese cylinder beads is simple to make and has time-less appeal. Using just two colors, weave a pattern of triangles easily without even charting it. In this bracelet, cylinder beads produce supple, slinky, and exquisitely beautiful peyote stitch because they are so uniform and linear.

Ingredients

3 g Japanese cylinder beads in each of two
    colors (A, B)
1 pair ⅜" (1 cm) silver-plated basket-weave crimp
    end findings
2 silver-plated 4mm jump rings
1 silver-plated ball-and-socket closure (see
    resources, page 232)
Beading thread
Solder
Flux
Glue

Tools

Size 10 beading needle
Flat-nosed pliers
Soldering iron

Setup

Pull a wingspan of thread from the spool or bob-bin and, rather than cutting it, mark the wing-span by folding an inch of masking tape over the thread. Thread the needle and slide it toward the center of the thread so it is nearly doubled, but use singly.

1 *Establish the width.* Pick up 8A. Allow the beads to fall down to the tape (Figure 1).

2 *Offset every other bead of Step 1 by a half step, producing high beads.* Pick up a new A. Skip the last bead of Step 1. Pass back through the second to the last bead. (Be careful—if you allow the first bead of Step 2 to fall down the thread and settle next to the beads of Step 1, you may accidentally pass back through the wrong bead.)

Mantra: *Pick up a bead, skip a bead, pass through the next bead.* Pick up 1A. Skipping the next bead of Step 1 and heading toward the tail, pass through the next A. Work across the row toward the tail and finish with the needle and thread exiting the very first bead (Figure 2). Every even-numbered bead of Step 1 has just become Row 1; every odd-numbered bead of Step 1 has become Row 2; and the beads added in this step are Row 3.

3 *Stitch each new bead into the next high bead of the previous row.* Pick up 1B. Pass back through the last bead added in the previous row. Pick up 1A and pass through the next high bead of this row, working toward the opposite edge. Make 2 more stitches with A, placing 4 new beads in this row (Figure 3).

Steps 1–3 produced 4 rows of beadwork.

4 *Continue to add 4 beads per row and begin triangle pattern as follows:*

Row 5: 3A, 1B
Row 6: 2B, 2A
Row 7: 2A, 2B
Row 8: 3B, 1A
Row 9: 1A, 3B
Row 10: 4B
Row 11: 4B
Row 12: 4B
Row 13: 1A, 3B
Row 14: 3B, 1A
Row 15: 2A, 2B

Row 16: 2B, 2A
Row 17: 3A, 1B
Row 18: 1B, 3A
Row 19: 4A
Row 20: 4A
Row 21: 4A
Row 22: 1B, 3A

Is the pattern obvious now, both in words and in beads (Figure 4)? It might help to read it aloud in a singsong way.

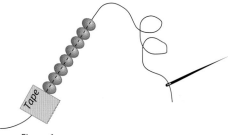

Figure 1

Figure 2

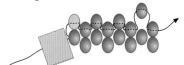

Figure 3

Figure 4

5 *Work until the end of the thread.* Repeat Rows 5–22 until 8" (20.5 cm) of thread remain, no matter which row you've completed. Remove the thread from the needle.

6 *Begin weaving from the other end.* Pull another wingspan of thread from the spool, and this time cut it. Slide off the tape and thread the newly cut end on the needle. Continue weaving the bracelet from this end, from the other end of Row 1. Follow the directions for Row 22, then repeat Rows 5–22. Stop when the bracelet is 1" (2.5 cm) short of the desired length, to allow for the crimp-end finding, jump rings, and ball-and-socket closure.

7 *Weave in the thread ends.* If the beads are so close together that the usual half hitches will not fit between them, skittle (see page 25) the tail through the beads.

8 *Add findings and clasp.* Use a jump ring to secure the ball half of the ball-and-socket-closure to one basket-weave crimp-end finding and another jump ring to secure the socket half to the other. Solder the jump rings closed (see page 20). Attach the basket-weave crimp-end finding to each end (see page 27).

Try this . . .

Rather than counting beads or working with a graphed pattern, consider weaving each row entirely in one color and change colors every row or two. Or arrange beads on the bead mat in a pleasing way, about the size of the intended bracelet, and pick up the arranged beads in order while weaving the bracelet.

Joy Squared Cuff

● ● ● ● ● ● ● ●

Experience the ease and efficiency of peyote-stitching cube beads and learn to create a space or intentional "hole" in the beadwork to accommodate a square-stitched toggle. Choose a palette of seven colors that bring you joy.

Ingredients
40 g 4mm cube beads, divided among seven
   colors (A, B, C, D, E, F, G)
Fireline 10# beading thread

Tools
Size 10 beading needle

Setup
Mise en place (see page 8)

1 *An even number of beads establishes the width of the work.* Pick up 1B, 1C, 1B, 1C, 1B, 1C. Allow the beads to fall down to the tail.

2 *Offset every other bead of Step 1 by a half step, producing high beads.* Pick up 1D. Skip the last bead of Step 1 and pass back through the second-to-last bead. (Careful—if you allow the first bead of Step 2 to fall down the thread and settle next to the beads of Step 1, you may accidentally pass back through the wrong bead.)

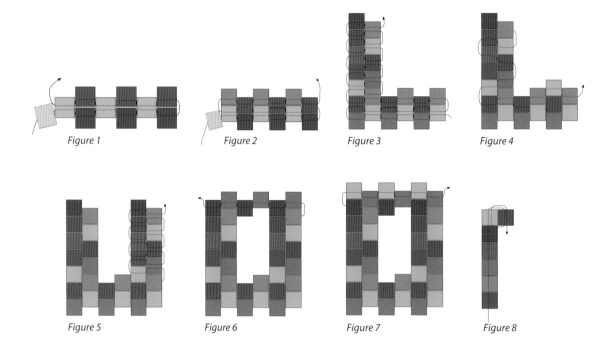

Figure 1

Figure 2

Figure 3

Figure 4

Figure 5

Figure 6

Figure 7

Figure 8

Mantra: Pick up a bead, skip a bead, pass through the next bead. Pick up 1D. Skip the next bead of Step 1, heading toward the tail, and pass through the next one. Repeat, adding 1D and finishing with the needle and thread exiting the first bead (Figure 1).

3 *Stitch each new bead into the next high bead of the previous row.* Pick up 1E. Pass back through the last bead added in the previous row. Pick up 1E and pass through the next high bead of this row, working toward the opposite edge. Add 1E making a total of 3 new beads added in this row (Figure 2). Repeat Step 3, changing bead color every row (or occasionally repeating a row as you desire), until the ends meet around your wrist.

4 *Weave a hole for the closure.* Weave 1A. Pick up 1C and pass back through the A just added. Pick up 1G and pass back through the C just added. Continue to weave a 2-bead column of short rows, adding E, F, C, C, B, and D, for 9 beads total (Figure 3). Weave the thread down this 2-bead column, keeping inside the beads, to the full row at the

base. Pass through the center bead of the row, add 1A, and pass through the last bead of the row (Figure 4).

Weave a second 2-bead column using 1C, 1G, 1E, 1F, 1C, 1C, 1B, and 1D, placing 9 beads total to match the first column (Figure 5). Pick up 1A and pass back through D (the last bead added). Pick up 1A, 1D, 1A, and pass through the high D of the first column (Figure 6).

Weave a row, placing 3F by passing back through each A of the previous row (Figure 7).

Weave another full row, placing 1E into each F of the previous row. Weave 2 more full rows of any color. Weave in your thread by passing through the beads diagonally, staying within the beads and placing no fewer than 4 half hitches. Cut the thread.

5 *Weave a toggle for the closure.* Cut another wingspan and thread the needle to square-stitch a bar toggle. (For more on square stitch, see page 138.)
Row 1: String 6 randomly chosen beads.
Row 2: Pick up a new bead (bead 7). Pass through the sixth bead again, and pass through bead 7

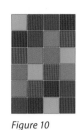

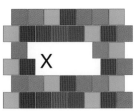
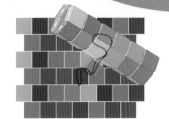

Figure 9   *Figure 10*   *Figure 11*   *Figure 12*   *Figure 13*

(Figure 8). Pick up another bead (bead 8), pass through the fifth bead again, and pass through bead 8 again. Repeat across the row, adding 6 beads for a total of 2 rows and 12 beads total (Figure 9). Flip the work up like the page on a wall calendar. Add Row 3 to Row 2 as you added Row 2 to Row 1. (It may help to ignore Row 1, think of Row 2 as Row 1, and follow those directions again.) Flip the work up again. Add a fourth row of square stitch (Figure 10).

Fold up the first row and the last row, forming a squared-off tube. Sew these 2 rows together by tying Bead 1 of the first row to Bead 1 of the last row. Sew Bead 2 of the first row to Bead 2 of the last row. Continue to weave the first row and last row together, one pair of beads at a time (Figure 11).

Weave the tail in, making half hitches. Weave the thread in and out of the beads and up and down the rows, making it secure and stiff, but don't cut it yet. The remainder of the thread will attach the toggle to the cuff.

6 *Attach the toggle.* Try the cuff on, allowing the ends to overlap. When attached, the toggle will rest along the edge of the hole closest to the end (Figure 12). Determine where you need to place the toggle. Pick up a bead that will serve as a shank for the toggle.

Pass through the bead of the cuff where the toggle is to be. Pass back through the shank and the toggle. Pass back through the toggle and shank and into the bead of the cuff (Figure 13).

Weave in the thread, making half hitches.

Try this . . .

You can use this short-row method to weave a hole into any peyote band and replace the square-stitched toggle with a button, bead, or beaded bead.

35

Carpet of Beads Bracelet

Peyote stitch done with two (or more) beads at a time, theoretically cuts the production time by half (or more). In this project, you'll learn to peyote stitch a loop that makes a distinctive closure for a simple band. You can also transform a simple band into the lavishly fringed variation! Gemstones and pearls make elegant fringe.

Ingredients
240 size 8° Japanese seed beads for bracelet band (A)
Less than 1 g assorted seed beads for loop closure (B)
Button or beaded bead (like Beaded Bead Toggle on page 40) for closure
Beading thread

Additional ingredients for fringed variation:
60–100 pea-size beads of any type, 3 beads for every 2 rows of the bracelet (H)
1 g size 11° seed beads (C)
6 g size 8° seed beads (D)
4 g size 6° seed beads (E)
Power Pro 10# beading thread

Tools
Size 10 beading needle

Setup
Pull a wingspan of thread from the spool. Do not cut it, but mark the wingspan by folding an inch of masking tape over the thread. Thread it on a beading needle and slide the needle toward the center of the thread so it is nearly doubled, but use singly.

1 *An even number of pairs of beads establishes the width of the work.* Pick up 4A.

2 *Offset every other pair of beads from Step 1 by a half step, producing high beads.* Pick up 2A. Working toward tail, pass back through Beads 2 and 1 of Row 1 (Figure 1).

3 *Stitch each new pair of beads into the next pair of high beads of the previous row.* Pick up 2A. Pass back through the 2A added in the previous row.

  Mantra: Pick up 2 beads, skip 2 beads, go through 2 beads.

  Repeat Step 3 until bracelet is the desired length—when the ends meet around the wrist—or until 8" (20.5 cm) of thread remains. Weave in the end of the thread, making half hitches. If the bracelet is not yet long enough, pull another wingspan from the spool and this time cut it. Slide off the tape, thread the needle with the newly cut end, and continue weaving the bracelet from this end (Figure 2). When it reaches the desired size and the ends meet around the wrist, make a few half hitches, but do not cut the thread.

4 *Weave a closure loop.* The closure is generally the most at-risk area of a piece of jewelry, so use a separate thread or secure the existing thread with a few half hitches before making the closure. This way, should the button or loop be pulled off, the rest of the piece remains intact and you simply need to sew the button or loop back in place.

  With the thread exiting a corner bead, pick up 1½" (3.8 cm) of B beads. Pass through the corner bead at the opposite edge of the bracelet. Work once around the loop with peyote stitch, varying

the number of beads and placing 1, 2, or 3 beads with each stitch (Figure 3). *Mantra: Pick up 1, 2, or 3 beads, skip 1, 2, or 3 beads, pass through the next 1, 2, or 3 beads.*

  Weave in the thread, making half hitches.

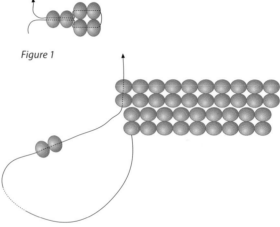

Figure 1

Figure 2

Figure 3

5 *Attach closure button or toggle.* Position the button or toggle ½" (1.3 cm) from the end of the bracelet opposite the loop end. If the button has a shank, sew the button in place with thread. If you are using a beaded bead or a shank-less button, create a shank (see page 22) by placing 1 or 2 size 8° seed beads between it and the bracelet. Travel through the beads to exit the spot where the button or toggle should be attached. Pick up the bead that will serve as a shank. Pass up through the center of the button or toggle (Figure 4).

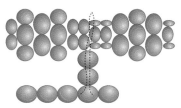

Figure 4

Pass back through the button or toggle, shank, and into a bead of the bracelet. If the toggle falls off, it is because the thread failed to catch a cross thread of the toggle as it passed back through. Try again, or you may opt to use a turning bead (see page 22). Sew back up through the shank and button or toggle and back down again before weaving the thread in.

6 *Fringe the surface (optional).* Take some time to select small lampworked beads, crystals, vintage, pearls, or gemstones from your collection. Don't leave the design of your lavishly fringed masterpiece entirely to chance—sort them by color or size, then arrange them into a landscape that you want to capture in the finished piece. For example, if you're working with several green leaf beads and 7 yellow flower beads, arrange them on the bead mat in a patch that is similar in size to your cuff with the yellow flower beads dispersed among the green leaf beads in the way they should appear in the finished piece, then use them in order.

Fringed variation

When adding fringe, be careful not to catch the thread. Each successive fringe offers greater opportunity to snag or catch the thread without realizing it. Keep your attention focused, and work with ample lighting to avoid unhappy surprises. Try to cup the fringed areas inside your nondominant hand, revealing only the area being worked.

Thread a double wingspan of Power Pro and fold masking tape over the midpoint. Slide the needle near the center of one half, or about one-fourth the length of the thread. Drape the bracelet over the index finger of your nondominant hand. Pass the needle and thread through an edge bead near the center, pointing inward rather than outward.

Create three fringes per row, one between every pair of beads in the bracelet, with none coming directly out the edge. Alternate between rows of plain fringe and "hoo-hah" fringe (one with a pea-size bead). Avoid adding fringe to the rows that surround the button, beaded bead, or toggle, as the loop must be able to freely slip over and beneath it.

Plain fringe

Pick up 4D and 1C (turning bead). Pass back through the 4D and into the next A in this row in the bracelet (Figure 5).

Hoo-hah fringe

Pick up 4D, 1H, and 1C (turning bead). If the C falls into the hole of the H, remove the C and add 1E before the turning bead. Pass back through the E (if you used one), H, and 4D, and into the next A in this row (Figure 6).

Continue to hold the work draped over your finger to expose and isolate the area being worked. When finished, weave in the thread and tail, making half hitches.

Figure 5   *Figure 6*

Try this . . .

If the bracelet's base beads (A) can accept one more pass of thread, you may embellish the edges after the bracelet is completed, which adds decades of longevity to this piece. To add beads to the edges, repeat the *mise en place* and, working from the underside, exit an edge bead. Pick up 3 or 5B. Turn and pass back toward the interior through an edge bead of the next row. Weave across the row to exit the opposite edge. Repeat.

It is also possible to embellish the edge as you place the fringe. At the end of each row, when exiting an edge bead, you would pick up 3 or 5B before turning to pass back toward the interior through an edge bead of the next row (Figure 7). This saves time but will not add to the durability of the piece.

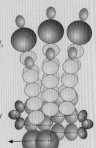

Figure 7

Your Basic Beaded Bead or Toggle

• • • • • • • • • • • • • • • • • • •

Combine one, two, and even three-drop peyote stitch to weave this small rectangle. When rolled up, the first and last row "fit" together, yielding a seamless join—an invisible seam when they are stitched together. Make one to use as a toggle or single bead; make a pair for earrings; make several to string into a necklace or bracelet. You'll use this seamless method of making tubes of any dimension and with any number of beads.

Ingredients
2 g of size 8° seed beads in three colors (A, B, C)
Beading thread

Tools
Size 10 beading needle

Setup
Mise en place (see page 8)

1 *An even number of beads establishes the width of the work.* Pick up 2A, 3B, 1C, 1A, 1C, 1A, 3B, 2A.

2 *Offset every other bead or group of beads of Step 1 by a half step, producing high beads.* Pick up 2A and pass back through all 3B of the previous row. Pick up 1A and pass through the next C of the previous row. Pick up 1A and pass through the next (second) C of the previous row. Pick up 3B and pass through the last 2A (closest to the tail) of the previous row (Figure 1).

3 *Stitch each new bead or group of beads into the next high bead or beads of the previous row.* Pick up 2A and pass back through the last 3B added to the previous row. Pick up 1C and continue through the next A of the previous row. Pick up 1C and continue through the next A of the previous row. Pick up 3B and continue through those last 2A of the previous row.

Alternate between Steps 2 and 3 for eight rows or other desired number, being sure to end with an even number of rows (Figure 2).

4 *Zip the ends together.* Be sure that the tail exits one corner of the beadwork and the working thread exits the catercorner, so that by curling the

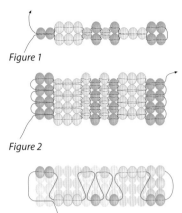

Figure 1

Figure 2

Figure 3

5 *Embellish the toggle (optional).* While weaving through the beads to secure the threads and stiffen the toggle, come out of an end bead, pick up 3 beads, and pass into the adjacent bead to make a *picot.* Repeat, placing 2 picots at each end of the toggle. Or place the picot across the end rather than into an adjacent bead. Make another using a Japanese drop as the center bead of the 3-bead picot. The possibilities!

first and last rows up to meet you can join them seamlessly into a tube. Notice that the beads of one edge fit within the beads of the opposite edge, reminding you of a zipper. The needle and thread exit the last row away from the work. Direct them back toward the work and pass through the first 2 high beads of the first row (Figure 3).

Pass through the next high beads of the last row. Pass through the next high beads of the first row. Repeat this staggering from first to last row as you sew across the work, weaving a seamless join. When the thread exits the last bead, there are 2 beads that have not been seamlessly joined. Make a U-turn with the thread and pass back through the last beads of the opposite edge. Now each bead is connected to another, and each bead of the first row is connected to a bead of the last row.

Weave in the thread and tail, making half hitches. If you won't need the thread to embellish the bead, cut it.

Try this . . .

To make a pair of earrings, you'll need 2 beaded beads, 4 beads whose diameter is larger than the beaded beads', a pair of earring wires, and a pair of 1½" head pins. Place one of the 4 beads on a head pin, followed by a beaded bead and another of the 4 beads. Use round-nose pliers to form a loop with the extended head pin. Place the loop on the earring wire. Repeat for second earring.

Weaving can resume off either edge of a zipped tube, using herringbone stitch (see Chapter 10), brick stitch (see Chapter 11), African polygon (see Chapter 12), or African helix (see Chapter 13). Brick stitch will achieve a look of longer rows of peyote stitch.

Zipped Tube vs Tubular Peyote Stitch

There are several important distinctions between a tube of zipped-up flat peyote and tubular peyote (which you'll learn beginning on page 28). Tubular peyote stitch is developed from successive rounds of beads woven onto an initial ring of beads, so the edges, being the first and last rounds, display peyote stitch's characteristic high beads. The zipped tube has even edges. Compared side by side, the beads of a tubular peyote-stitched tube are each perpendicular to the beads of a zipped tube. Though neither is flexible, zipped tubes are less so than tubular.

Tubular   Zipped

Dewdrop Diagonal Bracelet

• • • • • • • • • • • • • •

Delight in this method of beading "on the bias" and its supple results. In diagonal peyote stitch, each added row is the same length, but every other row begins with one increase and ends with one decrease. Create a beautiful bracelet of perfect Japanese seed beads peppered with color-lined drop beads, providing the look of dewdrops. The distinctive closure features an open tab and a woven toggle that is delicately fringed—you may want to weave two extras to wear as earrings.

Ingredients
17 g size 8° Japanese seed beads (A)
1 g size 11° Japanese seed beads (B)
2 g lined Japanese drop beads in single
    or assorted colors (C)
Size D or Fireline size 6# beading thread

Tools
Size 10 beading needle

Setup
Mise en place (see page 8), leaving a 12"
    (30.5 cm) tail

1 *An even number of beads establishes the width of the work.* Pick up 16A. To assess the bracelet's actual width, hold the 16A diagonally rather than vertically (Figure 1). This row is actually over 1½" (3.8 cm) but produces a bracelet of less than 1" (2.5 cm) wide.

2 *Offset every other bead of Step 1 by a half step, producing high beads.* Make the first stitch with a 1B and each of the following 7 stitches with an A (Figure 2). Each row is 8 stitches. *Mantra: Pick up a bead, skip a bead, go through a bead.*

technique
Diagonal peyote stitch
increasing on edge

3 *Weave a row that begins with an increase and stops one bead short of the edge.* Pick up 1A, 1B, 1A, and slide them close to the work. Skip the A and B just strung and pass back through the first A of this group (Figure 3). This is the first stitch of this row. Weave 7 stitches with A, stopping after placing the 8 beads total in this row.

4 *Weave a regular row that begins with B.* Pick up 1B and pass back through the last bead added in the previous row. Pick up 1A and continue through the next high bead. Place all 7A likewise.

Repeat Steps 3 and 4, alternating between a row that starts with an increase and stops one bead short of the edge, and a row that starts with 1B and then places 7A by stitching a new bead into the next high bead of the previous row.

Occasionally substitute a lined drop (C) for an A. When beading in the vicinity of a drop, rotate the work so every drop's plumpness appears on one surface of the work. Adjacent beads stabilize the drop.

Continue to weave until the tapered ends meet around the wrist. Put the work down for a moment.

5 *Weave a distinctive toggle.* Repeat the *mise en place* and make another diagonal peyote piece, this one half as wide. Follow Steps 1–4, but start with 8A and place 4 new beads in each row, stopping when you've woven about 1" (2.5 cm). Substitute a C for an A here and there.

6 *Fringe the toggle.* Use the remaining thread to produce several fringes of varying length off the point. Pick up 3, 5, 7, or 9B, and 1C. Pass back through all the B beads and the A bead of the toggle (Figure 4). Repeat as desired. Weave in the thread and tail making half hitches. Set the toggle aside.

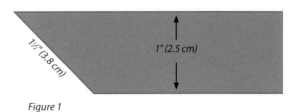

Figure 1

Figure 2

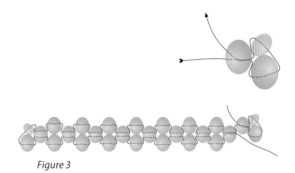

Figure 3

Answer the Phone, Return to the Work, and Know Where You Are!

Examine the work. If the thread is coming from the edge that the tail is on, start the row with an increase (1A, 1B, 1A) to produce an increase on this edge.

If the thread is coming from the edge without the tail, simply weave across the row, making the first stitch with 1B and the rest with 7A. Be careful not to add too many beads in the row. The number of beads added in each row should be half of the number strung in Step 1.

Figure 4

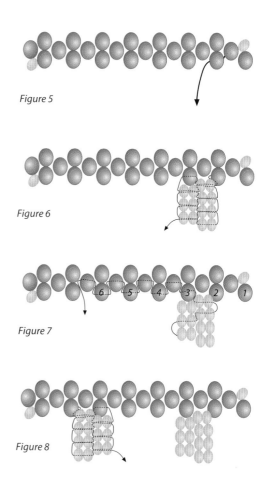

Figure 5

Figure 6

Figure 7

Figure 8

7 *Add a tab-style loop closure.* The loop side of the closure is a tab with a square hole to accommodate the toggle. Weave through the beads to exit the second high bead of the end, following the existing thread path (Figure 5). Pick up 2B and pass through the next A. Do not continue across the row. Instead, *pick up 2B, turn, and pass back through the previous 2B. Repeat from *, adding 7 pairs of B (Figure 6). This is the first strip.

Weave down to the base, following the thread path, and across the last row of A beads to exit the low bead following the sixth high bead (Figure 7). Pick up 2B, turn, and pass back through the sixth high bead. Repeat to add 7 pairs of B (Figure 8).

Pick up 2B, 1A, 2B, 1A. Pass through the sixth, fifth, and seventh pair of B in the first strip added in this step (Figure 9).

Turn, pick up 2B, and pass back through 1A. Pick up 2B, skip 2B, pass through 1A. Pick up 2B, skip the next 2B and pass through the sixth, fifth, and seventh pair of B (Figure 10).

Weave across the row twice more, substituting a drop for 2B if desired and treating the A as though it were a pair of B. Travel through the beads into the A beads of the bracelet.

8 *Add the toggle.* Slide the tape off the bracelet's tail. Thread the tail on a needle. Pick up 2B and pass through the A and both B again (Figure 11). Continue to weave a 2B-wide length of ladder stitch: *Pick up 2B. Pass through the previous 2B again and the new 2B (Figure 12). Repeat from * until the shank for the toggle is ½" (1.3 cm) long. Fold it over and weave the end into the A at the base (Figure 13).

Weave through the beads, following the same thread path, halfway up the ladder. Weave into an A in the center of the toggle and back into the B of the shank. Weave into an A at the toggle's center and again back down into the shank. Weave the thread in, making half hitches.

technique
Diagonal peyote stitch
increasing on edge

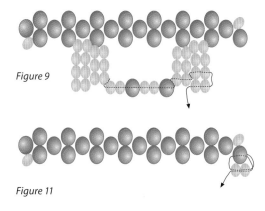

Figure 9

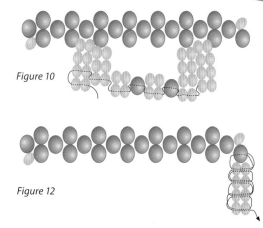

Figure 10

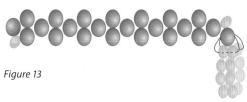

Figure 11

Figure 12

Figure 13

Try this . . .

Succumb to the temptation to make another pair of toggles to use as earrings. Having used the increase and decrease technique four times, diagonal peyote and this method of increasing have become part of your DNA! To use the toggle as an earring, thread its tail on a needle and pick up 6 beads before weaving it in. The loop of beads can then be strung on an earring wire.

In the bracelet recipe the B beads are smaller than the A beads, producing a delicate edge. To make a slightly more jagged edge, use a bead for B that is same size as A; for a very jagged edge, use a pearl or other larger bead for B.

Bookend Beaded Beads

• • • • • • • • • • •

When placing the last bead in every other row of odd-count peyote stitch, there is no high bead available. Though it's possible to anchor the thread by snagging the thread of the previous row, a better technique is to weave down into beads of the previous rows and back up to emerge from the necessary bead to resume. Sample a single-needle method to produce the first bead, then sample another method using two needles for the second bead.

Ingredients
1 g each of three colors Japanese cylinder beads
   (R, Y, B)
Beading thread

Setup
Mise en place (see page 8), using only 1 yd
   (91.5 cm) of thread

Tools
2 size 10 beading needles

technique
Flat odd-count peyote
stitch, single needle

Single-Needle Method

1 *An odd number of beads establishes
the width of the work.* Pick up 2R, 3Y, 3B, 3Y, 2R.

Figure 1

2 *Offset every other bead of Step 1 by a half
step, producing high beads.* Pick up 1R, skip
the last R of the previous row, and pass through
the next bead. *Mantra: Pick up a bead, skip a bead,
pass through a bead.* Add 1Y, 1Y, 1B, 1Y, and 1Y in this
manner. To finish the row, pick up 1R (even though
there is no bead to anchor it) and slide it down to
the work. Make a U-turn with the needle and pass
through the bead below the new R (Figure 1). Pass
diagonally up through the next 2 beads (Figure 2).
Change direction by entering the bead below the
bead just exited. Continue diagonally up through
the next bead (Figure 3). Pass down through the
next bead diagonally. Change direction by passing
up through the bead above it (Figure 4).

Figure 2

Figure 3

Figure 4

3 *Stitch a new bead into the next high bead of
the previous row.*
Row 4 and every even-numbered row: Weave across
the row, adding 1R, 1Y, 1B, 1B, 1Y, 1R. Every bead
placed has a bead to anchor it.

Navigating Through the Beads

When weaving the thread
through the beadwork, travel
diagonally until you mean to
change direction. To change
direction, make a U-turn and
enter a bead that is side by
side with the one exited.

Figure 5

Figure 6

Figure 7

Row 5 and every odd-numbered row: Weave across the row adding 1R, 1Y, 1Y, 1B, 1Y, and 1Y. Pick up 1R, even though there is no bead to anchor it. Slide the new R down to the work. Make a U-turn and pass back through the bead below the new R and the next one diagonally (Figure 5). Change direction by entering the bead above this one and down the next one, diagonally (Figure 6). Change direction once again. Pass through the bead above (the new R), positioning the needle so it is ready to weave across the row (Figure 7).

Weave 20 rows and stop.

4 *Zip up tube.* Roll the first row up to meet the last row and weave it seamlessly (see page 24). Weave in the thread and tail, making half hitches.

Double-Needle Method

Did you notice while weaving the single-needle sample that every other row requires the anchoring maneuver? All those extra thread passes occur along the same edge of the work. Although the

technique
Flat odd-count peyote
stitch, double needle
zipped

beadwork appears symmetrical, it is unbalanced in weight and structure. I prefer the balance and lean thread passes of the method using two needles.

1 *An odd number of beads establishes the width of the work.* With another yard of thread, place a needle on each end of the thread. With one needle, pick up 2R, 3Y, 3B, 3Y, 2R, and center them on the thread.

2 *Offset every other bead of Step 1 by a half step, producing high beads.* Use the same needle to pick up 1R, skip the last R of the previous row, and pass through the next bead. *Mantra: Pick up a bead, skip a bead, pass through a bead.* Add 1Y, 1Y, 1B, 1Y, 1Y in the same manner. To finish the row, pick up 1R, even though there is no bead to anchor it. Slide the "homeless" R up to the work, where it belongs. Put aside—retire—that needle and thread for now, and pick up the other one. Pass back through the homeless R with this new needle (Figure 8).

3 *Stitch a new bead into the next high bead of the previous row.*
Row 4 and every even-numbered row: Continuing with the second needle, weave across the row using 1R, 1Y, 1B, 1B, 1Y, 1R.

Row 5 and every odd-numbered row: Weave across the row, placing 1R, 1Y, 1Y, 1B, 1Y, 1Y, and homeless R (requiring the needle swap).

 Alternately weave a regular row (each even-numbered row) and back again (each odd-numbered row), swapping needles at the end.

4 *Zip up tube.* Roll the first row up to meet the last row and weave it seamlessly (see page 40). Weave in the thread and tail, making half hitches.

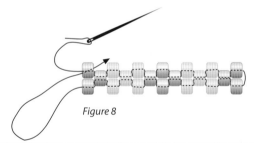

Figure 8

Try this . . .

Weave ten of these beaded beads to string as a beautiful slinky strand of beadwork, as shown here. Or, combine the lessons of the first five projects! Using the techniques from this project, weave a 13-bead-wide band with a border and centered diamond pattern. Close it with the basket-weave crimp finding from the Band of Triangles or weave your own closure with a hole from the Joy Squared Bracelet or a loop from the Carpet of Beads Bracelet, paired with a toggle from the Joy Squared Bracelet, a Symmetrical Beaded Bead, or a toggle from the Dewdrop Diagonal Peyote Bracelet.

Fat Little Embellished Beaded Bead

● ● ● ● ● ● ● ● ● ● ● ● ● ● ● ●

Incorporate various bead sizes and styles in this tasty exercise in two-needle odd-count peyote. A term borrowed from quilters, "stitch in the ditch" is a technique used to decorate the surface of the beaded bead with additional beads.

Ingredients
1 g size 11° Japanese seed beads (A)
1 g size 8° Japanese seed beads (B)
1 g Japanese drops (C)
Beading thread

Tools
2 size 10 beading needles

Setup
Cut 1 yd (91.5 cm) of thread and put a needle on each end.

techniques
Two-needle odd-count
peyote stitch
Stitch in the ditch

1 *An odd number of beads establishes the width of the beadwork.* Pick up 1A, 1B, 1A, 1C, 1A, 1B, 1A. Center the beads on the thread.

2 *Offset every other bead of Step 1 by a half step, producing high beads.*
Row 3: Weave across the row using 4A as follows: Pick up 1A, skip the last A of the previous row, and pass through the next bead. *Mantra: Pick up a bead, skip the next bead, and pass through the following bead.* Weave 3A and pick up the fourth A, though there is no bead to anchor it. Slide the "homeless" bead up to the work. Put aside that needle and thread for now and pick up the other one. Pass back through the "homeless" bead with the second needle.

3 *From now on, stitch a new bead into the next high bead of the previous row.* When the last bead of a row has no high bead, swap needles.
Row 4: Weave 1B, 1C, 1B.
Rows 5–12: Rep Rows 3 and 4.
    To confirm that 12 rows have been woven, be sure that there are six beads on each edge of the work.

4 *Zip up the tube.* Roll the first row up to meet the last row and weave it seamlessly (see page 40). Weave in the thread and tail, making half hitches.

5 *Stitch in the ditch.* Pass one of the needles and thread through 1A and 1B. Pick up 1C (Figure 1). Pass through the center C straight ahead (Figure 2), allowing the new C to settle into the ditch between 2A and in the space between the B and C.
    Pick up 1C before passing through the B straight ahead. Change direction by making a U-turn into the adjacent B. Repeat this embellishment until 12C are spaced evenly between pairs of B in the original tube.
    Weave in the thread and tail, making half hitches.

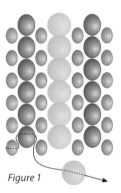

Figure 1

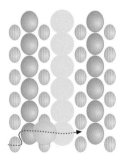

Figure 2

Can't Stop Beading Bracelet

• • • • • • • • • • • • •

You *could* pick up an odd number of beads, pass through the first of them again, pulling them into a ring, then peyote weave ad infinitum . . . or you could follow the recipe presented here. It offers a spiraling design, an opportunity to work with three bead sizes and styles at once, an evening of mindful meditation, *and* a beautiful bracelet. Stitch a Beaded Bead or Toggle (page 40) for the closure.

Ingredients
7 g size 8° seed beads in each of two colors (A, B)
7 g size 6° seed beads (C)
7 g size 8° color-lined triangle seed beads (D)
Beading thread
Bead, button, or toggle bar (either purchased or
   following recipe on page 40)

Tools
Size 10 beading needle
Pencil, dowel, or knitting needle

Setup
Mise en place (see page 8)

1 *An odd number of beads establishes the diameter of the tube.* Pick up 1A, 2D, 2B, 2C, 2B, 2D, 2B. Pass through 1A again to pull the beads into a ring. You may find it easier to work around a pencil, dowel, or knitting needle—slip the ring of beads onto one that fits inside without spreading the beads apart (Figure 1). It may also help to tape the tail down.

2 *Offset every other bead of Step 1 by a half step, producing high beads.*
Mantra: Pick up a bead, skip a bead, go through a bead.
   Weave across the row, using 1A, 1D, 1B, 1C, 1B, and 1D as follows (Figure 2):
   Pick up 1A, skip the next bead (1D), and pass through the following bead (1D).
   Pick up 1D, skip the next bead (1B), and pass through the following bead (1B).
   Pick up 1B, skip the next bead (1C), and pass through the following bead (1C).

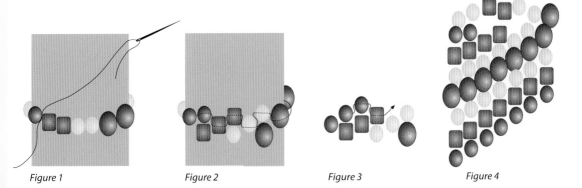

Figure 1   Figure 2   Figure 3   Figure 4

Pick up 1C, skip the next bead (1B), and pass through the following bead (1B).

Pick up 1B, skip the next bead (1D), and pass through the following bead (1D).

Pick up 1D, skip the next bead (1B), and pass through the following bead (1B).

3 *Stitch each new bead into the high beads produced in the previous row (Figure 3).*

Pick up 1B and pass through the next high bead (1A).

Pick up 1A and pass through the next high bead (1D).

And so it continues—pick up a bead like the bead just passed through. Pass through the next high bead. Succumb to the rhythmic repetition that distinguishes peyote stitch. But be careful: your brain will default to picking up a bead like the next high one, rather than the one just passed through.

4 *Size and finish the bracelet.* Weave until the tube is long enough to fit around your wrist. Following the directions for the Carpet of Beads Bracelet (on page 36), weave a loop for the closure, then weave in the thread making half hitches. Thread the tail on a needle, pick up several beads for a shank, and attach a beaded toggle bar for a closure, or attach the purchased button or toggle of your choice. Weave in the tail, making half hitches.

Did you notice . . .

If you examine the work, you'll see that the beads are aligned vertically and offset one-half step horizontally. The initial ring established the diameter of the tube, with every subsequent bead stacked on previously added beads. The beads are stacked, but the rows/rounds are not—in fact, there are no rows/rounds! Though stripes can be produced vertically, they cannot be made horizontally. There is no identifiable end bead (Figure 4). The work spirals around and around without end. To make a piece with horizontal stripes or finite rows/rounds, start with an even number of beads and step up at the end of each row/round (as in the Starry Night Card Case on the next page or the Undulating Peyote Tube or Bead on page 60).

Try this . . .

Instead of attaching a loop and toggle for a closure, weave a bangle to slide over your hand. When the piece is long enough to fit around your wrist, weave one more inch (2.5 cm). Generally, that extra inch is all that is necessary to slide the bangle over your hand. To measure for fit, curve the bangle and measure the inside diameter. When the piece is long enough, curve the tube to meet end to end, matching the spiral design. Zip up the ends seamlessly (as in the Your Basic Beaded Bead or Toggle on page 40).

Starry Night Card Case

· · · · · · · · · · ·

Start with a ring of beads, and after many hours of bead bliss, you'll have a beautiful card case and an understanding of charted designs, in flat and tubular peyote stitch. Practice decreasing along an edge by tapering the last few rows.

Ingredients
45 g Japanese cylinder beads in sky colors (A)
5 g Japanese cylinder beads in star color (B)
Fireline 6, 8, or 10# or size D beading thread

Tools
Size 10 beading needle
Index card
Masking tape
Ruler/measuring tape

Setup
Mise en place (see page 8)

1 *An even number of beads establishes the diameter of the tube.* Pick up 106A. Recount them—it is crucial to start with the correct number, as tubular peyote stitch done with an odd number of beads will produce a continuous spiral and eliminate the distinct rows necessary to create this piece. Fold an index card in half and lay the strung beads in the crease, aligning the string of beads so that you will be able to pass through them again easily. Hold the piece with the tail end toward you and the needle end away from you. Bring the needle around, passing under the index card and towards you, then up to the crease. Pass the needle through all the beads again, and check to see that none were skipped. Slip the beads off the card and pull them into a circle. Roll up the card and slide the ring of beads onto it, pulling them tight so that no more than one bead's width of thread shows. Tape the tube to retain this size.

Using the tube for support makes it easier to hold the work and helps maintain even tension. Tension should be tight enough to hold the beads firmly in place, yet loose enough to allow the beads to roll on their thread, creating the slippery and fluid feel of beautifully executed peyote stitch beadweaving. (No thread should be visible except along the edge of flat peyote stitch.)

Pass your needle through the very first bead strung—the one with the tail extending from it—a third time. Be sure the tail exits to the right, if you'll be working in a clockwise direction. If this is not the case, slip the beadwork off the card, flip it over, and remount it on the tube, or simply turn the tube upside-down. If you prefer to bead counterclockwise, be sure the tail exits to the left.

Every even-numbered bead of the original 106 will become Round 1, and the 53 odd-numbered beads become high beads, forming Row 2 when Row 3 is added.

2 *Offset every other bead of Step 1 by a half-step, producing high beads.* Pick up a bead, skip the next bead of the original ring, and pass through the following bead. Pick up another bead, skip the next bead and go through the following bead.

Mantra: Pick up a bead, skip a bead, go through a bead. When you have added 53 beads, notice that there is no space for a fifty-fourth bead. This signals the end of the round. Pass the needle up through the first bead of this round without adding one to come up to the new level to start a new round. This maneuver of passing up through the first bead of the newest round, without addition of a bead, is called a *step up*. Step up before you commence each new round. Notice that each successive step up occurs one bead to the left of the previous round's (Figure 1).

3 *Stitch each new bead to the next high bead from the previous round. Rounds 4–6:* Fill each next space with 1A, securing it by passing

Figure 1

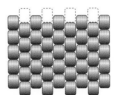

Figure 2

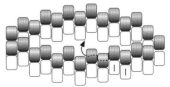

Figure 3

Working Round 3 produces Rounds 1, 2, and 3 at once.

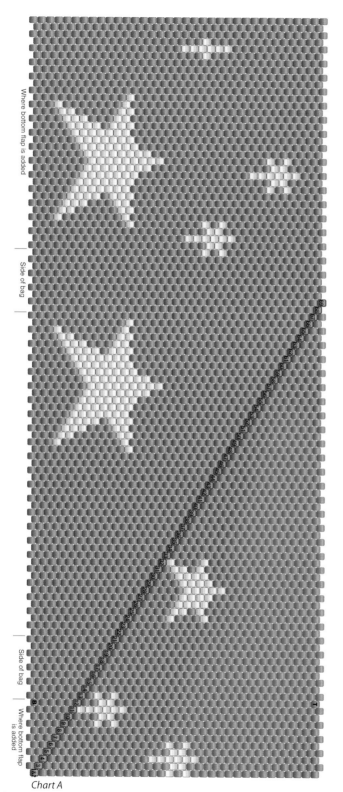

through the next high bead (Figure 2). Add 53 A per round, then step up (Figure 3).

Rounds 7–63: Using the same technique as Round 4, begin to use B and A to follow the graphed design (Chart A).

Using Peyote Graph Paper

Photocopy Chart A and roll it into a tube so that the first and last rows of charted beads meet. Clip it in position and find your place, where the beadwork you've made matches the graph. The first bead in Round 7 is the bead labeled 7 and corresponds to the bead you will add next.

Unclip Chart A and lay it down. Place a straightedge beneath Round 7. Locate the bead labeled 7 again, indicating the start of that round. Place each bead in that round, counting only those beads that appear whole along the straight edge, or every other bead. This round starts with 20A, then 1B, followed by 7A, 1B, 7A, 1B, 7A, 1B, 8A for a total of 53 beads. Step up through the first bead of this round (the bead labeled 7), and you're ready to start Round 8.

Continue to follow the design laid out in the chart through Round 63. Remember that each successive step up occurs one bead to the left of the previous round.

Rounds 64–104: Weave all rows of A beads, substituting an occasional B bead for sparkle.

When row 104 is complete, remove the tube form (if you haven't already).

4 *Weave a bottom for the case.* A short flap, worked back and forth in rows on the bottom rim, will serve as the case's bottom when seamlessly woven into the opposite side of the rim.

Refer to Chart A. Count 11 beads to the left of the bead labeled 1 and find a bead labeled B. Repeat the mise en place. Pass through bead T and exit it from the left.

Row 1: Pick up 1A and make a U-turn with your needle. Place the new A on bead B and secure it by passing through the adjacent high bead to the right. Continuing to the right, add a total of 22 A.

Row 2: Turn and weave across the row, adding 22 A.

Rows 3–16: Repeat Row 2, back and forth.

Lay your bag down, centering the flap, and flatten it. You will notice that the bag extends 4.5 beads' width to each side of the centered flap. Bring the flap over to meet the beads on the opposing edge. If the high beads of the flap appear to fit between the high beads on the opposite side, you're ready to join the bottom. If not, weave a seventeenth row onto the flap. Seamlessly connect the opposing pairs of 22 beads (as in the Your Basic Beaded Bead or Toggle on page 40). Skittle the thread (see page 25) into the body of the bag and trim it close.

5 *Weave a flap from the top rim (optional).* You will make the design upside down, as it will fall over the front of the bag and thus appear right side up. Locate the bead labeled T (the top bead in the column of beads that starts with bead B). Repeat the mise en place. Pass through bead T and exit it from the left. (When the flap is completed, you will remove the tape and weave the tail into the flap.)

Rows 1–23: Weave 23 rows, following the directions for the bottom flap.

Row 24: Begin the design, referring to Chart B. Remember to read the chart back and forth, as you're working flat. After completing the 59 charted rows, add another row of A. Take the time to weave decreases along the edge, starting at Row 60 as follows, tapering the flap.

Decrease

At the conclusion of the row, anchor the thread by wrapping it around the thread that holds the bead you last exited and the one beneath it, then pass back through the last bead placed. Weave across the row, producing one fewer stitch in this row.

6 *Finish the case.* Skittle the thread and any remaining tails into the body of the bag and trim them close.

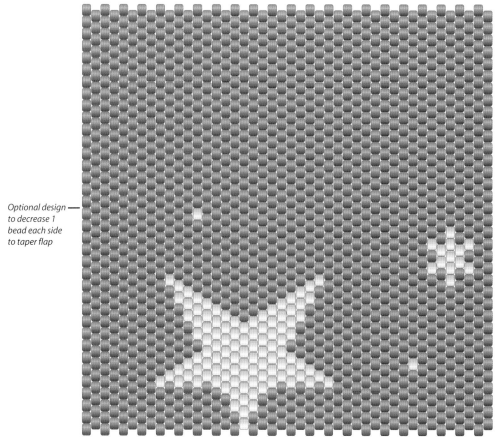

Optional design to decrease 1 bead each side to taper flap

Chart B

Did you notice . . .

Both odd-count and even-count tubular stitch have beads aligned vertically and offset a half step horizontally. While odd-count continues without end because it has no finite rounds, even-count produces level rounds, each with a beginning and an end. This makes it possible to weave striped rows. Remember that the rows are established by every other bead, making 2 or 3 rounds necessary to produce a stripe rather than dots.

In previous projects, rectangles were woven using flat peyote stitch and rolled up and seamlessly joined to form tubes. Their rims are smooth. This project created a seamless tube composed of rows of beads stacked on the initial ring of beads, and its rims are the alternating high and low beads characteristic of peyote stitch.

Undulating Peyote Tube

· · · · · · · · · · · ·

This project couples the precision of peyote stitch with a variety of graduated bead sizes to produce a tube that undulates and spirals with each successive row. It offers both the trance-inducing repetition we love about peyote stitch and the thrill of changing beads with every stitch!

Ingredients

2 g size 14°/15° Japanese seed beads in each of two colors (A, B)
3 g size 11° seed beads in each of three colors (C, D, E)
5 g size 8° seed beads in each of two colors (F, G)
6 g size 6° seed beads (H)
Fireline 6# beading thread

Tools

Size 12 beading needle
Pencil or dowel for support (optional)

Setup

Mise en place (see page 8)

1 *Establish the circumference of the tube.* Pick up 2F, 2G, 2H, 2G, 2F, 2E, 2D, 2C, 2B, 2A, 2B, 2C, 2D, 2E. Tie the thread and tail in a knot, but do not pull the thread tight—allow 2 beads' width worth of slack, which will be taken up when the beads are displaced into 2 rows in Step 2. Pass through the first 2 beads (2F) again. You may find it easier to work on a dowel or pencil—slip the ring onto a diameter that nearly occupies it.

2 *Offset every other bead of Step 1, producing high beads.* Pick up a bead just like the one just passed through (F). Skip the next bead—the first of the 2G—and pass through the one following it, the second of the 2G. Pick up a bead just like the one just passed through (G). Skip the next bead (the first of 2 H) and pass through the one following it (the second of 2 H). Continue in this manner to the last 4 beads of the initial round. Pick up a D, skip the next E and pass through the second E, pick up an E, and step up through both F (Figure 1).

3 *Continue weaving by picking up a bead like the one just passed through, passing through the next high bead, and stepping up at the end of every round (Figure 2).*
   Mantra: *Pick up a bead, skip a bead, go through a bead.*

Figure 1

Figure 2

Remember the warning from the Can't Stop Beading Bracelet on page 52—your brain will default to picking up a bead like the one you are *going* to pass through, despite your intention to pick up a bead like the one you *just* passed through. Step up at the end of every round by passing through both F beads. (Identify this spot by the tail coming out of the bottom of this stack of beads.) Keep the tension tight. The tube is awkward to hold and bizarre-looking until an inch is completed. Be patient.

4 *Finish the piece.* Weave 11 inches (28cm). Weave the thread and tail into the work to slide onto any rope necklace as shown opposite, or just weave one inch (2.5 cm) to use as a beaded bead.

Try this . . .

The severity of the undulation depends on the disparity of bead sizes. If there is only one bead of the largest size, the broadest part of the spiral will have a sharp peak. If there are two or three beads in the largest size, a flattened band results.

When using a graphed design, continue to pick up a bead the same *size* as the one just passed through and use the *color* indicated in the graphed design.

Weave a sufficient length to join seamlessly and slip it over your hand like Suzanne Golden's Crayola-colored and black-and-white bangles that she's noted for.

Supple, Shiny, and Shapely Bracelet

• • • • • • • • • • • • • • • •

Tubular peyote stitch is stiff. One foot of tubular odd-count peyote nearly bursts from the effort required to curve it into an endless bangle. A supple fluidity can be achieved in tubular peyote by adding an extra bead carried between stitches. I call this technique "peyote-carry-one." These extra beads, joints between immovable beads, are simply carried and not woven into. You'll encounter carried beads again in Dutch Spiral on page 69.

Ingredients
15 g each size 8° seed beads in matte metallic (A)
   and opaque brown (B)
25 g color-lined magatamas (C)
Sterling silver toggle clasp
Beading thread

Tools
Size 10 beading needle
Skewer, knitting needle, or
   straw support (optional)
Setup
Mise en place (see page 8)

1 *Establish the circumference of the rope.* Pick up 1A, 1C, 1B, 1A, 1C, 1B. Pass through the first bead once again, pulling it into a ring. (Some beaders find this easier to handle if placed on a skewer for the first few rounds.)

2 *Offset every other bead of Step 1, producing high beads.* Pick up 1C, 1B, and pass through the next B of the ring. Pick up 1A and pass through the next A (without skipping beads). Pick up 1C, 1B, and pass through the next B, allowing the C to sit atop the previous C. Pick up 1A and pass through the next A (Figure 1).

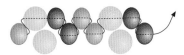

Figure 1

3 *Continue weaving the rope until you reach the desired length.* Pick up 1C, 1B, and pass through the next high B. Pick up 1A and pass

through the next high A. *Mantra: CB into B, A into A, CB into B, A into A . . .* Avoid holding the work flat; for the rope to develop allow the rounds to accumulate on top of each other. Repeat until the ends nearly meet around the wrist.

4 *Finish the bracelet.* Pick up A beads equal to half the length of the bar of the toggle closure. Sew around the loop of the bar toggle and into the beads several times. Weave back down through the A beads before weaving in the thread, making half hitches.

Slide the tape from the tail, thread the tail on a needle, and sew the other end of the toggle in place. Weave the tail in, making half hitches.

Did you notice . . .

See the swirling pattern that emerges? In other beadwork, swirls or spirals are left in the wake of the weaving, trails of sorts. Here, the spiral forms in front of the new bead.

Try this . . .

Because the extra beads are only passed through once, this technique presents an opportunity to use beads with small holes (such as pearls, Czech size 12° seed beads, and smaller beads). You could also produce dramatic texture by using drops or other shaped beads. Make another piece using smaller beads and increasing the sequences from 2 to 3, starting with 1A, 1C, 1B, 1A, 1C, 1B, 1A, 1C, 1B. Make another using a dagger for C for a spiky, almost Goth look.

Peyote Mandala

● ● ● ● ● ● ●

A mandala is a geometric symbol of the universe used in meditation. Bead-weaving a mandala is in itself meditation. Surrender to the hypnotic experience of weaving concentric circles of larger circumferences. To produce flat circular beadwork, each round must be large enough to surround the previous round.

Ingredients
1 g size 8° seed beads in each of
    five colors (A, B, C, D, E)
Beading thread

Tools
Size 10 beading needle

Setup
Mise en place (see page 8)

Follow the bead-by-bead tutorial or, if you are comfortable with peyote stitch, skip ahead to the "recipe in a nutshell."

Bead-by-Bead Tutorial

1 *Form ring base.*
Round 1: Pick up 3A and pass through first A again, pulling them into a ring. (The tail extends from one end of the first A and the thread from its other end.)

2 *Add rounds outside first ring.*
Round 2: Pick up 2B and pass through the next A of the ring. Do this for all 3A of the ring, producing a 6-bead round. Step up by passing into the first B of the first 2B of this round (Figure 1).

3 *Pick up 1C and pass through the next B of Round 2.* Do this for all 6B, producing a 6-bead round. Step up by passing into the first C of this round (Figure 2).

4 *Pick up 2E and pass through the next C of Round 3.* Do this for each C, producing a 12-bead round. Step up by passing into the first E of the first 2E of this round (Figure 3).

5 *Pick up 1A and pass through the next E of Round 4 (the second of the pair of E), pick up another A and pass through the next E of Round 4.* Do this for each of the 12E. Step up by passing through the first A of this round (Figure 4).

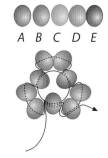

A B C D E

Figure 1

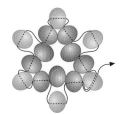

Figure 2

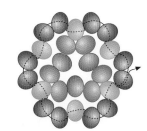

Figure 3

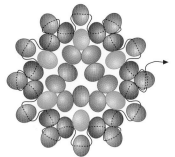

Figure 4

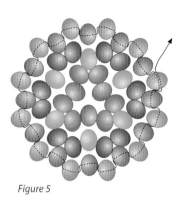

Figure 5

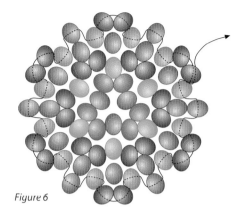

Figure 6

6 *Pick up 1D and pass through the next A of Round 5.* Do this for each of the 12A of Round 5, producing a 12-bead round. Step up by passing through the first D of this round (Figure 5).

7 *Pick up 2E and pass through the next D of Round 6 and then pick up 1A and pass through the next D.* Repeat this series for each D bead of Round 6, producing an 18-bead round. Step up through the first E of the first 2E of this round (Figure 6).

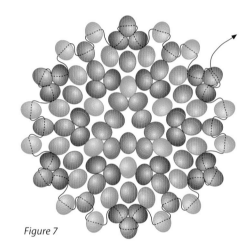

Figure 7

8 *Pick up 1A and pass through the next E (the second of the pair of E) from Round 7, and pick up 1C and pass through the next A of Round 7, and pick up 1C and pass through the next E of Round 7.* Do this series 6 times, weaving into each of the 18 beads, producing an 18-bead round. Step up through the first A of this round (Figure 7).

9 *Pick up 1A and pass through the next C of Round 8 and pick up C and pass through the next C of Round 8 and pick up 1A and pass through the next A of Round 8.* Do this series 6 times, weaving into each of the 18 beads, producing an 18-bead round. Step up through the first A of this round (Figure 8).

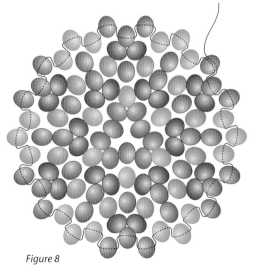

Figure 8

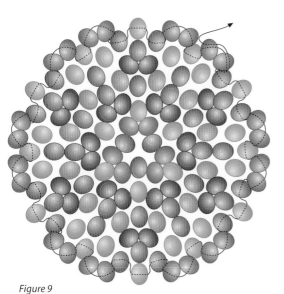

Figure 9

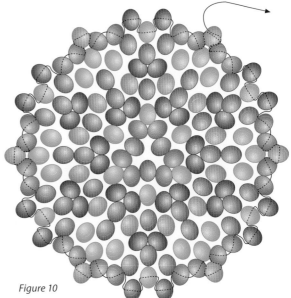

Figure 10

10 *Pick up 2B and pass through the next C of Round 9, and pick up 2B and pass through the next A of Round 9 and pick up 1C and pass through the next A of Round 9.*

Do this series 6 times, working all 18 beads and producing a 30-bead round. Step up through the first 2B of this round (Figure 9).

11 *Pick up 1D and pass through the next 2B of Round 10 and pick up 1E and pass through the next C of Round 10 and pick up 1E and pass through the next 2B of Round 10.*

Do this series 6 times, producing an 18-bead round. Step up through the first D of this round (Figure 10).

12 *Pick up 2B and pass through the next E of Round 11, and pick up 2A and pass through the next E of Round 11, and pick up 2B and pass through the next D of Round 11.*

Do this series 6 times, producing an 18-pair round (Figure 11).

Weave in the thread and tail, making half hitches.

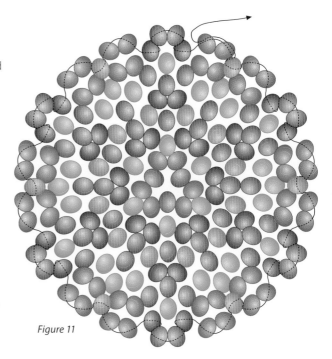

Figure 11

Recipe In a Nutshell

Round 1: Pick up (PU) 3A. Pass through (PT) the first A again to form a ring of beads.

Round 2: *PU 2B, PT next A of the previous rnd; rep from * 2 more times. Step up (Figure 1).

Round 3: *PU 1C, PT next B of the previous rnd; rep from * 5 more times. Step up (Figure 2).

Round 4: *PU 2E, PT next C of the previous round; rep from * 5 more times. Step up (Figure 3).

Round 5: *PU 1A, PT next E of the previous round; rep from * 11 more times. Step up (Figure 4).

Round 6: *PU 1D, PT next A of the previous round; rep from * 11 more times. Step up (Figure 5).

Round 7: *PU 2E, PT next D of the previous round, then PU 1A, PT the next D of the previous round; rep from * 5 more times. Step up (Figure 6).

Round 8: *PU 1E, PT next high bead of the previous round, PU 1C, PT next high bead of the previous round, PU 1C, PT next high bead of the previous round; rep from * 5 more times. Step up (Figure 7).

Round 9: *PU 1A, PT next high bead of the previous round, PU 1C, PT next high bead of the previous round, PU 1A, PT next high bead of the previous round; rep from * 5 more times. Step up (Figure 8).

Round 10: *PU 2B, PT next high bead of the previous round, PU 2B, PT next high bead of the previous round, PU 1E, PT next high bead of the round; rep from * 5 more times. Step up through 2B (Figure 9).

Round 11: *PU 1D, PT next high bead of the previous round, PU 1E, PT next high bead of the previous round, PU 1E, PT next high bead (both B, when they appear in pairs) of the previous round; rep from * 8 more times. Step up (Figure 10).

Round 12: *PU 2B, PT next high bead of the previous round, PU 2A, PT next high bead of the previous round, PU 2B, PT next high bead of the previous round; rep from * 8 more times. Step up (Figure 11).

Weave in the thread and tail, making half hitches.

Did you notice . . .

The recipe offers a place to start and will only guarantee flat beadwork for the first few rounds. Thereafter, the beads' dimensions dictate how each round must proceed to remain flat.

Tubular beadwork is circular beadwork with each round the same size as the one before, allowing the rounds to "stack" with their sides perpendicular to the base. Shapes and forms of incredible finesse are achieved by varying the size of each round. If the size of the round is larger than the previous one but falls short of circumnavigating the previous one, a form with sloping sides results. If the round is smaller than the previous round, the sides will incline inwards, like a ginger jar.

Two

Dutch Spiral

||||||||||||||||||||||||||||||||||||||||||||||||||||||||||||||||||||||||||||||||||||||||||||||||||||||||||||||||||||||||

You may recognize this curvy, open, and textural stitch, known as Dutch Spiral, as a variation of tubular peyote stitch. The basic stitch is illustrated easily in three seed bead sizes—use a medium size for the spiraling band of peyote stitch, punctuate it with a large seed bead or crystal at its edge, and bridge the spiraling beads with segments of small seed beads.

Taste the classic stitch in the Sparkle, Dash, and Dot Bracelet on the next page, an elegant contrast of matte beads with bicone crystals. Spice it up in the Bam! Kick that Dutch Spiral Up a Notch! Bead on page 73 by enlarging the peyote panel and adding pearls and drops.

One inch (2.5 cm) or so of Dutch spiral works beautifully as a beaded bead or earring, while longer ropes are wonderful for bracelets, necklaces and lariats.

Sparkle, Dash, and Dot Bracelet

● ● ● ● ● ● ● ● ● ● ● ● ● ● ●

Think of this project as a curling ribbon of peyote stitch, bordered by a band of "ladder rungs" of three size 11° seed beads and punctuated by a line of crystals. Weave a tube composed of black seed bead "dashes," a narrow band of "dots," and a spiraling swath of crystals. Secure it around the wrist by passing a fringed end through an opposing looped end.

Ingredients
4 g size 11° black opaque seed beads (A)
5 g size 8° green matte seed beads (B)
126 4mm green bicone crystals (C)
Power Pro 10# beading thread

Tools
Size 10 beading needle

Setup
Mise en place (see page 8), leaving a 24"
   (60 cm) tail

1 *Establish the rope's diameter.* Pick up 1C, 2A, 2B. Pass through them all again from the tail forward, then pass through C yet again, forming a ring (Figure 1).

2 *Offset every other bead, producing high beads.* Pick up 2A, 1B. Pass through the first B of the previous round. Pick up a second B and pass through the second B of the previous round. Pick up 1C and pass through the C bead of the previous round (Figure 2).

Note: In this pattern, never weave into A. Just pick them up and forget 'em. They're just along for the ride, though their presence makes this weave flexible.

3 *Continue for the desired length.* Pick up 3A, 1B. Pass through the first B of the previous round. Pick up 1B and pass through the high B of the previous round. Pick up 1C and pass through the C of the previous round.

Repeat Step 3 until the ends of the tube meet around the wrist.

4 *Taper this end of the bracelet by gradually decreasing the number of A beads per segment.* Pick up 2A, 1B. Pass through the first B of the previous round. Pick up a second B and pass through the second B of the previous round. Pick up 1C and pass through C of the previous round. Pick up 1A, 1B. Pass through the first B of the previous round. Pick up a second B and pass through the second B of the previous round. Pick up 1C and pass through C of the previous round.

5 *Weave tassel end of closure. Fringe 1:* Pick up 2A, 12B, 1C, and 3A. Pass back through C and the nearest B. * Pick up 1A, 1C, 3A. Pass back through C, A, B (Figure 3).

Repeat from *, producing a branch fringe after every B, 7 more times. Pass back through all the B and both A and into a bead of the rope. Make half hitches.

Fringe 2: Pick up 4A, 10B, 6A, 1B, 1C, 1A, 1C, 1A, 1C. Pass back through B and 6A. Pick up 3A, 1C, 1A. Pass back through C and 3A. Pick up 5A, 1C, 1A. Pass back through C and 5A, 10B, 4A (Figure 4). Make

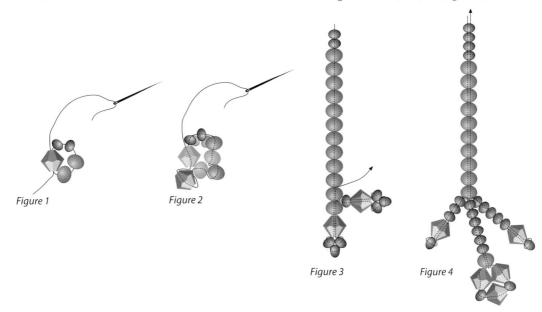

Figure 1

Figure 2

Figure 3

Figure 4

71

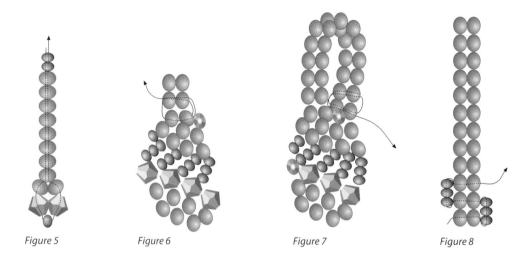

Figure 5   Figure 6   Figure 7   Figure 8

half hitches on the thread connecting the fringe to the rope.

Fringe 3: Pick up 2A, 9B, 1C, 1A, 1C, 1B. Allow the ninth B, C, A, C, and B to form a loop while passing back through the 8 remaining B and 2A (Figure 5). Make a half hitch knot here too.

Produce six fringes total.

6 **Weave loop end of closure.** Slide the tape from the tail and thread it onto the needle. Pick up 2B and pass through the last 2B of the rope again (Figure 6).

Pass through the newly strung 2B again. Pick up 2B and pass through the previous 2B and these new 2B. Repeat until you have a ladder-stitched strip 12 beads long. Pass through the 2B opposite the start of the loop (Figure 7).

Pick up 3A. Pass through the last 2B (Figure 8). Work back and forth, embellishing the edges of the loop, ending at the other end. Weave in the thread.

Did you notice . . .

Each new bead confronts the spiral, as you pick up a bead or beads just like the next high bead. Compare this with the Undulating Peyote Tube, where you picked up a bead just like the one exited, and then proceeded to the next high bead, with the spiral trailing behind. The spinner in me (of yarns, not extreme stationary bicycling) wants to describe these opposing spirals in the terms used to compare the twist in a yarn: spun clockwise ("S") versus counterclockwise ("Z").

Try this . . .

As a variation, increase the number of A used, either all at once or 1A at a time, stitch by stitch. Or replace the segment composed of 3A with B-A-B-C-B-A-B and substitute the C with an A.

Bam! Kick That Dutch Spiral Up a Notch! Bead

• •

Use an array of beads to explore the capacity of Dutch Spiral. Weave an entire necklace length or just a beaded bead with this recipe, whose peyote-stitched band is seven size 11° beads wide, bordered by rice-shaped pearl rungs and punctuated by Japanese drops. As you work, consider other beads and proportions and invent your own recipe. String the resulting collection of beaded beads.

Ingredients
3 g each of size 11° seed beads in seven colors (A,
    B, C, D, E, F, G)
30 Japanese 3.4mm drops (O)
30 rice-shaped 4×6mm pearls (P)
Beading thread

Tools
Size 12 beading needle

Setup
Mise en place (see page 8)

Note: The girth of the pearls may cause them to crowd and buckle. To avoid this, every other time a P is called for while weaving, substitute 3 seed beads for 1P.

1 *Establish the diameter of the tube and the width of the curling-ribbon peyote panel.* Pick up 1O, 1P, 1A, 1B, 1C, 1D, 1E, 1F, 1G. Pass through the O again, forming a ring.

2 *Produce high beads.* Pick up 1P (or 3 size 11° seed beads; see note above) and 1A and pass through the A of Round 1. Pick up 1B and pass through the B of Round 1. Pick up 1C and pass through the C of Round 1. Pick up 1D and pass through the D of Round 1. Pick up 1E and pass through the E of Round 1. Pick up 1F and pass through the F of Round 1. Pick up 1G and pass through the G of Round 1.

3 *Weave into the high beads created in the previous round.* Pick up 1O and pass through the O of the previous round (Figure 1). Pick up 1P and 1A and pass through the A of the previous round. Pick up 1B and pass through the high B (this is peyote stitch). Pick up 1C and pass through the high C of the previous round. Pick up 1D and pass through the high D of the previous round. Pick up 1E and pass through the high E of the previous round. Pick up 1F and pass through the high F of the previous round. Pick up 1G and pass through the high G of the previous round.

Repeat Step 3 until the desired length is reached. The sample bead is 1⅝" (4 cm) long. Weave in the tail and thread.

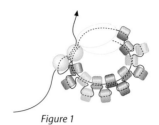

Figure 1

Try this . . .

Revisit this stitch, using your peyote skills to full advantage. Graph an elaborate design for the peyote panel. Rather than creating stripes by weaving each round in the same order, weave the graphed design using each high bead of the peyote panel.

Remember how and why you alternated a pearl in one round with something narrower, like 3 seed beads, in the next round. This will inform how you incorporate high profile beads in other beadwork. Substitute a triangle bead for a bead of the same size.

Keep a pencil on hand to document the ideas that come to you for the next one!

String the accumulated samplers, or make one long enough to wrap around the wrist and finish the same way as the Sparkle, Dash, and Dot Bracelet (see page 70). If these projects whet your appetite for more Dutch Spiral, explore the creative possibilities for altering the segments in the recipe.

Three

Netting

|||||||||||||||||||||||||||||||||||||||||||||||||||||||||||||||||||||||||||||||||||||||||||||||||||||||||||||||||||

Literal scholars could argue that all off-loom beadweaving is netting, as it connects beads with thread that passes through previously added beads or thread. But to beadworkers, "netting" generally refers to the open, flexible fabric created by adding bead segments to the midpoint of previously placed bead segments. It is worked either vertically or horizontally, as opposed to right-angle weave, cross-needle weave, or other weaves worked in multiple directions.

Though any beads can be used, netting is so much easier to do if the beads are designated as *main* or *contrast*. The contrast beads will become the high beads, those that will be woven into.

A single main bead (3-bead netting) produces a dense weave. Longer main bead sequences (5- or 7-bead netting) produce a more open and lacy weave (see below).

Allow me to introduce the concept of odd and even count to netting. If the netting begins with an even number of *main* bead sequences, just turn at the end of the row and weave back across, producing diamond-shaped rows with half-diamonds along the edges. An odd count requires a special flourish before weaving back across the row, also producing diamond-shaped rows of diamond-shaped units, with spiky edges.

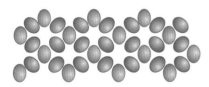

3-bead netting

5-bead netting

Netting transitions easily from many other stitches (including peyote stitch, right-angle weave, daisy, and chevron) as well as the edges of fabric and bead strands. Horizontal netting—netting worked across the fabric, bead strand, or edge—is recognizable because the contrast beads lie horizontally. Vertical netting adds a strand of several bead segments to weave back across (and back across and back across) and is recognized by vertical contrast beads (below, right).

If you are familiar with peyote stitch, netting might feel like peyote stitch with additional beads before and after each bead.

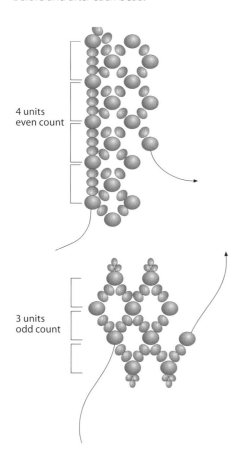

4 units
even count

3 units
odd count

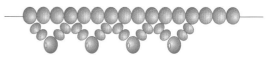

Horizonal netting with horizontal contrast beads

Vertical netting with vertical contrast beads

Peppered Netted Rope

Whip up a bracelet or necklace while dabbling in horizontal netting in the round. To both understand the stitch and create an elegant pattern, limit the beads to two colors of the same size.

Ingredients
10 g size 11° seed beads, main color (M)
5 g size 11° seed beads, contrasting color (C)
Beading thread
10mm ring half of a sterling silver toggle clasp

Tools
Size 10 beading needle

Setup
Mise en place (see page 8)

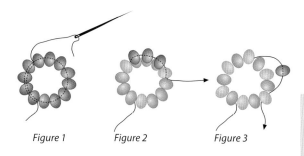

Figure 1   Figure 2   Figure 3

1 **Establish the diameter of the rope.** Pick up 3M, 1C, 3M, 1C, 3M, 1C. Pass through the first 4 beads again (3M and 1C), pulling the beads into a ring (Figure 1).

2 **Build the foundation for the beadwork to fol-low.** Pick up 1M, 1C, 1M and pass through the next C of the previous round (Figure 2).

Repeat twice more. Pass through the first 2 beads of this round (M and C), to step up.

3 **Repeat for the desired length.** Pick up 1M, 1C, 1M, and pass through the next C of the previous round.

With so many Cs, it can be hard to tell which one you should pass through. Here's an easy trick: Skip those that have an X of thread passing through them. If there is only one thread passing through the C, it's your bead! But if there are 2 threads cross-ing each other through the C, skip it and look for the next one.

Repeat Step 3 until you reach the desired length (to fit around neck or wrist).

Last Round: Pick up 1M and pass through the next C of the previous round, for all three C (Figure 3).

4 **Finish the rope.** Pass through all the beads in the last round again, making half hitch knots between every other bead. Pick up 6M and sew around the loop of the toggle bar several times. Pass back through 5M. Pick up an M and pass through an M of the last round, opposite the other connection of the 6M. Weave through the beads, making half hitches. Pass back through the 6M, sew again around the loop of the bar and pass back down the 6M beads. Weave the thread in with half hitches and cut.

Slide the tape of the thread. Thread the tail on a needle and attach the ring half of the toggle. Make half hitches around the loop. Weave back down into the beadwork, making half hitches.

Step Up or Not? Toss a Coin

To step up at the end of Round 2 and each additional round, pass through the first M and C of the round just completed. Or exercise the unusual option of not stepping up. Recall that even-count tubular peyote stitch requires a step-up at the end of each row and odd-count tubular peyote stitch presents no opportunity to step up. Tubular netting works whether there is a step-up or not. A tube with a step-up yields an even number of contrast beads around its circumfer-ence, and one without the step-up has an extra contrast bead around its circumference, making it an odd number.

Tangy Credit Card Case

Create an open weave by flanking each contrast bead with two main beads, creating a five-bead horizontal netting, as opposed to the denser three-bead netting of the previous project. Produce a gusseted bottom by transitioning from tubular netting to flat netting and closing the bottom with a seamless join. Repeat that transition on the opposite end to create a flap closure. Taper it by decreasing at the start of each row.

Ingredients
3 g each of twelve different colors 11° seed beads
1 button or toggle for closure
Fireline 8# beading thread

Tools
Size 12 beading needle

Setup
Mise en place (see page 8), leaving a 5'
(153 cm) tail

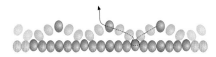

Figure 1

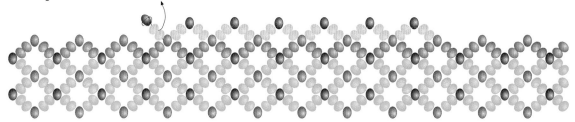

Figure 2

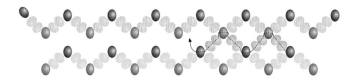

Figure 3

1 *Establish the diameter of the tube.* Choose two colors of seed beads (Ca and Cb) that will be used for contrast throughout. The other ten colors will be used as main colors (M) and change in each round.

Pick up 16 sequences of 1Ca, 2M, 1Cb, 2M. Pass through them all again. Pass through the first Ca a third time. *Note:* Hereafter, any C can be a or b.

2 *Provide the foundation for the beadwork to follow.* Pick up a set of 2M, 1C, 2M, and pass through the Ca bead of Round 1.

Do this 16 times. Step up by passing through the first 2M and 1C (Figure 1).

3 *Repeat to reach the desired size.* Pick up 2M, 1C, 2M, and pass through the C bead of the previous round. Do this 16 times. Step up by passing through the first 2M and 1C of this round.

Continue for the entire height of the card case, using a different-colored bead for M bead on each round.

4 *Make a flap to weave seamlessly into the opposite edge for the bottom.* Weave across the row, adding only 6 sets of 2M, 1C, 2M. Pick up 2M and a 1C like the C bead in the edge row, for a turning bead. Pass back through the second M (Figure 2).

Weave back and forth across the row this way 3 times, until there are 2 turning beads on each end.

5 *Close the bottom.* To connect the flap to the opposite edge, pick up 2M and pass through the C bead of the opposite edge (Figure 3). Repeat for each C bead along both edges.

At the final C bead, pass through 2M, a turning bead, and the edge's C bead. Pass through the other turning bead and into the edge's M bead (Figure 4).

Weave through the beads across the row to exit the opposite end of the flap. Connect the turning bead, the remaining C bead of the edge, and the last turning bead as above. Weave the thread in and cut it.

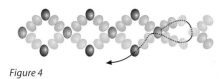

Figure 4

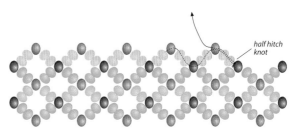

half hitch
knot

Figure 5

6 *Begin to weave a flap closure.* Remove the tape and thread the tail on a needle. Identify seven centered sets at the top edge that will be the base of the flap. Weave seven sets of 2M, 1C, 2M. Pick up 2M, 1C and a new set of 2M, 1C, 2M. (Select a new color combination for 2M, 1C, 2M for each row.) The 2M and 1C at the beginning of each row is the setup to turn the row (which you might recognize if you are familiar with crochet). Weave 6 sets total. Turn the row again by starting with same colors of 2M and 1C that were just used. To taper the flap, decrease one set per row as follows.

7 *Decrease to taper the flap.* After placing the last unit, instead of picking up a half unit (2M, 1C) and the next new row's unit (2M, 1C, 2M), make half hitches and pass back through the last 4 beads placed: the C bead just passed through and the M-M-C just added (Figure 5). This decrease creates a step-up to start the next row. (You may recall from the Starry Night Card Case on page 54 that peyote stitch is decreased similarly: The thread is anchored so that you can pass back through the beads and resume weaving one stitch fewer each row.)

From this step-up, pick up a new set (2M, 1C, 2M) and weave across the row, placing five sets of beads.

Turn by stepping up into the middle of the last set (decrease), and weave back across the row, adding 4 sets. Repeat decreases until the row is two sets long.

8 *Finish the case.* Pick up 2M, 1C, and enough beads to fit over the bead or toggle. Pass through the C bead again. Pick up 2M and weave into the remaining C bead of the flap. Weave in the thread and cut. With a small amount of beading thread, sew on the bead or toggle opposite the closure loop, picking up a few beads to use for a shank if necessary.

Did you notice . . .

The bottom flap was woven six sets wide to allow space for the turning beads that would close all four sides of the bottom. The turning bead introduced at the edge of the bottom flap provides a taste of a netting variation that is edged with picot, which you'll learn in greater detail in the next project, the Lacy, Spiky Bicone Bracelet.

Lacy, Spiky Bicone Bracelet

• • • • • • • • • • • •

Instead of using a smooth curve of beads to transition at the end of a row, as in even-count-sequence netting, the end of the row in odd-count is punctuated by a turning bead. This project employs picots at the edges of a stretchy bracelet that twinkles with the sparkle of Swarovski bicone crystals. Unlike many other stitches, the first step in odd-count netting does not establish the width of the piece, and the subsequent steps are not worked across entire rows, as you'll see below.

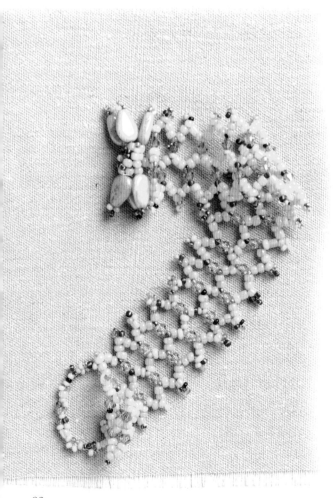

Ingredients
8 g size 6° or 8° seed beads (A)
3 g size 11° seed beads (B)
40 bicone 4mm crystals (C)
6 flat, drop-shaped beads,
      12×8mm, drilled lengthwise (D)
Power Pro 10# beading thread

Tools
Size 12 beading needle

Setup
Mise en place (see page 8), allowing a 14"
      (36 cm) tail

1 **Pick up one less segment than the desired width.** Pick up a B-C-B, 2A, B-C-B, 3A, 3B (the picot). Pass back through the last A bead (Figure 1).

2 **Complete one lobe and begin the next.** Pick up 2A, B-C-B, 2A, and pass back through the corresponding B-C-B of the previous row (Figure 2). Pick up 3A, 3B. Pass back through the last A bead.

Repeat Step 2 until ends meet around the wrist.

3 **Weave a toggle.** Repeat the *mise en place* and pick up 4A. Peyote stitch 8 rows (see Chapter One for instructions on peyote stitch). Roll the piece into a tube and zip it shut (see page 40). Pass through the center of the toggle to the other edge.

*Pick up 1D, 3B, and pass back through 1D and the toggle (Figure 3).

Repeat from *, placing a total of 3 drop beads at each end of the toggle. Weave in the tail and cut it. Before weaving in and cutting the thread, exit the toggle at the mid-line between rows 2 and 3 of

the 4 rows of beads. Pick up 1A and weave into the 2A in the center of one end of the bracelet. Weave through the beads to circle back to the 1A just added (Figure 4).

Pass back through 1A and into the toggle again. Weave back down into the bracelet. Weave in the thread, making half hitches.

4 **Weave the closure loop.** Slide the tape from the 14" (35 cm) tail. Thread the tail on a needle. Weave through the beads, making half hitches, and exit the second or third B-C-B from the end. Pick up 1⅝" (3.8 cm) of A and B beads randomly. Pass through 2A, 4 picot-tipped spikes back from the end (Figure 5).

Weave through the beads, making half hitches, to exit at the start of the loop. Peyote-stitch across the loop (as in the Carpet of Beads Bracelet on page 36), adding more beads as you wish. Weave in the thread, making half hitches.

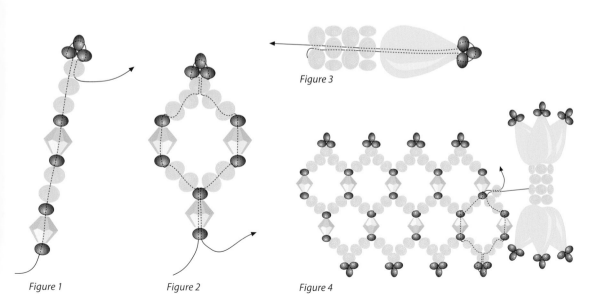

Figure 3

Figure 1

Figure 2

Figure 4

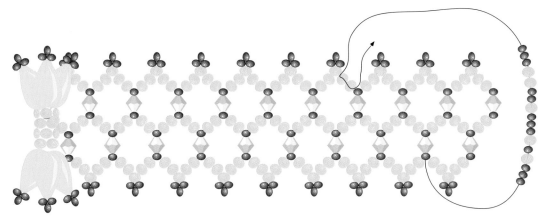

Figure 5

Did you notice . . .

Each crystal is flanked by a B to protect the thread.

This piece is 3 (odd-count) sequences wide (Figure 6). Broken down: (S) start with two less sequences than the desired width (here, C-M-C), (Step 1) pick up M-C-turning bead(s) and pass back through this C bead, (Step 2) pick up M-C-M and pass through the corresponding C bead (repeat Step 2 for every corresponding C bead there is). Alternate between Steps 1 and 2.

This odd number of sets displaces adjacent units by a half step, as in peyote stitch. This does not occur in rows of even numbers of sets. Don't let your head hurt thinking about it, just an interesting structural note.

Try this . . .

Make more renditions of this recipe, but try the following variations: Substitute a pearl and turning bead for the picots along one edge. Substitute the B-C-B with 2 alternating cubes or with a size 6°. Increase the 3A on the opposite edge to 5A. Substitute the picot along this edge with 5 drops. Make it long enough to wrap around your throat. See how it assumes a curve as you weave.

This is a versatile and inexhaustible stitch in its flat state. You can connect the turning beads of one edge to create beaded doilies or mandalas or connect the turning beads at both edges to create sculptural forms as diverse as geodesic domes, baskets, and bezels. Make a beautiful variation by substituting a bugle bead for the 2A.

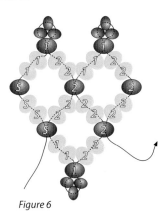

Figure 6

84

Mardi Gras Beaded Netted Bead

• • • • • • • • • • • • • • • • • •

Some accomplished beaders flaunt strands of beaded beads composed of only a few colors or single-color beads resembling gumdrops. I can't recall ever making anything in a single color, so here is a recipe that uses between two and seventeen colors. Using an odd number of sequences, weave a netted band that reaches around the circumference of a wooden base bead. Gather the edges, wrap the netting around the base bead, and sew the first and last rows together.

Ingredients
5 g size 11° seed beads divided among one to
    sixteen colors (M)
2 g size 11° seed beads or optional size 8° seed
    beads in a color that contrasts with M (C)
1 g size 15° Japanese seed beads for the picot in
    the color of your choice (P)
⅞" (2.2cm) wooden or other round bead
Beading thread

Tools
Size 10 beading needle

Setup
Mise en place (see page 8)

1 *Produce two-thirds of a row.* Pick up 1C, 2M, 1C, 2M, 1C, 2M, 1C, 2M, 1C, 2M, 1C, 2M, 1C, and 3P. Pass back through the last C bead picked up.

2 *Finish the first row and begin the next.* Pick up 2M, 1C, 2M. Skipping the next C bead, pass back through the third-from-last C bead of the previous row. Pick up 2M, 1C, 2M. Skipping the next C bead, pass back through the fifth-from-last C bead of the previous row. Pick up 2M, 1C, 2M. Skipping the next C bead, pass back through the seventh-from-last C bead of the previous row, in this case the first C bead strung (Figure 1). Pick up 2M, 1C, and 3P. Pass back through the C bead.

3 *Continue until the netting is wide enough to wrap around the core bead.* Pick up 2M, 1C, 2M. Notice that the previous row produced diamond shapes of netting with 1C in each corner.

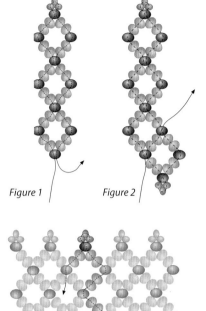

Figure 1   Figure 2

Pass through the middle C, the high bead of the 5-bead sequence (Figure 2). Do this twice more. Pick up 2M, 1C, and 3P. Pass back through the C bead.

Repeat Step 3 until netting is wide enough to reach around the wooden bead.

4 *Join ends of netting.* Pick up 2M and pass through the middle C bead on Row 1. Pick up 2M and pass through the middle C bead on the last row. Repeat, alternating between first and last rows, across the width (Figure 3).

5 *Gather the edges of the netting.* Pass through 2P, exiting the middle one. Pass through all the middle P beads along that edge (Figure 4). To control the gathering and the size of the hole in the finished bead, you may want to place one or more beads between each middle P bead.

6 *Wrap the wooden bead.* Insert the wooden base bead in the cup formed by the netting, aligning the hole in the bead with the gathered edge of the netting. Repeat Step 5 to enclose the base bead in the netting.

Weave in the thread and tail, making half hitches.

Figure 3

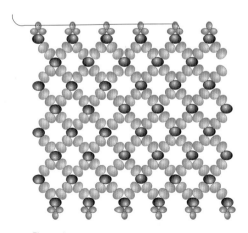

Figure 4

Try this . . .

Make another version of this project, but as you connect the middle P bead of each picot along one edge, add one seed bead between each P bead. Next hone weave one or more rows of peyote stitch (see page 28) off this ring of new beads.

Or, follow Steps 1–3 to weave a longer piece, varying the size or bead type across the row and placing the largest beads in the center. By graduating the size of the beads across the row the band will curve, making for a comfortable and stunning beaded collar.

Classically Feminine Pearl Collar

Make this piece an heirloom by stringing the first row on beading wire, ensuring that it will hold up well for many years of wear. This design features a magnetic clasp, available in many styles. They hold the piece securely but are easy and safe to wear because of their ability to "break away" when tugged. Make two versions, an elegant creamy collar of round beads and a dramatic dark piece with larger pearls and the sparkle of faceted beads.

Ingredients

Creamy necklace:
30 g size 11° Ceylon seed beads (M)
5 g size 8° Ceylon seed beads (C)
100 pearls 4–6mm (P)
Power Pro 10# beading thread

Dark necklace:
30 g size 11° brown iris 3-cut seed beads (M)
5 g size 8° brown iris seed beads (C)
52 4 × 10–13mm top-drilled brown pearls (P)
Power Pro 10# beading thread colored with black permanent marker

Both versions:
Magnetic clasp
24" (61 cm) of medium 0.019 or 0.018" beading wire
2 crimp beads large enough to accommodate doubled wire

Tools
Crimping pliers
Size 12 beading needle
Wire cutters
Masking Tape

Setup
Mise en place (see page 8)

Creamy Necklace

1 *Establish the size of the collar.* String a crimp bead, 2C, and half the clasp on one end of the beading wire. Pass the wire back through the 2C and the crimp bead. Crimp (see page 26). String 1C, 2M, 1C, 2M, and so on for 22" (56 cm), ending with 1C.

Don't string the second crimp bead yet, but fold a piece of masking tape over the beading wire ¼" (6 mm) from the end of the beads to hold everything in place.

2 *Offset the beads of Step 1 in preparation for the rest of the weaving.* You will use your needle and thread to weave the necklace off the strung base row, beginning at the tail and avoiding the crimp because it may cut the thread. Pass through the M bead after the C bead next to the crimp bead, toward the C bead. Pick up 2M, 1C, 2M, and pass through the next C bead of the base row. Continue in this manner across the row (Figure 1). (If one set is unused when you make the last complete stitch, ignore it for now.)

3 *This step produces a complete row. (Repeat this step for each desired row.)* To turn the row, pick up 2M, 1C, in addition to 2M, 1C, 2M and pass back through the waiting C bead from the previous row. To weave across the row, pick up 2M, 1C, 2M, and pass through the next waiting C bead of the previous row (Figure 2). Weave across the row this way.

Repeat Step 3 for one more row.

4 *Introduce dangles to the collar.*
Row 5: *Pick up 2M, 1C, 2M, 1P, 1M. Pass back through 1P, 2M, 1C. Pick up 2M and pass through the waiting C bead (Figure 3). Repeat from * across the row.

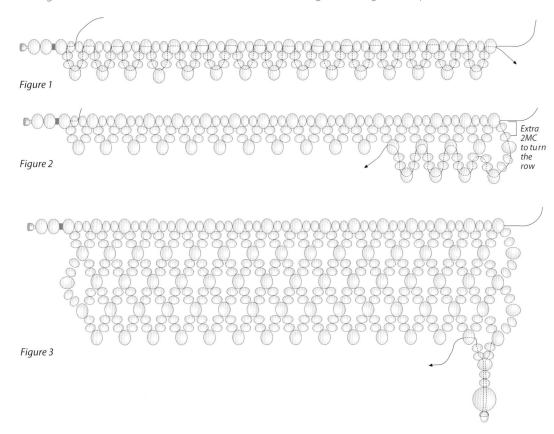

Figure 1

Figure 2

Extra
2MC
to turn
the
row

Figure 3

5 *Finish the collar.* Weave in the thread and tail. Remove the tape from the beading wire. String the second crimp bead, 2C, and the other half of the clasp. Pass the beading wire back through the 2C and crimp bead. Before crimping the second crimp bead, finesse the strung components to be sure that there is no gap between the beads, but there must be enough play in the beads so that the strand is flexible. When you are confident, crimp the second crimp bead. Trim any excess beading wire.

Dark Necklace

1 *Establish the size of the collar.* String a crimp bead, 2C, and half the clasp on one end of the beading wire. Pass the wire back through the 2C and the crimp bead. Crimp (see page 26). String 1C, 5M, 1C, 5M, and so on, for 18" (46 cm), ending with 1C. Don't string the second crimp bead yet, but fold a piece of masking tape over the beading wire ¼" (6 mm) from the end of the beads to hold everything in place.

2 *Offset the beads of Step 1 in preparation for the rest of the weaving.* You will use your needle and thread to weave the necklace off the strung base row, beginning at the tail and avoiding the crimp because it may cut the thread. Pass through the M bead after C bead next to the crimp bead, toward C bead. Pick up 5M, 1C, 5M, and pass through the next C bead of the base row. Continue in this manner across the row (similar to Figure 1). (If one set is unused when you make the last complete stitch, ignore it for now.)

3 *This step produces a complete row.* To turn the row, pick up 5M, C in addition to 5M, 1C, 5M and pass back through the waiting C bead of the previous row. To weave across the row, pick up 5M, C, 5M and pass through the next waiting C bead of the previous row. Weave across the row this way (similar to Figure 2).
Repeat Step 3 for one more row.

4 *Introduce dangles to the collar.*
Row 5: Pick up 5M, 1C, 5M, 1P, 3M. Pass back through the first 2M of this step and the C bead. Pick up 5M and pass through the waiting C bead. Repeat this sequence across the row.

5 *Finish the collar.* Follow directions for Step 5 of the Creamy Necklace to attach the other half of the clasp.

Did You Notice . . .
When a "netted" piece is finished, it is very difficult to tell whether it was woven vertically or horizontally. (Though by following the recipes here you will create collars like the ones pictured, the examples were actually woven vertically.) To identify whether a piece was woven horizontally or vertically, look closely and determine whether the threads pass through the C bead horizontally or vertically. If working solely with thread, choose vertical netting over horizontal to make strong and enduring beadwork. But if the first row is strung on beading wire, select horizontal over vertical.

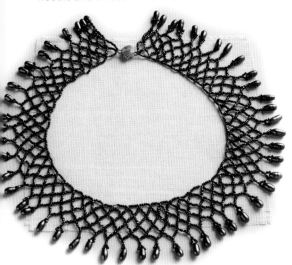

Oglala Bracelet

· · · · · · · ·

Named for the beadworkers of the Lakota nation in South Dakota who are credited with this stitch, the ruffled lace produced in this recipe is simply consecutive rows of radical increases of horizontal netting. For the closure on your bracelet, choose a button that will fit within the peyote-stitched loop, or weave a Beaded Toggle (see page 40), Mardi Gras Beaded Netted Bead (see page 85), or Winged Bead (see page 198).

Ingredients

2 g size 11° seed beads in each of two colors (A, B)
1 g size 15° seed beads (C)
7 or 11 pistachio-size (12×6×6mm) beads (D)
Button, bead, or toggle for closure
Beading thread (for weaving)
Power Pro 10# beading thread (for assembly)

Tools

Size 10 beading needle

Setup

Mise en place (see page 8)

1 **Build the base of the bracelet.**
Row 1: Pick up 1A, 2B, 1A, 2B, and so on, for twice the desired length of the finished bracelet.
Row 2: Pick up 3A and pass back through the last A bead of the previous row. Weave across the row, adding 3A between each A bead of the previous row (Figure 1).

2 **Weave a closure loop.** Pick up 32A and/or B. Pass through the first of these A beads again, forming a loop. Work peyote stitch around the loop, making four evenly spaced increases by using two beads in place of one every four stitches (Figure 2). (See page 28 for instructions on peyote stitch.) Work another round of peyote stitch without increasing. Slide the tape off the thread. Thread the tail on a needle, and weave the tail into the loop's beads.

3 *Weave consecutive rows of radical increases.*
Row 3: Pick up 5A and pass through the center
A (high bead) of each set of 3A of the previous row.
Weave across the row this way, adding 5A between
every high bead of the previous row.
Row 4: Pick up 7B and pass through the center A
(high bead) of each set of 5A of the previous row
(Figure 3).
Row 5: Pick up 3C, skip the last B bead of the
previous row, and pass through the following one.

Weave across the row this way, adding 3C at a time,
skipping a B bead, and passing through the next B
bead. (Just ignore the A beads.)

4 *Add the bridge.* Repeat the *mise en place*, and
enter the first pair of B of Row 1 of the bracelet
(Figure 4).
  *Pick up 3B, 1D, 3B (this is the bridge). If the B
slips into D's hole, substitute a larger seed bead for
B in the bridge. Count back 6 pairs of B on Row 1

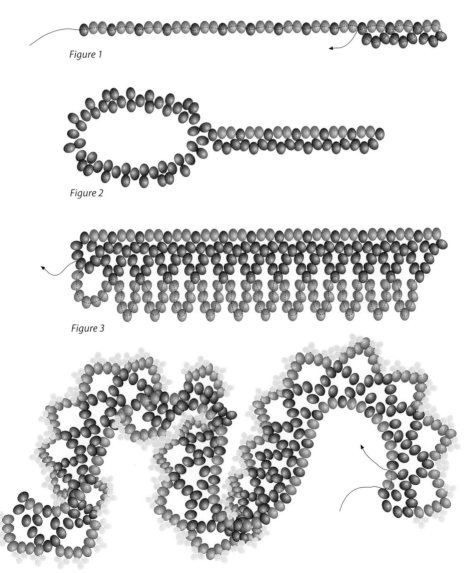

Figure 1

Figure 2

Figure 3

Figure 4

91

and pass back through all. Pass through the bridge again (Figure 5). Pass down through the sixth pair of B again.

Repeat from * for the length of the bracelet. Weave in the thread with half hitches, but save what remains to attach the closure before cutting it.

5 *Size the bracelet.* Before attaching the button, toggle, or winged bead closure, determine if the bracelet is too long, too short, or just right. If the loop doesn't reach the other end of the bracelet around your wrist, you'll need to place the closure on a "stem" of beads to cover that length (Figure 6). To make a stem of beads, simply string enough beads to add the desired length to the bracelet, and add the closure. Weave back and forth through the stem to strengthen. Or, if the loop overlaps the bracelet, you'll need to place the closure on the surface of the bracelet rather than the end (Figure 7).

6 *Attach the bead or toggle for closure.* Pass the Power Pro through the beads to exit where the closure will be attached. Pick up a few seed beads and the closure. Pick up a turning bead. Pass back through the closure and seed beads. Weave in the thread and trim close. (If you are using a button with a shank, omit the seed beads and simply pass through the shank and back into the bracelet.)

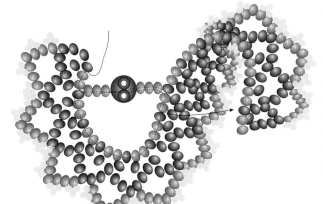

Figure 5

Figure 6

Figure 7

Try this . . .

If weaving row upon row of radical increases thrills you, start another piece by making Row 1 about 6" (15 cm) long. Weave Row 2 off of Row 1 twice. Weave a Row 3 onto each of the Row 2s. Weave a Row 4 onto each of the Row 3s. Embellish the edge of each Row 4, following the directions for Row 5. Flutterby Oglala!

Starlight and Snowflakes

• • • • • • • • • • • •

Circular netting begins with a ring of beads. A round of netting is built off that ring. Each successive round must be larger to remain flat. Make stars or snowflakes by altering the number and sequences of beads that will repeat in a round. Use them to adorn a velvet dress or cashmere sweater. Stiffen them with a dunk in acrylic floor treatment and hang in a window or on a tree.

Ingredients

Star (5 points or units):
1 g each in two colors of size 11° seed beads (A, B)
1 g size 8° seed beads (C)
1 g size 15° seed beads (D)
Beading thread

Snowflake (10 points or units):
2 g each size 11° seed beads in 2 colors (A, B)
30 Swarovski 4mm bicones (C)
1 g size 8° seed beads (D)
Power Pro 10# beading thread

Tools
Size 10 beading needle

Setup
Mise en place (see page 8)

Star

1 *Create the initial ring of beads.*
Round 1: Pick up 1A and 1C five times. Pass through the first A again, pulling the beads into a ring.

2 *Begin weaving the star.*
Round 2: Pick up 2A, 1C, 2A. Pass through the next A of the ring. Repeat all around the ring, placing 5 units. Step up by passing through 2A and the high C (Figure 1).
Round 3: Pick up 3B, 1C, 3B. Pass through the high C bead of the previous round. Repeat for all 5 units. Step up through 3B and the high C bead (Figure 2).

Round 4: Pick up 7A, 1C, 7A. Pass through the high C bead of the previous round. Repeat for all 5 units. Step up *only* through 7A, stopping short of the high C bead (Figure 3).

3 *Embellish star.* Pick up 3B and pass through 7A, C, and down into the 3B and the C bead of Round 2 (Figure 4). Pick up 7D. Enter the high C bead of Round 4 in the same direction.
  *Pick up 3D, pass *down* through the fourth, third, second, and first of the 7 D (Figure 5). Pass through the C bead of Round 2 again, plus 3B, 1C (of Round 3), down into 3B and the C bead of Round 2. Pick up 7D.

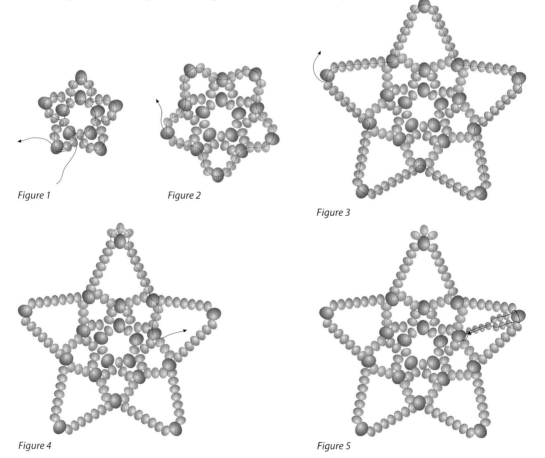

Figure 1

Figure 2

Figure 3

Figure 4

Figure 5

Pass through the C bead of Round 4. Pick up 3B and pass through the C bead of Round 4 again.

Repeat from * for all 5 units. (For the last unit, the 3B are already in place, so do not add any—just pass through the 3 already there.) Weave in the ends, making half hitches.

Snowflake

1 *Create the initial ring of beads.*
Round 1: Pick up 1A, and 1C ten times. Pass through the first A and pull into a ring (Figure 6).

2 *Begin weaving snowflake.*
Round 2: Pick up 2A, 1B, 2A, and pass through

the next A of the ring. Repeat for all 10 units. Step up by passing through 2A and the high B bead (Figure 7).
Round 3: Pick up 1B, 2A, 1C, 2A, 1B. Pass through the high B of the previous round. Repeat for all 10 units. Step up by passing through B, 2A, and high C bead and beyond through 2A, (Figure 8).
Round 4: Pick up 1D. Pass through 2A. Pick up 5B to loop above high C bead. Pass through next 2A. Repeat for all 10 units. Step up through 1D, 2A, first 3 of the 5B, exiting the high B bead (Figure 9).
Round 5: Pick up 7A, 1C, 7A. Pass through the next high B bead of the previous round. Repeat for all 10 units. Step up by passing through 7A, stopping short of the C bead.

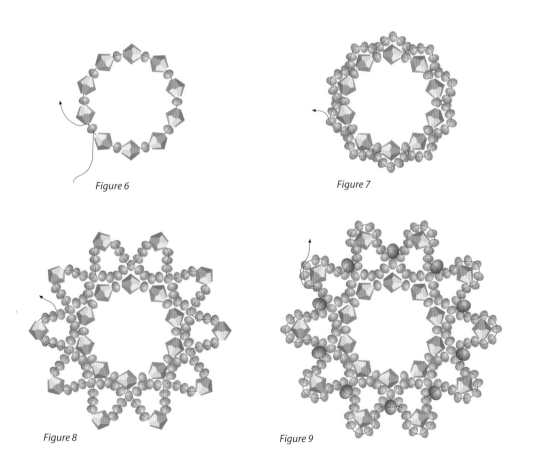

Figure 6

Figure 7

Figure 8

Figure 9

95

3 *Embellish snowflake.* Pick up 5B to loop over the high C. Pass through the first 5A (of the 7). Pick up 1D. Pass through the last 5A (of the 7). Repeat for all 10 units. You can opt to finish the snowflake by weaving in the thread and cutting now or continue weaving. For a larger snowflake, add more rounds by repeating Round 5 with additional A beads, using 9 in place of 7. Repeat the embellishment, weaving through 7A instead of 5. Consider adding even more rounds, finishing the piece by weaving in the thread when the piece is as large as you like.

Try this . . .

Circular netting can be regarded as horizontal netting with each round larger than the preceding round. A similar result can be produced with vertical odd-count netting by gathering the points or picots along one edge. Work up this little bead doily to illustrate the point. You'll need 2 g of ⅜" (1cm) bugle beads (B) and 1 g size 11° seed beads (C)
Step 1: Pick up 1C, 1B, 1C.
Step 2: Pick up 1B, 4C. Pass back through the first C bead of the 4C.
Step 3: Pick up 1B, 1C, 1B. Pass through the high C bead of the previous row.

Step 4: Pick up 1B, 1C, 1B, 1C, 1B. Pass through the high C bead of the previous row.

Repeat Steps 2–4 until ten 4C units are produced (Figure 10). Pass through the single C beads (Figure 11). Connect the beginning and end by picking up 1B and passing through the corresponding C bead of Row 1. Pick up 1B and pass through the corresponding C bead of the last row. Repeat, alternating between the first and last rows until linked.

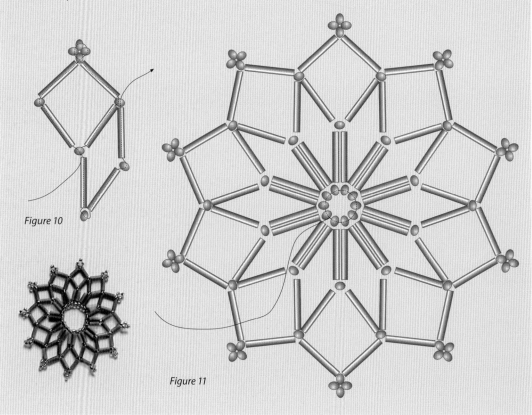

Figure 10

Figure 11

Fandango Beaded Scarf

• • • • • • • • • •

Beading the ends of a silk scarf enhances the drape of an otherwise weightless fabric, causing it to swing and sway with the wearer's movements. Shiny glass beads are also the perfect contrast to matte, plush velvet, as the two textures underscore and enhance each other when paired.

Ingredients
Silk or velvet scarf to embellish
40 g size 11° or 8° seed beads,
      either a single color or "bead
      soup" mix (M)
20 g size 11° or 8° seed beads, one
      color that contrasts with the M
      beads (C)
Drop beads or fire-polished beads
      (about 4mm), 3 per linear inch
      (2.5 cm) along the edge of the
      scarf (D)
Sewing or beading thread to
      match scarf

Tools
Size 10 beading needle

Setup
Mise en place (see page 8), using
      sewing thread

1 *Attach the picot base* (This step is optional, as the vertical netting can be done directly from the scarf's edge. To omit the picot base, anchor the thread at the corner of the scarf and skip ahead to Step 2.)

Anchor the thread to the corner of the scarf using a knot. Pick up 3M. Sew through the edge of the scarf one bead's width away. Pass back through the last bead. Pick up 2M. Sew through the edge of the scarf a bead's width away. Pass back through the last bead (Figure 1). Repeat for entire edge. Before finishing the last inch, count the number of picot high beads. Fit the necessary number of picots in that last inch to leave a number divisible by three or four plus one extra (because the first one doesn't count) so that the netting will end on the last high bead. Step up into the high bead to begin netting.

2 *Make the netted fringe.*
Row 1: Pick up 5M, 1C five times, then *pick up 1D (or 3M for a decorative picot at the point of your netting). Pass back through the last C bead (Figure 2).

Row 2: Pick up 2 sequences of 5M, 1C, 5M. Skip the next C bead and pass back through the third-to-last C bead of the previous row. Pick up 2 more sequences of 5M, 1C, 5M. Skip the next C bead of the previous row and pass through the following C bead. Pick up 5M. If you started with the picot edging and the number of high beads is divisible by 3, skip the next 2 high beads of the picot edge and pass through the third one; if the number is divisible by 4, skip the next 3 and pass through the fourth one. If you skipped the picot edging, pass through the scarf edge ½" (1.3 cm) from the last stitch through the fabric.

Row 3: Pick up 5M, 1C, 5M. Pass through the corresponding C bead. Pick up 5M, 1C, 5M. Pass through the corresponding C bead. Pick up 5M and 1C and repeat from* across the edge of the scarf (Figure 3).

Weave in the thread.

Figure 1

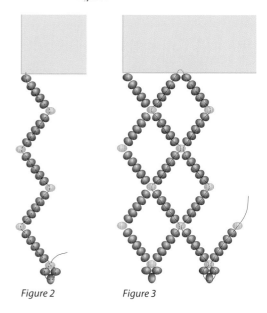

Figure 2   Figure 3

Four

Spiral Rope

Spirals are a commonly occurring motif in tubular beadwork, but this stitch, named for the beloved spiral, is not tubular at all. From its appearance you would guess it's a strand of beads embellished with descending and spiraling bead loops. But appearances can be deceiving.

Spiral rope is woven with 1 base bead and one segment at a time, growing by 1 base bead per stitch. Their proportion to each other determines how full or sparse the result will be.

If the segment is slightly shorter than the base unit, the spiral will be lush. If the segment is longer than the base unit, leggier results reveal more of the base. Of course, wider beads in a segment produce fuller results.

Start by picking up a base unit (we'll say 4A) and a segment (B-C-B) and pass through the base unit again (Figure 1). Take this opportunity to compare the length of the base unit to the length of the segment.

Hereafter, *pick up 1 base bead and a segment. Pass through the top 3 base beads and the new base bead (Figure 2).

Push the new segment to one side before repeating from *. In a perfect world, you'd expect the base beads to be linear, for zippity-do-dah beadwork. Ah, life is beautiful but not perfect, so

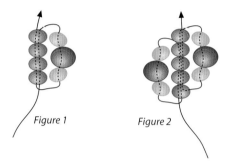

Figure 1   *Figure 2*

don't expect the base beads to align. This stitch is satisfying anyway.

At the end of each stitch, you'll push each new segment aside. It doesn't matter whether you move it left or right as long as you're consistent. Otherwise, the segments will not spiral. If you resume beading from the beginning, push each new segment in the opposite direction.

Make a perfectly beautiful necklace while experimenting with spiral stitch: Assemble a palette of beads and weave an inch of spiral, using a base of your choice and a similar size segment. Every inch or so, change a bead or two or the entire segment as shown at left. After a few inches, replace the base bead with a different color of the same size. In 4 stitches, the base will be entirely the new color. Weave a few inches with a leaf-shaped bead in the segment. Replace the leaf with a lentil, drop, tulip, or dagger bead. Or make a picot, loop or fringe mid-segment for several stitches.

If you're planning to combine several stitches in the same piece, finish by weaving three more segments into the same base beads without adding a new base bead. Use the "top" bead of each of the four new segments as the first round of tubular peyote stitch (see page 28) or tubular herringbone stitch (page 161). Add a loop/toggle clasp.

Spiraling Fire-Polished Rope Lariat

· · · · · · · · · · · · · · · · · · ·

Weave faceted beads and two sizes of seed beads into an opulent rope that works well at any length for earrings, bracelets, necklaces, or lariats. Try this tasseled, fringed lariat, then accessorize by weaving 1" (2.5 cm) to hang from an earring wire or weaving enough to meet around your wrist, using the tail and thread to attach a finding.

Ingredients

6 g size 11° seed beads (A)
25 g size 8° seed beads (B)
12 fire-polished faceted 4mm beads
    per inch (2.5 cm) of desired finished
    piece (about 400 for a lariat) (C)
1 g size 15° seed beads (D)
Beading thread
Focal bead (choose one to
    hang vertically)
2 M&M-size (6 x 10mm)
    beads (M)
Beaded toggle (like in the Saturn
    Bracelet on page 139 or
    Your Basic Beaded Bead or Toggle
    on page 40)
2" (5 cm) medium diameter (0.018"
    or 0.019") beading wire
2 crimp beads, to fit doubled
    beading wire

Tools

Size 10 beading needle
Crimping pliers

Setup

Mise en place (see page 8)

101

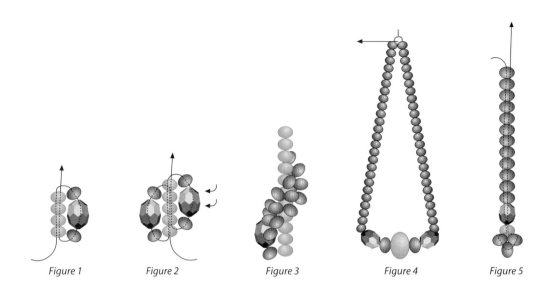

Figure 1   Figure 2   Figure 3   Figure 4   Figure 5

1 *Place one full unit of the base with one segment.* Pick up 4B (base) and A, C, A (segment).
Pass through 4B again (Figure 1). Push the segment
to one side. Choose either side—but stick with it.

2 *Add one bead to the base and a segment with
each stitch.* Pick up one base bead (B) and a
segment (A, C, A). Push the new beads close to the
work. Pass up through the top 4 base beads—the
top 3B of the work and the new B (Figure 2). Push
this new segment to the chosen side. ***Mantra: Pick
up a base bead and a segment. Push them close to
the work. Pass through the top beads of the base,
plus the new base bead. Push the segment aside.***

Repeat until the rope measures 29" (75 cm).
Weave 7 more stitches using 3A as the segment
(Figure 3).

3 *Weave closure loop.* Weave the thread through
the beads, making half hitches, and exit a B
bead ½" (1.3 cm) from the top. Pick up 40D. Pass
through 1B bead again. Weave a round of circular
peyote stitch (see page 28) off this loop that's large
enough to accommodate the toggle.

4 *Add the focal bead and fringe tassel.*
Prepare the focal bead by creating a finding
(see page 26). Attach the focal bead at the end of
the spiral. Thread 2' (61 cm) beading thread on a
needle and fold tape over the tail. Pass through the
loop of wire that extends from the bottom of the
focal bead. (Each of the following fringes will pass
through this loop.) Add fringe until the tassel looks
lush, sampling each of the methods below at least
once.

Looped fringe
Pick up 1" (2.5 cm) of D, 1C, 1A, 1M, 1A, 1C, and another 1" (2.5 cm) of D. Pass through the loop again
(Figure 4). Pick up 1" (2.5 cm) of D, 1A, 1B, 1C, 1B, 1A,
and another 1" (2.5cm) of D. Pass through the
loop again.

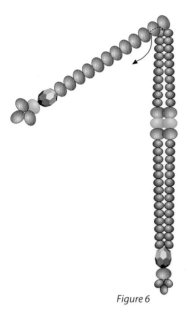

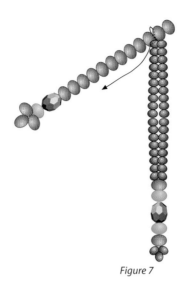

Figure 6   *Figure 7*   *Figure 8*

Straight fringe

Pick up 12A, 1C, 1B, 3A. Pass back through 1B, 1C, 12A (Figure 5).

Pointed loop fringe

Pass through the first A of the straight fringe. Pick up 10D, 1B, 1A, 1B, 13D, 1C, 1A, 3D. Pass back through 1A and 1C. Pick up 13D, 1B, 1A, 1B, 10D. Pass through the first and second A bead of the straight fringe (Figure 6). Pick up 18D, 1A, 1B, 1C, 1B, 1A, 3D. Pass back through 1A, 1B, 1C, 1B, 1A. Pick up 18D. Pass through the next A bead of the straight fringe (Figure 7).

Branched Fringe

Pick up 11D, 1A. Pass back through the last 4D. Pick up 4D, 1B, 3D. Pass back through 1B, 4D, and the seventh through first of the initial 11D (Figure 8).

When you have finished placing the fringe, weave in the thread, making half hitches, and trim close.

5 Attach the toggle. Remove the tape from the tail. Thread the tail on a needle. Pick up several A beads for a shank, the toggle, and another A turning bead. Pass back through the toggle and seed beads and through several beads of the lariat. Pass up through the beads and toggle several more times before weaving in the tail, making half hitches, and trimming the thread close.

> ## Try this . . .
>
> There is an alternative to pushing the new beads close to the work before passing through the required number of base beads and the new base bead: after picking up the base bead and new segment, pass up through the requisite base beads, pull the thread, placing the new beads, and now pass through the new base bead. Though this seems to require an additional step, some beaders prefer it.

Double Spiral Roll-On Bangle

Why settle for one spiral, when you can design two compatible spirals to chase each other around your wrist? This produces a heftier rope but grows only one base bead in length for every two segments added. For an exciting piece, consider making the two segments very different from each other. This bangle is flexible, making it a breeze to slide on and a pleasure to wear.

Ingredients
75 each of two colors 4mm faceted, fire-polished beads (A, B)
110 size 6° seed beads (C)
300 each of two colors size 11° seed beads to complement A and B (a, b)
Focal bead, 1–1½" (2.5–3.8 cm) wide from hole to hole and ½" (1.3 cm) tall
Power Pro or Fireline beading thread
3" .019 beading wire
2 crimp beads

Tools
Size 10 beading needle
Crimping pliers

Setup
Mise en place (see page 8)

1 *Place one full unit of the base with both segments.* Pick up 4C (base). Pick up 2a, 1A, 2a (Segment A). Pass through 4C (base) again (Figure 1). Push Segment A to the left. Pick up 2b, 1B, 2b (Segment B). Pass through 4C again (Figure 2).

2 *Add a base bead and a segment A.* Rotate the work so that Segment A is on the right of the base and segment B is on left.

Pick up 1C (one base bead) and a Segment A (2a, 1A, 2a). Push them close to the work.

Pass through the top 3C of the base and the new C (Figure 3). Because the base was 4 beads, pass through 4 base beads each time a Segment A is added.

3 *Add Segment B without adding a base bead.* Rotate the work so that Segment B is on the right of the core and Segment A is on left. Pick up a Segment B (2b, 1B, 2b), without a C. This places Segment B on the same level as Segment A, so that both segments arise from the same base beads. Pass up through the top 4 base beads.

Repeat Steps 2 and 3 until the piece reaches your desired length, allowing for the additional length of the focal bead. In general, 1" (2.5 cm) plus the wrist measurement is ample to slide on and a pleasure to wear. For example, if the wrist measures 6¼" (16 cm), the inside diameter of the work needs to be 7¼" (18.5 cm) to slide over the hand. If the focal bead is ¾" (2 cm) long, 6½" (16.5 cm) of beadwork must be woven to equal a finished piece of 7¼" (18.5 cm).

4 *Attach the focal bead to finish the bangle.* Prepare the focal bead by creating a finding (see page 26). Pass through one wire loop of the finding,

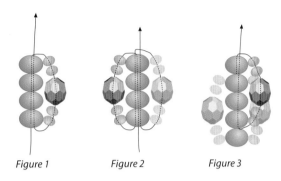

Figure 1   *Figure 2*   *Figure 3*

then pass back into the beadwork and weave the thread in. Slide the tape off the tail. Thread the tail on a needle. Pass through the other wire loop, then pass back into the beadwork and weave the tail in, making half hitches.

Try this . . .

My student, Susan, alternated segments A and B, but pushed them each to the same side. The single spiral with alternating segments was interesting and not what she expected. Mistakes are fodder for creativity. Welcome each "oops."

Don't try this . . .

My student, Jill, tried pushing each A segment to the right and each B segment to the left. For 1" (2.5 cm) or so it was interesting, but the beadwork became so crowded that it was self-limiting.

Luscious Leafy Pearl Bracelet

• • • • • • • • • • • • • •

Combine several shapes and sizes of leaves and pearls in a free-form weave, adding multiple segments into the same base beads. The loss of the full spiraling effect is a small price to pay for the full and opulent bracelet that results from placing as many segments as possible in each set of base beads.

Ingredients
5 g size 11° seed beads (A)
8 g size 8° seed beads in a complementary color (B)
60 leaves in many styles and finishes (L)
60 pearls, drilled both lengthwise and widthwise (P)
Beaded toggle bar of your choice. (Directions for
    the toggle shown here appear on page 40).
Power Pro 10# beading thread

Tools
Size 12 beading needle

Setup
Mise en place (see page 8)

1 *Place one full unit of the base with one segment.* Each of the segments in this piece will be either 2A, 1L, 2A, or 2A, 1P, 2A. Pick up 4B (base) and one segment. Pass through the 4B again (Figure 1).

2 *Add a base bead and a segment.* Pick up 1B and a segment. Push them close to the work. Pass through the top 3B of the core and the new B.

3 *Add extra segments to the same base in a free-form fashion, at will.* Pick up a segment (without a B) and pass through the top 4B (base beads). Push each new segment to the right before adding another (Figure 2).

Repeat Steps 2 and 3 until bracelet reaches your

desired length, placing two or more segments on the same core beads before adding another core bead. With the thread exiting from the top of the last core bead, pick up at least 2B to use as a shank and pass through the toggle. Turn and pass back through the toggle and shank, catching threads of the toggle to attach it. Pass through the shank and toggle several more times until it is secure, then weave in the thread, making half hitches.

4 *Weave a closure loop.* Remove the tape from the tail. Thread the tail on a needle. Pick up 5A, 1B, 2A, 1B, 2A, 3B, 2A, 1B, 2A, 1B, 2A. Pass through the base to exit the end of the bracelet.

Weave tubular peyote stitch (see page 28) around the loop. Weave in the tail, making half hitches.

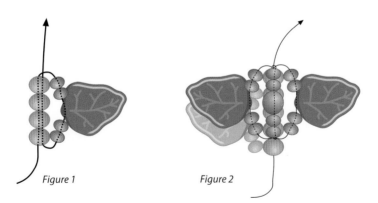

Figure 1   *Figure 2*

Try this . . .

In a free-form spirit, consider making fringe between base beads, as in the Carpet of Beads Bracelet on page 36!

Five

Right-Angle Weaves

There are two types of right-angle weave that produce the same finished bead-work. They do, however, use very different thread paths. Cross-needle weaving, or double-needle right-angle weave, is made using two needles on opposite ends of the same length of beading thread. Single-needle right-angle weave passes through the beads in alternating circular paths.

Some beaders who find it confusing to change directions with each stitch, as in single-needle right-angle weave, prefer to weave all their right-angle work using two needles.

On the other hand, I prefer single-needle right-angle weave to cross-needle weave. For the first two years that I experimented with Fireline, the only times it broke were in cross-needle weave. I couldn't determine the cause: It could be that the thread was split when crossing the needles. It could be that Kevlar factor—the thread will sever itself when crossed. It could be a nick in the bead edge or a sharp hole. It didn't, however, happen in identical work in single-needle right-angle weave.

Weaving with a single needle involves traveling in paths that alternate between clockwise and counterclockwise. Double-needle may work up faster, but it doesn't provide sufficient passes through the beads to hold them together should the thread break.

Try both methods in this chapter, beginning with cross-needle and progressing to single-needle right-angle weave (beginning on page 118), and see which one you prefer.

Cross-Needle Weaving

This simple stitch will make you yearn for ambidexterity. To start the stitch, center a finding or 1 bead on a wingspan of thread with a needle at each end. Pick up a bead on each needle, then cross the needles in yet another bead; repeat for desired length. This fast, friendly, and versatile weave produces a single row of right-angle weave.

When only 8" (20.5 cm) of thread remains on the needles and you need to add new thread, center another wingspan in the last common bead. Weave the abandoned threads into the work.

Enjoy these three simple and rewarding projects, using gemstones, glass, pearls, and crystals; they're wonderful for whipping up gifts to suit anyone's taste.

Embellishing cross-needle woven work leads to exciting necklace designs and adds the extra advantage of reinforcing the work. A plain chain of beads becomes an exotic and long-wearing lacy necklace if you create fringe and loops between the beads (Figure 1). You can also make the work curve gently—wonderful for short necklaces—by weaving a slightly smaller bead between each bead along one edge and a slightly larger one along the other edge (Figure 2).

It's easy to make an appealing diagonal pattern by using one color for a "north" bead of one unit, a "south" bead of an adjacent unit, and the bead they share, then using another color in the next unit (Figure 3).

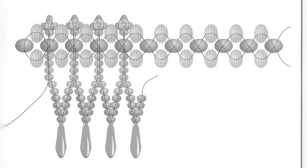

Figure 1

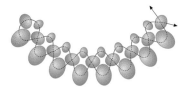

Figure 2

Figure 3

Cross-Needle Caution

Be sure to keep the stitch's name in mind and cross the needles in the bead—in a cross-needle weave class, there is always one beader who passes the needles through in the same direction (see below). The resulting beadwork is beautiful and reminiscent of the first rows of peyote or, depending on the number of beads per needle, netting. It is not, however, what was intended. It is essential that the needles pass through the common bead in opposite directions, making the sides perpendicular, to form a true cross-needle weave.

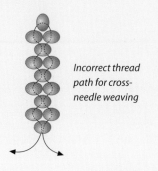

Incorrect thread path for cross-needle weaving

Dazzling Crystal Bracelet

· · · · · · · · · · · ·

 Practice working this weave with both hands—just thread a wingspan of thread with a needle on both ends, and you're off and running. Just about any bead works well with this stitch, but in this project we'll succumb to the bling of crystal bicones, benefiting from their perfect fit within this stitch.

Ingredients

Embellished pink version:

90 bicone-shaped 4mm crystals (C)

Beaded toggle of your choice in complementary colors

Plain green version:

72 fire-polished 4mm beads (F)

4 size 8° seed beads (B)

Bead tube connector finding with jump rings and lobster claw clasp

Both bracelets:

1 g size 11° seed beads in one or more colors (A)

Power Pro 10# beading thread

Tools

2 size 10 beading needles

Setup

 Follow directions for *mise en place (see page 8)*, omitting the tape. Place a needle on each end of the thread and slide them to 12" (30.5 cm) from the ends.

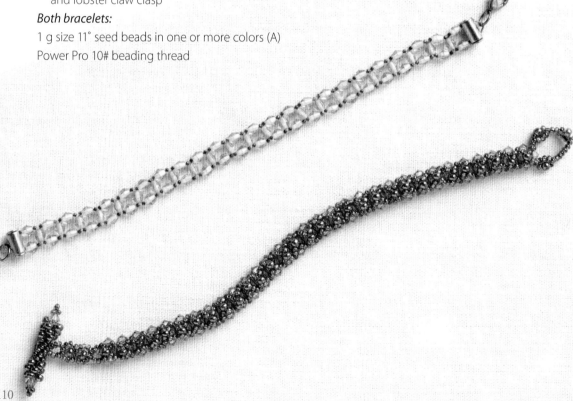

Figure 1

Figure 2

Figure 3

1 *Place the first end of the closure and prepare for the first unit.* **Pink bracelet:** Pick up 24A and center them on the thread. Pick up 1C with one needle and cross through it with the other needle. Pull this into a loop of beads with both threads extending from the C bead in opposite directions (Figure 1). Pass through all the beads again with one needle (or, if you wish, weave a round of peyote around the loop).

Green bracelet: Pick up 2B and center them on the thread.

2 *Place a unit with separate and shared beads.* **Pink bracelet:** With both needles extending from the C (common bead) in opposite directions, pick up 1C with each needle. Pick up another C bead with one needle and cross through this C bead with the other needle (Figure 2).

Repeat Step 2 until the piece is 1" (2.5 cm) short of the desired length of the bracelet.

Green bracelet: Pick up 1A, 1F, 1A with each needle. Pick up another F with one needle and cross through it with the other needle. Repeat until the bracelet is ½" (1.3 cm) short of the desired length. On the last unit, pick up and cross the needles through 2B.

3 *Embellish the bracelet (optional).* Look ahead and follow the directions on page 117 to embellish the top of the bracelet (as for the pink bracelet shown on page 110 and the pearl version on page 112) with another layer of cross-needle weave.

4 *Attach the closure and finish the bracelet.* **Pink bracelet:** Measure the finished length of your beaded toggle. Pick up 2A on each needle. Pair the needles and pick up enough A beads to equal half the length of the toggle bar. With both needles held together, pass through the middle of the toggle bar (Figure 3). Catching the thread between the beads (rather than using a turning bead), pass back through the toggle bar and the seed bead shank.

Working with one needle at a time, weave the ends into the work, making half hitches.

Green bracelet: Weave in the threads, using half hitches. Open one end of the bead tube finding and slip it onto the 2B. Close the end using pliers. Repeat at the other end.

Attach a jump ring to one loop on one finding. Attach a jump ring and lobster claw clasp to the other end.

Try this . . .

To make a variation on this bracelet, weave another piece, but this time, with crossed threads extending from a common C, pick up ½–1" (1.3–2.5 cm) seed beads on each needle before crossing them in another C. Resume weaving a 4C unit. Alternate between weaving seed bead and 4C segments.

To make the pearl version shown here, follow the directions for the pink bracelet, but substitute 4 to 6mm pearls for C and choose pearly seed beads for A.

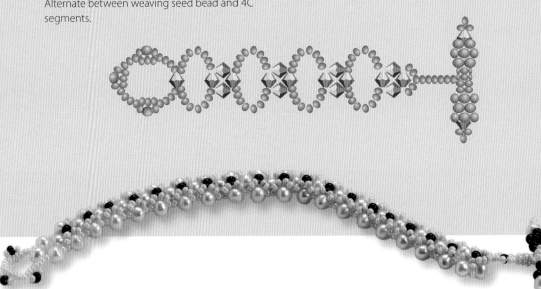

Gemstone Zigzag Bracelet

• • • • • • • • • • •

A zigzag pattern results when you purposefully cross-needle weave off-center. Uniform accent beads of a single color show it to greatest advantage. Choose a simple silver toggle closure to complement the movement of the beads.

Ingredients
45 6mm faceted fire-polished
    beads (C)
5 g size 8° seed beads (A)
Power Pro 10# beading thread
Sterling silver toggle clasp

Tools
2 size 10 beading needles
Permanent marker

Setup
Follow directions for *mise en place (see page 8)*, omitting the tape. Place a needle on each end of the thread and slide them to 12" (30.5 cm) from the ends.

1 *Place the ring half of the toggle clasp.* Fold the thread one-third of the way from one end and pass the fold into the loop of the toggle ring. Pass both ends of the thread through the fold, making a lark's head knot (Figure 1). Adjust the thread as necessary to ensure that the toggle is placed one-third down the distance from one end—the other end is twice as long, or two-thirds of the total. Using the permanent marker, mark 4" (10 cm) from the end of the short thread.

2 *Prepare for and weave the first unit.* Pass both needles through 1A, pick up 2A on each needle, and pick up 1C with one needle and cross through it with the other.

3 *Place additional units off-center.* Pick up 1A with the short thread; pick up 1A, 1C, 1A with the long thread; and pick up 1C with one needle and cross through it with the other (Figure 2).

    Repeat Step 3 until the beaded section of the piece is 1" (2.5 cm) less than the desired length of the bracelet.

4 *Attach the bar half of the clasp.* Pick up 2A with the short thread. Pick up 1A, 1C, 2A with the long thread. Holding both needles together, pick up 3A (or enough A to equal half the length of the bar). Remember that the bar will be folded along the shank, and both must pass all the way through the ring of the toggle before the bar is released to catch the ring. If the shank is absent or too short, the bar will not clear the ring to do its job.

    With each of the threads, make an individual half hitch knot on the loop of the bar closure. Weave back down the stem and into the beadwork, making half hitches (Figure 3).

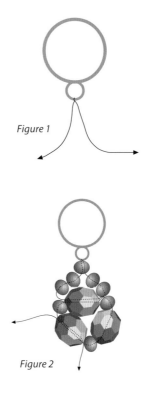

Figure 1

Figure 2

Try this . . .

This project works up easily in nearly any combination of accent bead and seed beads. The short thread always picks up a seed bead. The long thread always picks up a seed bead, an accent bead, a seed bead, an accent bead. Cross the short thread through the last accent bead.

Figure 3

Band of Pearls Ring and Crayola Beaded Rope Bracelet

Cross-needle weave a base to embellish with another layer of cross-needle weave. Weave a band of fancy seed beads to wear around a finger, adorning one surface with pearls. Weave a long strip of seed beads to embellish on both surfaces, creating a solid bead rope bracelet of surprising suppleness.

Ingredients

Ring

30–36 size 6° seed beads (C)
1 g size 11° seed beads (A)
1 g size 15° seed beads (B)
10–12 round 3mm pearls (P)

Rope

35 g size 6° seed beads (C)
10 g size 11° seed beads (A)
15 g size 8° seed beads (B)
Beaded bead or beaded toggle bar
Power Pro 10# beading thread

Tools

2 size 12 beading needles

Setup

For both the ring and rope: mise en place (see page 8), omitting the tape. Thread a needle on each end of the thread and slide them to 12" (30.5 cm) from the ends.

Figure 1

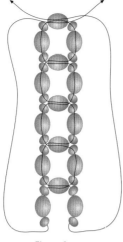

Figure 2

Ring

1 **Weave the base.** Center 1C on the thread. With each needle, pick up 1A, 1C, 1A. Cross the needles in a new C bead. Repeat Step 1 until the piece nearly fits around the finger (Figure 1).

2 **Close the ring.** Pick up 1A, 1C, 1A on each nee- dle. Cross the needles in the first C (Figure 2).

3 **Embellish the surface.** Pick up 2B on each needle. Pick up 1P and cross the needles in it (Figure 3). Pick up 2B on each needle. Cross the needles in the next C bead of the base (Figure 4).

Repeat this step all the way around the ring. Weave in the threads.

Bracelet

1 **Weave the base.** Center 3Cs on the thread. Pick up 1C with one needle and cross through it with the other (Figure 5). Pick up 1C on each needle. Pick up 1C with one needle and cross through it with the other.

Figure 3

Figure 4

Figure 5

Figure 6

Repeat until you reach the desired length. The rope portion of the bracelet shown here measures about 6½" (16.5 cm).

2 *Embellish the surface.* Pick up 2A on each needle. Pick up 1B with one needle and cross through it with the other needle. Pick up 2A on each needle. Cross them in the next common C bead (Figure 6).

Repeat for the length of the rope, flip it over, and repeat on the underside.

3 *Finish the bracelet.* Pick up 8A to create a shank and pass up through the beaded toggle. Turn and, catching a thread of the toggle, pass back through the toggle and the 8A. Weave in the thread, making half hitches. With a new length of thread on the opposite end, pick up enough B beads to make a loop that slides snugly over the toggle (or use peyote stitch, as on page 28) and pass back into the bracelet. Weave in the thread and tail, making half hitches.

Try this . . .

Even though this is the cross-needle weave chapter, consider this alternative approach to creating identical embellishment using a single needle. It works up faster and exercises your beady brain. After working the first step of the bracelet, follow these two steps to try this technique.

1 *Start to embellish the surface (the first pass). Work back across the piece toward the beginning.*
Pick up 2A, 1B, 2A and, if the thread is exiting the last C from right to left, enter the next C from right to left (Figure 7). Repeat for the entire length. When the first C is reached, flip the work over and repeat for the entire length on this surface.

2 *Finish embellishing the surface (the second pass).*
Pick up 2A and pass through B (from left to right, if you were previously working from right to left). Confirm that it was passed through in the correct direction by verifying that the hole is horizontal rather than vertical. Pick up 2A and pass through C (Figure 8). Continue down the bracelet's length. Weave in the thread and tail, making half hitches.

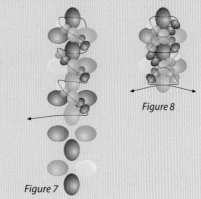

Figure 8

Figure 7

Single-Needle Right-Angle Weave

The squared and perpendicular composition of right-angle weave produces beadwork with the drape and flexibility of fine fabric that can nonetheless be structural and sculptural.

To envision how single-needle right-angle weave is created, envision two pairs of square-dancers facing off, the four points of a compass, or four sides of a square. Or remember the paper and pencil game connect-the-dots—beginning anywhere in the grid, one line connects two dots, and another is drawn at a right angle to the first. A third line perpendicular to the previous one creates a U shape. After a fourth line completes the square, a new square is built onto a side of the previous one. Adjacent beads lie perpendicular to each other.

Single Row

Start with 4 beads or sets of beads. (A set of beads is a sequence of beads that will repeat on each side of the unit.) Pass through all of them again, pulling them into a square ring. Pass through one or more again, exiting where another unit is to be added (Figure 1).

Pick up 3 more beads or sets of beads to add to the one just exited to make a new square. Pass through the bead from the original square, completing the new square. Pass through 2 of the new beads, exiting where another unit is to be added (Figure 2).

Additional Rows

To start a new row, pass through a bead at the bottom of a previously worked square; you will build off this bead, which becomes the top of the new

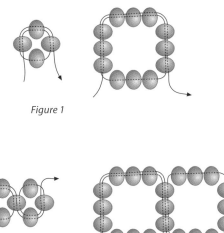

Figure 1

Figure 2

unit. Pick up 3 beads for the sides and pass through the base bead again (Figure 3). Each new unit in this row will have the top and one side already woven in. For the rest of the row, identify the 2 beads already in place and exit one. Pick up two new sides and pass through the two sides that were already woven in (Figure 4).

Try thinking of right-angle weave architecturally, as a bungalow motel. To double the size, build three walls onto one of the bungalow's existing walls. Add another unit by adding three walls to the far wall of the second unit. Repeat again and again, and in no time the bungalow becomes a hotel.

Never Go Straight

To travel through each side or each new bead, you will make a right turn. It is never an option to go straight. Correctly executed work has no thread passing through the center or between corners (see below).

With each side I pick up or pass through, I say in my head, "An up bead, an across bead, a down bead, an across bead, an up bead." *Mantra: up, across, down, across, up, across, down, across, up, across.* While it's not the trance-inducing repetition of peyote stitch or the zippity-do-dah of herringbone stitch (see page 161), it is fun to see where the next beads belong, then navigate through the work to get there and add what is necessary.

Right-Angle Weave in 3-D

For structural and sculptural constructions, a perpendicular unit can be built onto each unit (see below).

Connecting each of the perpendicular units results in solid beadwork, while other stitches may be flat, tubular, or hollow.

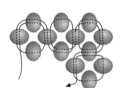

Figure 3

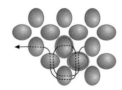

Figure 4

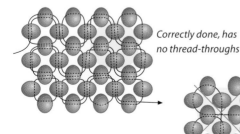

Correctly done, has no thread-throughs

Incorrectly done

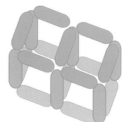

Three-dimensional right-angle weave

Round Beads in Right Angles Bracelet

Sample single-needle right-angle weave using big, round beads. Weaving with a single needle, you'll pass through several beads, going around one way before alternating and going in the opposite direction. Dizzying and fun.

Ingredients
5 g size 8° seed beads (A)
70 round 6mm beads (faux pearls, fire-polished or druk) (B)
Bead, button, or toggle for closure
Fireline or Power Pro 6# beading thread

Tools
Size 10 beading needle

Setup
Mise en place (see page 8)

120

Figure 1

1 *Place the first unit of Row 1.* Pick up B, A, B, A, B, A, B, A. Pass through the first 5 of these again, from the tail forward, and pull them into a ring. Regard the ring as square rather than round, with an A at each corner and a B at each side. The tail extends from a B, and the thread exits the opposing B of the ring (Figure 1).

Figure 2

2 *Add units to Row 1.* The thread exits the "far bead," where another unit will be added. From now on, one of the four sides of each unit will be already in place. For each new unit, you will add three sides to the one already present.

Pick up A, B, A, B, A, B, A. Enter the other end of the far bead, anchoring the 7 new beads to the far bead. Pass through 4 of the new beads, exiting the far bead (Figure 2).

Repeat for each additional unit until the bracelet reaches the desired length (allowing for the closure).

3 *Add Row 2.* Rather than exiting the far bead, exit a bottom bead. If you have woven an even number of units, the thread will exit on the right; with an odd number, the thread will exit on the left (Figure 3).

First unit: Exiting a bottom bead of previous row, pick up A, B, A, B, A, B, A. Enter the other end of the bottom bead, securing the 7 new beads to the bottom bead. Pass through 6 (if the first row contained an even number of units) or 2 (if there were an odd number of units) of the new beads again to exit the new unit (Figure 4).

Additional units: Until the end of the row, two sides of each new unit will already be in place. You will add two new sides each time.

Determine where to add the next unit. Exit one of the existing sides, identify the

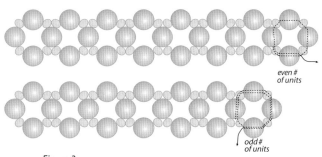

*even #
of units*

*odd #
of units*

Figure 3

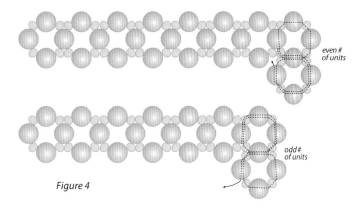

*even #
of units*

*odd #
of units*

Figure 4

121

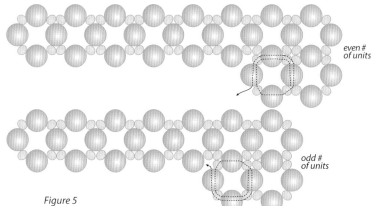

*even #
of units*

*odd #
of units*

Figure 5

second side, and pick up two new sides: A, B, A, B, A. Pass through the existing sides (Figure 5). Add an A between 2 B when necessary to maintain the pattern.

4 **Weave a slotted tab closure.** Exit an A from the end of the piece, toward the center. Pick up 1A and pass through the next A (Figure 6).

Pick up 3A, pass through the 3A of the previous row, and pass through the 3 new A again. Pick up 7A and pass through the 3A from the previous step and 6 of the 7 new beads again. This produces a row 5A wide (Figure 7). Weave 7 rows of square stitch (see page 138) off of these 5 beads.

Building on only the first 2 beads of the 5-bead base, work square stitch for 8 more rows (adding only 2 new beads in each row) (Figure 8).

Weave the thread down to the last row of the 5-bead square-stitch base and exit from a bead at the opposite side. Square-stitch 8 rows, building on the last 2 beads of this row and adding only 2 beads per row, to mirror the other side.

Finish the tab by square-stitching across both 2-bead columns (Figure 9) for 2 rows, adding 4 beads on both rows.

At the opposite end of the bracelet, slide the tape from the tail. Thread the tail on a needle and pick up 13A. Pass back through the other B on this end and the next A. Pick up 2A and pass through 3 of the 13A (Figure 10). Square-stitch 7A (Figure 11).

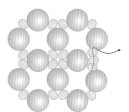

Figure 6

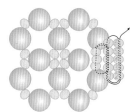

Figure 7

Figure 8

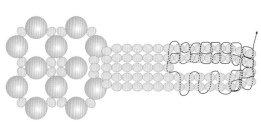

Figure 9

122

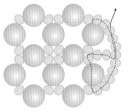

Figure 10

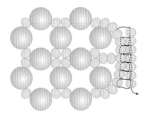

Figure 11

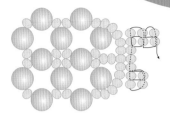

Figure 12

Figure 13

Square-stitch 2A. Weave through 5 beads and square-stitch 2 rows of 2A on the last 2A in the row. This creates a 3A-wide buttonhole-shaped opening, flanked by a 2-bead-wide row of square-stitch (Figure 12). Finish with 4 rows, 7 beads wide.

Pick up 5A and pass through the fourth and fifth again to square stitch the sixth and seventh beads just strung.

Pass through the sixth and seventh beads again to square-stitch them to the 2A of the previous row (Figure 13).

5 *Weave and attach a toggle.* Repeat the *mise en place*. Pick up 10A and peyote stitch 8 rows (follow the directions for Beaded Bead Toggle on page 40). Roll up the ends and zip shut.

From the midpoint of the toggle, pick up 2A (shank beads) and weave into the center bead of the fourth row of the narrow tab. Pass back up through the 2A and weave into the toggle. Pass through the center. Pick up 1B and a turning bead. Pass back through the B and the toggle bar, then pick up 1B and a turning bead. Pass back through the B and the toggle bar. Weave through the 2A shank and into the narrow tab, making half hitches.

Try this . . .

The alternate Step 2 offered at the end of the Band of Pearls Ring and Crayola Beaded Rope Bracelet projects on page 115 offers a single-needle method of duplicating the layered cross-needle weave

embellishment. The pearl piece shown below was embellished this way, using only one pass instead of two, down one row to place 22 rice pearls and 88 size 8° seed beads. The second row was embellished from the opposite direction to produce a mirror-image.

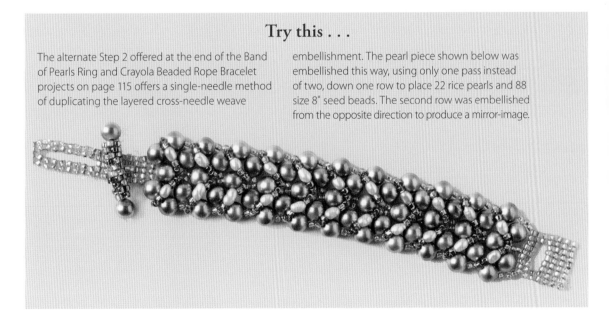

Jewels in R.A.W. Windows

• • • • • • • • • • • •

This is almost the inverse of the Round Beads in Right Angles Bracelet: Instead of weaving with jewels and embellishing with seed beads, weave little seed-bead windows to frame each jewel embellishment. Each side of the window is 3 beads long. Start with a ring of 12 beads, but think of it as a square rather than a circle. Add three sides onto one of the original sides, completing another window. In the first window the needle travels counterclockwise, and in completing the next window the needle travels clockwise.

Ingredients
8 g size 11° or 8° seed
    beads (A)
60–85 3–5mm crystals (B)
Power Pro 6# beading thread
Clasp or button

Tools
Size 12 beading needle

Setup
Mise en place (see page 8)

1 *Establish the first unit.* Pick up 12A, which will become four sides of 3A each. Pass through the first 9A again, pulling them into a square (Figure 1).

2 *Add units in Row 1.* Pick up 9A (3 sides of 3 beads each). Pass through the 3A from the far side of the previous unit again, securing the three new sides to the established side. Pass through two of the new sides, exiting the far side that will be part of the next unit (Figure 2).

Repeat Step 2 for the desired length of your bracelet, minus the measurement of your chosen clasp or closing, alternating between clockwise and counter-clockwise.

3 *Add another row.* Pass through last unit to exit a bottom side. Pick up 9A (3 sides of 3 beads each). Pass through the 3 beads that formed the bottom of the last unit again, securing the 3 new sides onto the existing one. Pass through the beads to exit the side where the next unit is to be.

4 *Weave across additional row.* From now on, because two sides are already in place for the next unit, pick up only 6A (2 sides of 3 beads each).

Pass through the 2 sides that are already in place, attaching the 2 new sides onto the 2 existing ones (Figure 3).

Repeat Step 4 across entire row, changing direction with every new unit. Pass through the beads to exit the far side where the next unit is to be. On some units it will be necessary to pass through 5 sides to arrive at the far side where the next unit is to be, while for others you will pass through 3 sides.

Weave Row 3 by repeating the directions for Steps 3 and 4.

Embellish with Crystals

Make several half hitches while weaving your way to one of the groups of 3 beads along the end of the bracelet.

Pick up 1A, 1B, 1A (the embellishment). Cross the "window" diagonally and pass through the opposite side of the window to exit in the identical corner of the next window (Figure 4).

Embellish the entire row this way, then embellish the other 3 rows this way. Follow the existing thread path to travel around the corner when you reach the end of a row to get to the next row.

Finishing

To finish the bracelets pictured here, one uses a basket-weave crimp end finding (see page 27), while the other is closed with a pair of flat disc beads sewn on one end with a seed bead shank (see the Stripy Bracelet on page 164) that fits within a loop of beads on the opposite end.

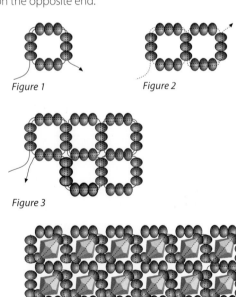

Figure 1

Figure 2

Figure 3

Figure 4

Fashion Magazine Earrings

• • • • • • • • • • • •

Mary came to class with a folder of fashion magazine pages filled with jewelry she wanted to interpret in beads. I asked her to choose one. Rendered in seed beads, this lovely pair of earrings, reminiscent of a gold pair in the Tiffany catalog, offers a wonderful exploration of right-angle weave. By the end of the first earring you'll be eager to whip up the second of the pair and have a deeper understanding of right-angle weave.

Ingredients
15 g size 8° seed beads (A)
Fireline 4# or 6# beading thread
2 earring wires

Tools
Size 10 beading needle

Setup
Mise en place (see page 8)

techniques
Right-angle weave, fringe,
square stitch, right-angle
weave increases

1 *Weave a row of right-angle weave three units long.* Pick up 4A. Pass through 3 of the A again. The tail exits from the bottom. The thread exits from the bottom of the far bead (Figure 1). Pick up 3A and pass through the far bead of the first unit again. Pass through 2 of the 3A just added, exiting the new far bead. Pick up 3A and pass through the far bead and 2 of the 3A just added.

2 *Weave a second row.* Pass through an additional bead of the third unit, exiting a bottom bead (Figure 2).

Pick up 3A and pass through the bottom bead of the first row again. Pass through one of the beads just added again. Remember that every single bead requires a 90° (or right angle) turn. Each bead is either an "up bead," an "across bead," or a "down bead."

Never go straight. To remember this rule, I say this mantra with each bead I pick up or pass through, **"across, up, across, down, across, up, across."**

Two sides of the next unit are already in place, so pick up only 2A. The far bead of the first unit of the row becomes the second bead of this new unit. Pass through the bottom bead of the second unit of Row 1 and the far bead of the previous unit (Figure 3). The 2A just added are now bottom and far beads of this unit.

Pass through these 2A and the remaining bottom bead of Row 1. Notice that it's necessary to pass through varying numbers of beads to exit the right spot (the far bead) to add a unit (Figure 4). Pick up 2A. Pass through the far bead of the previous unit and the last bottom bead of Row 1, then pass through the 2 new beads again.

3 *Make a fringe from each south bead.* Exiting the south bead of the unit just created, pick up 9A for the length of the fringe. Pick up 4 additional

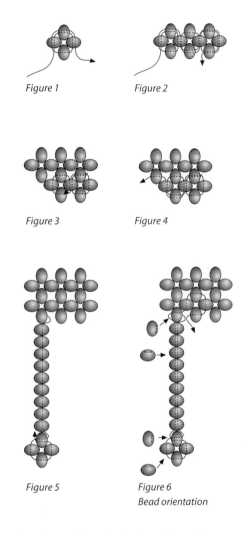

Figure 1

Figure 2

Figure 3

Figure 4

Figure 5

Figure 6
Bead orientation

beads and pass through the first of these four again (Figure 5).

Pass back through the 9A of the fringe beads, and pass through the bottom bead of the earring again through the opposite side of where you exited. Follow the thread path to weave through the beads of the second row to exit the next bottom bead (Figure 6).

Repeat Step 3 on each of the bottom beads to make 3 right-angle woven units. Weave down through the newest fringe to exit its bottom bead.

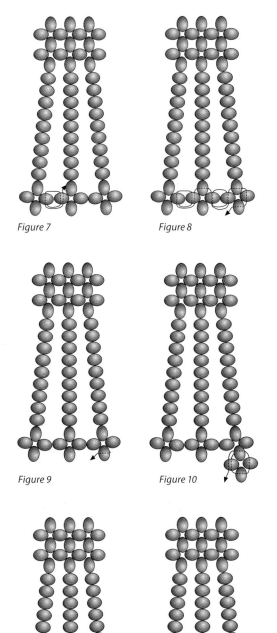

Figure 7

Figure 8

Figure 9

Figure 10

Figure 11

Figure 12

4 **Connect the units at the bottom of each fringe with single needle-ladder stitch (see page 153).** Align two adjacent units so that their side beads touch. Weave the thread to exit the bead touching the adjacent fringe's bead. Pass through the adjacent bead, linking them using ladder stitch (Figure 7).

Weave through the beads, following the thread path around the right-angle weave unit, and repeat (Figure 8).

5 **Weave a second row of right-angle weave off this row, with increases.** Note that the adjacent units in Row 1 do not share beads. In Row 2, you'll add a unit between each pair, resulting in 5 units in this row. Exit a bottom bead of Row 1 (Figure 9).

Pick up 3 beads and pass through the bottom bead again. Pass through one of the new beads (Figure 10).

You have added one unit. Make additional units in the spaces between the remaining units. To do this, pick up 3 beads and pass through the far bead again (Figure 11).

*Pass through 2 of the 3 new beads, exiting the far bead. Pass through the adjacent bottom bead from the previous row. As two sides of the new unit are already woven in place, pick up only 2 new beads.

Pass through the far bead of the previous unit, the bottom bead of the previous row, and one of the new beads again, exiting the far bead of the newest unit* (Figure 12).

To add an additional free-standing unit between the units already placed, pick up 3 beads and pass through the far beads again (Figure 13).

Repeat from * to * to create the fifth unit. Pass through and exit a bottom bead.

techniques
right-angle weave, fringe,
square stitch, right-angle
weave increases

Repeat Step 3, producing identical fringes off the 5 south beads from the previous row (Figure 14).

Repeat Step 4 to connect the 5 units at the bottom of the fringe.

Repeat Step 5 to weave a second row off the connected units, increasing by 1 unit between each existing pair, to create 9 units of right-angle weave.

Repeat Step 3, producing identical fringes off the 9 bottom beads. Weave in the thread, making half hitches.

6 *Use the tail to create a small loop to fit onto the earring wire.* Slip the tape off the tail. Thread the tail on a needle. Weave through the first row to exit the middle north bead. Pick up 3A, the earring wire, 3A. Pass through the middle north bead again (Figure 15). Weave in the tail, making half hitches.

Make a second earring to match the first.

Try this . . .

Make a pair using 3 strands of marcasite charlottes and a size 13 needle. The size of the beads makes it more challenging, but the resulting earrings are worth it.

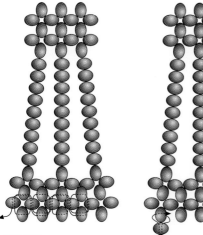

Figure 13

Figure 14

Figure 15

129

Six

Triangle Weave

||||||||||||||||||||||||||||||||||||||||||||||||||||||||||||||||||||||||||||||||||||||||||||||||||||||||||||||

This less-than-right-angle weave is composed of three-sided rather than four-sided units. Begin with three beads (or sets of beads). Pass through all of them again, pulling them into a triangular ring. Pass through one or more of the three sides to exit the side where another unit is to be added.

Make rows of triangle weave by adding two sides to a unit and passing through the new sides before adding another unit.

Triangle-woven circles are formed by adding two sides to a unit and then alternating between passing through only the first of the new sides again before adding another unit, and passing through both new sides again before adding another unit.

Each triangle is a wedge in a circle (think of pizza slices). Each triangle or wedge has three sides: two are spokes that join in the center, and the third is the outer edge or a portion of the circumference (Figure 1).

Row of triangle weave

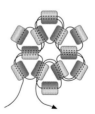

Circle of triangle weave (Figure 1)

Flaming Cocktail Ring

· · · · · · · · · · · ·

Four conjoined circles, each composed of five wedges of crystals, make a domed ring full of bling. You may decide to substitute a Japanese drop or magamata for the bicone crystals pictured here—the resulting bubbly-looking beadwork magnifies the light and color for a beautiful piece.

Ingredients
1 g orange size 11° seed beads (A)
3 g red-lined amber size 8° triangle seed beads (B)
20 bicone 4mm crystals (C)
1 round faceted 6mm bead (D)
Power Pro 6# beading thread

Tools
Size 10 beading needle
Setup
Mise en place (see page 8)

Note: A "side" in this project is a C or D bead. Sides are separated by B beads.

1 *Weave the first circle.*
Wedge 1: Pick up 1B, 1C, 1B, 1C, 1B, 1C (3 sides) and pass through the first 4 beads again to pull them into a triangle (Figure 1).
Wedge 2: The thread is exiting the first side of the unit (C) you're about to weave. Pick up 1B, 1C, 1B, 1C, 1B (2 sides). Pass through the first side (C) again. Pass through the 2 sides of the new unit (B, C, B, C) (Figure 2).
Wedge 3: The thread is exiting the first side of the next unit (C). Pick up 1B, 1C, 1B, 1D, 1B (2 sides). Pass through the first side (C) again. Pass through only 1 side of this new unit (B, C) (Figure 3).
Wedge 4: Repeat Wedge 2.
Wedge 5: Pick up 1B. Pass through the side (C) of the first triangle.

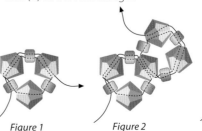

Figure 1   Figure 2   Figure 3

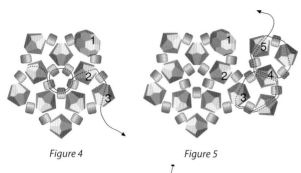

| Figure 4 | Figure 5 |

Figure 6

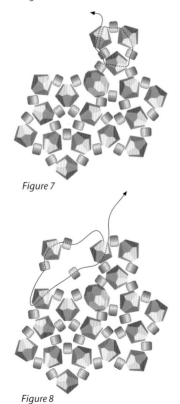

Figure 7

Figure 8

Pick up 1B, 1C, 1B (1 side). Pass through the last C and B beads to complete this unit. Pass through the 5B in the center—we'll call it "once around the inner circle."

2 Add a second circle.
Wedges 1 and 2: Consider the D bead to be the first of the five spokes that a new circle will be built around. You will notice that three spokes are already present, making up two wedges. After passing once around the inner circle, pass through the C labeled Spoke 2, and the B and the C beads labeled spoke 3 (Figure 4).

Wedge 3: The thread is exiting the first side of the next unit (C). Pick up 1B, 1C, 1B, 1C, 1B (2 sides). Pass through the first side (C) again. Pass through 2 sides (B, C, B, C) of this new unit.

Wedge 4: The thread is exiting the first side of the next unit (C). Pick up 1B, 1C, 1B, 1C, 1B (2 sides). Pass through the the first side (C) again. Pass through 1 side (B, C) of this new unit (Figure 5).

Wedge 5: Pick up 1B, 1C, 1B (1 side), and pass through 1D. Pick up 1B. Pass through the C bead labled spoke 5 in this unit and the next B and C beads (Figure 6).

3 Add a third circle.
Wedges 1–3: The first 4 spokes, making up 3 wedges, are already in place for this circle.

Wedge 4: The thread is exiting the first side of the next unit. Pick up 1B, 1C, 1B, 1C, 1B (2 sides). Pass through the first side (C) again. Pass through 1 side (B, C) of this new unit (Figure 7).

Wedge 5: Pick up 1B, 1C, 1B (1 side). Pass through the C bead that completes the circle. Pick up 1B. Pass through the opposite C bead (Figure 8). There are 2B at the end of this C. Skip the newest B and pass through the other B and C.

4 Add a fourth circle.
Wedges 1–3: The first 4 spokes, making up 3 wedges, are in place for this circle.

Wedge 4: The thread is exiting the first side of the next unit. Pick up 1B, 1C, 1B, 1C, 1B (2 sides). Pass through the first side (C) again. Pass through 1 side (B, C) of this new unit.

Wedge 5: Pick up 1B, 1C, 1B (1 side). Pass through the C that completes the circle. Pick up 1B. Pass through the fifth spoke C and the new B and C beads (Figure 9).

Weave around the periphery of the beadwork, pulling tight so that the piece forms a dome. Weave through the beads, making half hitches to anchor the thread. Weave once around each of 3 inner circles.

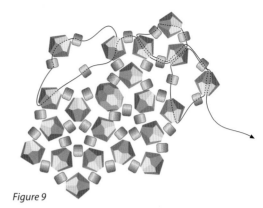

Figure 9

5 **Work the band of right-angle weave.** Exit a B at one end of the dome pointing outwards. Pick up 4B (side), 2B (across), and 4B (opposite side). Pass through both B at the end of the dome. Pass through 4B (side) and 2B (across) again (Figure 10). *Pick up side, across, and side segments (10B total). Pass through the last across segment, the new side segment, and the new across segment (10B). Repeat from * for desired length (to fit around wearer's finger) (Figure 11).

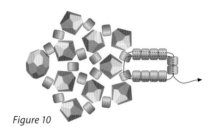

Figure 10

6 **Size the band.** Remove the last 6B. Pass through the 2B at the opposite end of the dome. Pick up 4B and pass through the last 2B across beads. Pass through the new side and both B of the dome again (Figure 12).

Pick up 2A, 1B, 2A, cross the strand diagonally across the unit, and pass through the next pair of across beads. Repeat this for entire length (Figure 13). Check the fit.

If the ring is a little too loose, pull out these diagonals and use a smaller set of beads such as A, B, A, or 4A. If it's a little too tight, allow the diagonal to be a little longer than 2A, 1B, 2A by adding a bead or two to the diagonal. The size can be finessed perfectly by executing the diagonals properly. When the ring fits perfectly, weave in the thread and tail, making half hitches.

Figure 11

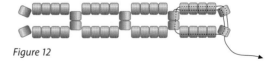

Figure 12

Figure 13

Five Easy Pieces Choker

● ● ● ● ● ● ● ● ● ● ● ●

Weave a circle composed of six wedges of triangle weave, with one wedge "gone missing." Weave more triangles off an edge, but before placing the sixth one to complete this conjoined circle, weave more triangles off an edge. Weave enough so the ends meet at your throat. Bead a toggle so beautiful you'll wear it in the front: a fringed, peyote-stitched bar to dangle through a crystal wheel like Amy's Fabulous Faux Pas (see page 135). Amy invented this while trying to make one of Nikia Angel's Sparkly Wheels from memory—a happy accident.

Ingredients

18 4mm faceted fire-polished beads per inch (2.5 cm) for your desired necklace length in two or more colors, used randomly (A)

10 g size 11° seed beads (B)

Fireline or Power Pro 6# or 10# beading thread

Tools

Size 10 beading needle

Setup

Mise en place (see page 8)

1 *Triangle weave an incomplete circle of 5 wedges.* Pick up 1B, 1A, 1B, 1A, 1B, 1A. Pass through the first B and A beads again, forming a triangle. Pick up 1B, 1A, 1B, 1A, 1B, and pass through the A being tied onto (Bead 1 in Figure 1). Pass through the first new B and A. Pick up 1B, 1A, 1B, 1A, 1B, and pass through the A being tied onto. Pass through new B, A, B, A. Pick up 1B, 1A, 1B, 1A, 1B, and pass through the A being tied onto. Pass

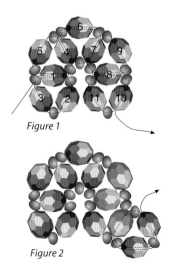

Figure 1

Figure 2

through the first new B and A. Pick up 1B, 1A, 1B, 1A, 1B and pass through the A being tied onto. Pass through the first new B and A (Figure 1).

2 *Triangle weave additional partial circles.* The fifth edge bead of the previous circle serves as the third spoke of the next circle*. Pick up 1B, 1A, 1B, 1A, 1B. Pass through the A being tied onto and the B, A, B, A just added (Figure 2). Pick up 1B, 1A, 1B, 1A, 1B. Pass through the A being tied onto and B, A of the new beads (Figure 3). Pick up 1B, 1A, 1B, 1A, 1B, and pass through the A being tied onto and the first B, A of the new beads (Figure 4).

Repeat from * until the piece measures 1" (2.5 cm) short of desired length to fit around wearer's neck.

3 *Weave Amy's Fabulous Faux Pas Wheel.* Exiting the last A of the work, pick up 3B, 1A, 3B, 1A, 3B, 1A, 3B, 1A, 3B. Pass through the A of the work again, forming a ring. Step up by passing through the next 2B to exit from the center B of the 3 (Figure 5). The center B is the high bead for the next round. Pick up 5B and enter the high bead in the next 5B set. Repeat 4 times. Repeat all around again

on the other side of the base row, making a second set (Figure 6).

Step up through 3 new B, exiting from a high bead. Pick up 1B, 1A, 1B, and enter the next high bead. Repeat all around. Step up through the following 3B of the second set, and repeat 4 more times (Figure 7) to mirror the first side. Weave the thread in, making half hitches. Set the choker aside.

4 *Peyote stitch a toggle bar.* Repeat the *mise en place.* Pick up 16B. Weave 8 rows of two-drop peyote stitch (see page 28). Seamlessly connect the first and last rows into a narrow tube. Add 3–4 strands of fringe to one end. For each fringe leg, pick up 8–12 A, 1B, and 1A (turning bead). Pass back through the B and As to the toggle. Remove the tape from the tail of the choker. Thread the tail on a needle. Pick up 5B for a shank, pass through the midpoint of the toggle, and pick up 1B (turning bead). Pass back through the toggle and shank and back into the first A of the choker. Weave the thread into the work, making half hitches. Weave in the thread and tail of the toggle, making half hitches.

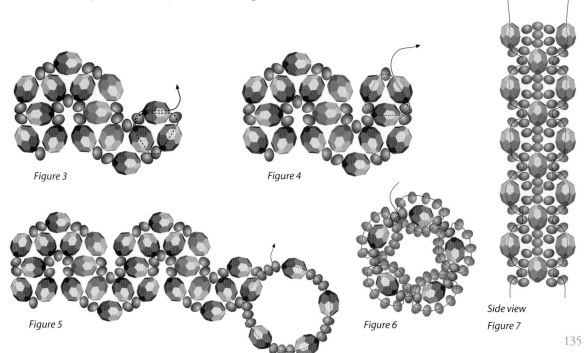

Figure 3

Figure 4

Figure 5

Figure 6

Side view
Figure 7

135

Penta-Petal Bead

• • • • • • • •

Six equilateral triangles woven into a round will lie flat. Omitting or adding units will make the beadwork convex or concave. To weave a nearly-round beaded bead, start with five triangles, then weave a second layer of triangles off the circumference beads. Fill the gap between circumference beads with a lined Japanese drop. Use the finished piece as you would any beaded bead.

Ingredients
15 fire-polished 2×4mm beads (A)
6 lined Japanese drops (B)
Fireline 10# beading thread

Tools
Size 10 beading needle

Setup
Mise en place (see page 8)

1 **Triangle weave a five-wedge circle.** Pick up 3A. Pass through the first and second again (Figure 1). * Pick up 2A. Connect them to the bead just passed through by passing through it (the bead of the first unit that your thread is exiting) again. Pass through the first A of the 2A just added again (Figure 2). Pick up 2A and connect them to the beads you just exited. Pass through both new A beads (Figure 3). Pick up 2A and connect them to the bead you just exited. Pass through 1 new A again (Figure 4). Pick up 1A and pass through the third side of the triangle, closing up the circle. Pass through both other sides of this newest triangle (Figure 5).

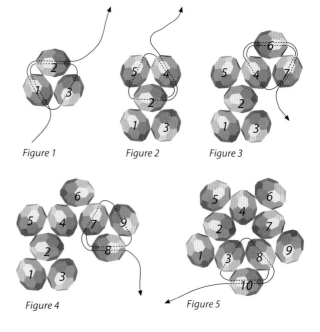

Figure 1   Figure 2   Figure 3

Figure 4   Figure 5

2 *Weave a second layer, sharing circumfer-ence beads.* Each circumference bead of the first layer becomes the base of a triangle for the second layer. Exiting a circumference bead, pick up 2A. Pass through the circumference A and the first new A again (Figure 6). Pick up 1A. Pass through the circumference bead and the previous bead. Pass through the A just added and the next circumference bead (Figure 7). Pick up 1A (the missing side of the next triangle to be made). Pass through the other 2 sides of this triangle and the new A (Figure 8).

Pick up 1A (the missing side of the next triangle to be made). Pass through the other 2 sides of this triangle, and the new A, and the next circumfer-ence bead (Figure 9). Pass through the other 2 sides of this triangle, which are already in place.

3 *Finish the bead by adding drops to the cir-cumference.* Exiting a circumference bead, pick up 1B and pass through the next circumference bead. Continue around the circumference, placing 4 more Bs in this manner. To place a drop in the center, pass through one of the spokes and pick up the last B, then pass through any other spoke. Weave in the thread and tail, making half hitches.

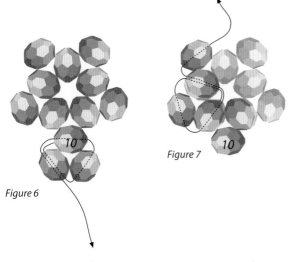

10

Figure 7

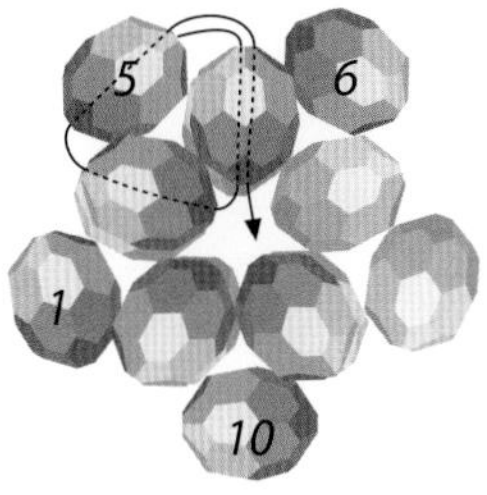

10

Figure 6

5   6

1

10

Figure 8

5   6

1   9

10

Figure 9

> ## Try this . . .
>
> To use this beaded bead as one half of a bead/loop clasp, pick up a shank bead, pass through the center of the beaded bead, pass through the center drop, and pass back down through the beaded bead and the shank. For earrings, hang dangles from an eye pin. Put the beaded bead on the eye pin, make a loop using the round-nose pliers, and slip it onto an earring wire. Make a matching or coordi-nating earring.

Seven

Square Stitch

|||||||||||||||||||||||||||||||||||||||||||||||||||||||||||||||||||||||||||||||||||||||||||||||||||||||||||||||||||||||||||||||||||||||||||||||

Almost any drawing, design, or graph can be rendered in beads with square stitch. Square-stitched beadwork is linear, square, and plumb, a reflection of the orientation of each bead, and closely resembles beadwork done on a loom.

It begins with a single strand of beads. All subsequent rows are added by weaving each new bead into position beside a previously placed bead, side by side. (The action may remind bead embroiderers of backstitch.)

The edge of the piece can be strung, as the beads are parallel with their holes aligned. The ends of the beadwork are appropriate base rows for many other stitches including brick, herringbone, and scallop stitches. The opposing edges of flat square stitch can be seamlessly connected, and you can also create tubular work from a base round.

The mantra for this stitch might be, "Pick up a bead, tie it on, pass through it, pick up a bead, tie it on, pass through it . . . " You will "tie on" a bead by passing through the bead next to it, and then passing through the new bead again.

Saturn Bracelet

• • • • • • •

Weave a band of randomly selected beads from a "bead soup" and finish the bracelet with a beaded closure. To make bead soup, select several colors from your stash of size 8° Japanese seed beads to make up your palette. Spill out a few grams of each color and mix them up—you've made bead soup. I like to include a range of light and dark in the mix. The bracelet's tapered ends provide opportunities to learn to increase and decrease. Embellish the bracelet with lampworked beads and colored wire.

Ingredients
18 g size 8° seed bead soup (A)
3 lampworked 12–20mm disc beads
1 rondelle, about 13–15mm
Beading thread
18" (46 cm) 20-gauge Artistic Wire

Tools
Beading needle
Round-nose pliers
Flat-nosed pliers
Wire cutters

Setup
Mise en place (see page 8)

Note: For lampworked discs, see Karen Ovington, Ghost Cow, and Harold Jargowsky in Resources on page 236.

1 *Establish the base row and the initial width.*
Pick up 4A.

2 *Start each additional row by placing two new beads next to the two last beads of the previous row, then weave one bead onto each subsequent bead on the previous row.* Pick up 2A. Pass through the second-to-last bead on the first row again. Pass through the second new bead (Figure 1).

   Pick up 1A. Pass through the bead from the previous row right next to the new bead. Pass through the new bead again. Repeat across the row (Figure 2).

3 *Increase one bead at each end of the previous row.* Pick up 3A (2A for the start of the row, plus 1A to increase). Pass through the last bead of the previous row and 3A just added (Figure 3).

   Pick up 1A, pass through the corresponding bead from the previous row, and pass through the 1A just added again. Repeat, placing 3 beads across the row. At the end of the row, pick up 2A to make another increase. Pass through the bead below and the one next to it and the last 2 beads of this new row (Figure 4).

Next row: Increase by 1A at each end of the previous row to result in an 8-bead wide row by picking up 3A

(2A for the start of the row, plus 1A to increase), then passing through the last bead of the previous row and 3A just added.

   Pick up 1A, pass through the corresponding bead from the previous row, and pass through the 1A just added again. Repeat, placing 5 beads across the row. At the end of the row, pick up 2A to make another increase. Pass through the bead below and the one next to it and the last 2 beads of this new row.

   Repeat Step 2, weaving without additional increases for the desired length minus 1¾" (4.5 cm) to allow for the decrease and closure.

4 *Decrease at each end of the row.* Pass back through 2A of the previous row. Pass through the second bead from the end of the last row worked. Square-stitch 6 beads in this row (repeating Step 2), stopping 1 bead before the end (Figure 5). Repeat the decrease on the next row, placing 4A.

5 *Weave a peyote-stitched loop closure.* Repeat the decrease row (Step 4), placing 2A. Square-stitch the next row, placing another 2A.

   Pick up 14A. Pass through the last row and 9A again (Figure 6).

   Pick up 20A. Pass through beads 6–9 of the initial

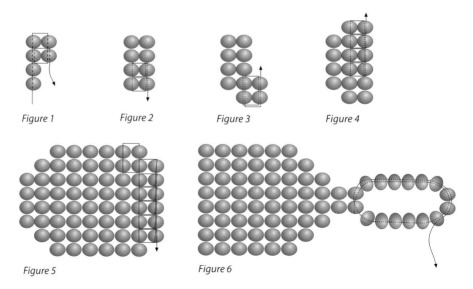

Figure 1   *Figure 2*   *Figure 3*   *Figure 4*

Figure 5   *Figure 6*

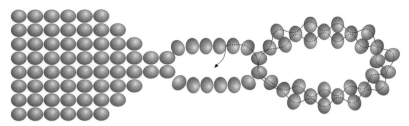

Figure 7

Figure 7

14A loop and 2 new beads of the 20A loop.

Weave around the loop in peyote stitch (see page 28). Pass through beads 6–11 of the 14 bead loop (Figure 7).

Pick up 1A, the rondelle, and 1A. Pass through beads 3, 2, 1 of the 14-bead loop.

Weave in the thread, making half hitches.

6 ***Weave a peyote-stitched toggle bar.*** Repeat the *mise en place*. Pick up 14A and work in peyote stitch for 6 rows. Roll up the piece into a tube and connect the first and last rows seamlessly as in Your Basic Beaded Bead or Toggle Bar on page 40. Weave the thread throughout the toggle bar to stiffen it.

Slide the tape from the tail. Thread the tail onto a needle and square-stitch the middle 2 beads of the beginning of the bracelet to the seventh and eighth beads of any row in the toggle. Weave the tail into the work, making half hitches.

7 ***Wrap the wire attachments for disc beads.*** Divide the wire into 6" (15 cm) lengths. Use the tip of round-nose pliers to make a tiny loop. Hold the loop flat within the jaws of flat-nosed pliers. Coil half the wire's length around the loop, making larger and larger rounds to make a flat spiral. Repeat for the two remaining lengths of wire (Figure 8).

Bend back the end of the wire at a right angle from the coil. Pass the wire through one disc bead and the spot on the bracelet where the disc is to be placed. Pass the wire back through the bracelet ½–1" (1.3–2.5 cm) away. Make another coil on this end, wrapping until the coil meets the surface of the bracelet.

Did you notice . . .

Woven across its width, the bracelet is flexible and sleek when wrapped around the wrist. If the same bracelet were woven across its length, it would also be flexible at the peril of sleekness, since the bead edges lift.

Looking down the length of the bracelet, the stitch emphasizes the texture of the beads. Looking across the width, against the rows, the color and design are more visible than the texture. Which aspect you want to emphasize may inform how you make and wear a piece.

Figure 8

Annealing the Wire

Manipulating the wire changes the structure and hardens, or anneals, it. The coil is not only a design feature—it also offers greater strength. ***Caution***: too much hammering, coiling, or bending leads to metal fatigue, causing the wire to break. You may have experienced this when you've bent a piece of wire back and forth rapidly, causing it to break. Sometimes the wire becomes too hot to handle in the process.

Beader's I.D.

● ● ● ● ● ●

Use regular graph paper to design your own square-stitched beadwork, or use charted needlepoint and loom designs, which translate flawlessly into square stitch. For this project, uniform and straight-sided beads are more satisfying to work with and produce work that appears less thready than rounder, plump or donut shaped beads. Japanese beads in general, and more specifically cylinder and even hex beads, are good choices.

Ingredients
15 g total 3.3mm Japanese cylinder beads
  (or size 8 hex) in three or more colors
Beading thread

Tools
Size 10 beading needle
Graph paper and pencil

Setup
Mise en place (see page 8)

1 *Chart your name badge.* Write your name in pencil on graph paper. With a colored pencil, fill in each cell that contains a pencil mark. These are the name cells. Fill in the cells surrounding the name cells with a contrasting color. Create a frame around the area by coloring the cells in 2 vertical and 2 horizontal lines that meet in the corner.

2 *Establish the width.* Pick up the entire row of beads, following Row 1 of the graphed design (Figure 1). (To make the example shown on page 142, pick up 3 gold, 19 amber, and 3 gold.)

3 *Form additional rows.* Use a ruler or some other straight-edge device to lay along the row in the chart you're working on, so you can keep your place in the graph. Follow the directions in Step 2 of the Saturn Bracelet on page 139 to add each row of beads (Figure 2). Keep in mind that rows of square stitch go back and forth, so you will need to read your chart right to left for one row and left to right for the next. If you lose your place and don't remember which direction you're going, compare the placement of beads in the chart to the placement of beads in your project.

4 *Finish the badge.* Weave in the thread and tail, making half hitches.

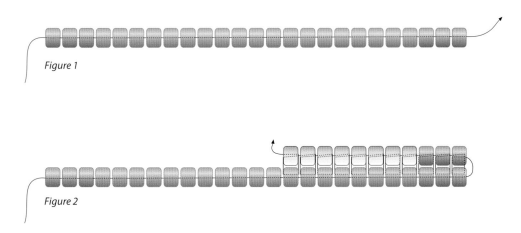

Figure 1

Figure 2

Eight

Daisy Chain

IIIIIIIIIIIIIIIIIIIIIIIIIIIIIIIIIIIIIIIIIIIIIIIIIIIIIIIIIIIIIIIIIIIIIIIIIIIIIIIIIIIIIIIIIIIIIIIIIIIIIIIIIIIIIIIIII

I suspect someone dizzied by right-angle weave came up with daisy chain.
The flower's center bead bridges the opposing sides and brings the needle to
where another unit will be added, without the dizzying changes of direction.
Very clever!

Think of a flower made up of a ring of beads, with another bead for the center. It is useful to imagine the petals as the sides of a square—top, bottom, left, and right. In most cases, opposing sides will have an equal number of beads (Figure 1).

Grab a needle, thread, and a few beads to see what I mean by making a four-petal daisy. Pick up 4A and pass through the first A again. Pick up 1 bead in a size smaller than A, and pass through the opposite A in the same direction (Figure 2). See? You're ready to add another unit without making a direction change.

Weaving Adjacent Daisies That Share Side Petals

1 *Establish the petal count of the daisy.* Pick up the number of petal beads. Pass through the first one again, pulling them into a ring (Figure 3).

2 *Cross the daisy center while placing a bead.* Pick up a center bead. Pass up through the opposing bead on the opposite side (Figure 4).

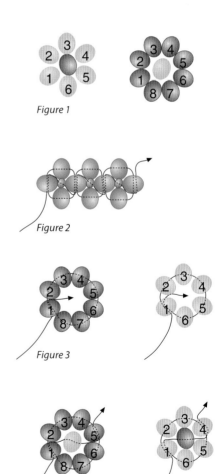

Figure 1

Figure 2

Figure 3

Figure 4

144

Figure 5

3 *Add sufficient petals to existing petals to create a new daisy.* Because one side's worth of beads is already in place, pick up only the other three sides' worth of beads to add another daisy. Pass through Bead 1 of the ring again (Figure 5).

Repeat Steps 2 and 3 for desired length.

Figure 6

Weaving Separate Adjacent Daisies With 2-bead Sides

1 and 2 *Work Steps 1 and 2 as above.*

Figure 7

3 *Add the first 2 beads of the separate flower with one peyote stitch.* Pick up a bead and pass down through the bead below (Figure 6). Pick up a bead, and pass back through the bead just added (Figure 7).

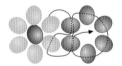 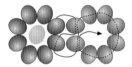

Figure 8

4 *Add petals to the existing petals to create a new daisy.* Because one side is already in place, pick up only the other three sides' worth of beads to add another daisy. Pass through position 1 of the ring (Figure 8). Pick up a center bead and pass up through the opposing bead on the opposite side (Figure 9).

Repeat Steps 3 and 4 for desired length.

Figure 9

Choosing Thread Path

Direction determines the stitch choice for adding beads between units. Coming *up* out of a unit is the proper start to weaving another unit in the same row. When weaving additional beads between the units, consider which method will preserve or reverse the direction of subsequent beading.

If you need to restore the needle's direction to up, use one peyote stitch to be ready to add another unit.

Square and ladder stitches reverse direction with each row.

Peyote stitch restores needle direction to "up," while ladder and square stitch reverse with each row.

Double Daisy Drop Bracelet

• • • • • • • • • • • • •

Enjoy the texture and drama of lined drop bead centers in a row of daisy chain, and learn to weave an additional row off a daisy chain. Refresh your peyote-stitch skills by weaving a matching dumbbell-shaped toggle bar and closure loop.

Ingredients
20 g size 8° seed beads (A)
8 g Japanese drops (B)
2 g size 11° seed beads (C)
Beading thread

Tools
Size 10 beading needle

Setup
Mise en place (see page 8)

1 *Weave a daisy chain.* Following Steps 1–3 on pages 144 and 145, weave a daisy chain with shared sides, using 6A for the petals and 1B for the center, until the ends just meet around the wrist.

2 *Add a second row of daisy chain.* When adding a row onto daisy chain (as in right-angle weave, chevron, triangle, and netting), you will build each unit in a new row from the bottom bead(s) of a unit in the previous row. This would be bead 6 in a 6-petal flower, or beads 8 and 7 of an 8-petal flower.

Repeat the *mise en place*. We will use a new thread to maintain the same dance through the beadwork and thread path of the flower-centers by beginning the second row next to the beginning of the first row. Pass through bead 6 of the first daisy of the previous row.

Pick up 5A. Pass through bead 6 again and 4 of the A just added. Pick up 1B and pass up through bead 4 of the new daisy (Figure 1).

*Pass through the next bead 6 of the previous row. Pick up 3A. Pass through position 1 of this new daisy. Pick up 1B and pass up through position 4 of the new daisy (Figure 2).

Repeat from * across entire row.

3 *Weave a loop closure.* Pass through positions 5 and 4 of the last daisy of the first row. Pick up 17A. Pass through the 4A at the bracelet's edge (beads 5 and 4 of the top row, and 5 and 4 of the bottom row). Weave a row of peyote stitch around this loop (see page 28): pass through 2A, pick up 2C, skip 1A, pass through 2A, pick up 2C, skip 1A, pass through 4A, pick up 2C, skip 1A, pass through 1A, pick up 2A, skip 1A, pass through 1A, pick up 2C, skip 1A, pass through A and into the bracelet. Weave the thread in, making half hitches.

4 *Weave a dumbbell toggle bar.* Repeat the *mise en place*. Pick up 1C, 1A, 1B, 1A, 4C, 1A, 1B, 1A, 1C. Peyote stitch 10 rows by adding 8 rows of 1C, 1B, 1C, 1C, 1A, 1A. Seamlessly weave the first and last rows together (see page 40).

5 *Attach the toggle bar and finish the bracelet.* Remove the tape from the tail of the bracelet. Thread the tail on a needle. Pick up 8C. Pass up through the toggle's midpoint. Pass back down through the toggle, catching a thread of the toggle to secure it, and 5A. Pick up 3A and weave into bead 2 of the bottom row. Weave in the thread, making half hitches.

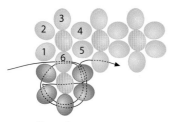

Figure 1

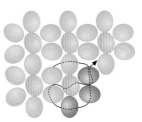

Figure 2

Springtime Chain Bracelet

• • • • • • • • • • • • •

Warm up by weaving a few green daisy chain units. Sneak in an occasional floral-colored bead. Then break out into full-blown daisy chain, incorporating everything you know and a few new hints given here. Start by practicing six-petal and eight-petal units. Give each unit in its own color, separate from adjacent units. Use either ladder stitch or square stitch to add additional beads between units.

Ingredients
15 g seed beads in assorted colors and sizes
2 g Japanese lined drops (for centers)
3–5 Czech pressed-glass leaf beads (to embellish the edges)
Beaded bead, toggle bar, or button
Power Pro beading thread

Tools
Size 10 beading needle

Setup
Mise en place (see page 8)

1 *Make a loop for the closure.* Pick up 2" (5 cm) of seed beads. Work peyote stitch once around the loop using assorted sizes and colors of seed beads.

2 *Weave the remaining length of the bracelet.* Practice 6-petal daisy chain (see page 145). Rather than sharing sides in common, as in the previous two projects, weave each unit in its own color. Use ladder stitch or square stitch to add beads between units (see page 149).

Ladder Stitch Between Units

Pick up 2 seed beads. Pass through the side beads of the unit (the bead next to the bead-just passed through, and the last bead-just-passed through) and both new beads (Figure 1).

Square Stitch Between Units

After completing your last daisy, pick up a contrasting bead. Pass through the bead last exited again, plus the new bead. Pick up another bead and pass through the bead beneath the bead just passed through, plus newly added bead (Figure 2).

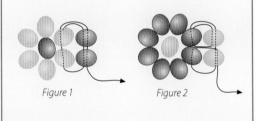

Figure 1   *Figure 2*

Change bead size and color with each unit. Weave a unit off the top or bottom of a unit. Allow 2 smaller stacked units to replace one regular-size one (Figure 3, far right).

Design as you go or duplicate the sample using this sequence:

Weave 3 entirely green 8-petal daisies with shared sides, then 1 salmon 11-petal daisy with a yellow center. Peyote stitch 1 purple size 8° or work 2-drop peyote stitch using size 11° green beads 7 times. Then add 1 peach 8-petal daisy with a blue drop center and 1 yellow 8-petal daisy with a yellow drop center. While adding positions 7 and 8, pick up 3 green seed beads, 1 leaf, and 3 green seed beads,

and pass through positions 7 and 8 again. Weave 1 orange size 15° 8-petal daisy off of position 5, a blue 8-petal daisy off of positions 7 and 8 of the orange daisy (Figure 3). Follow with 6-petal daisies: a coral size 6° daisy with blue center, 1 peach size 8° daisy with a copper center, 1 yellow size 8° daisy with a blue center, and 1 size 6° coral 8-petal daisy with a pink e-bead center. Return to 6-petal daisies in yellow with blue center, purple with yellow center, 2 green with a leaf added as above, peach with yellow center, purple with blue center, and 1 yellow 8-petal with blue center.

3 *Finish the bracelet.* Weave a few more units with small green beads. Weave the thread in, making half hitches. Slide the tape from the tail and make 4 half hitches. Sew through the button, beaded bead, or toggle, and make another 4 half hitches.

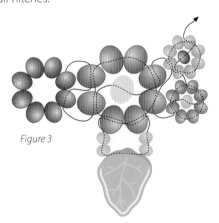

Figure 3

Hot Chili Pepper Collar

• • • • • • • • • • • •

Weave a length of daisy chain, and take advantage of the single beads along the edge to dangle a glass chili pepper, veggie bead, or other glass charm from every third bead.

Ingredients

20 g size 11° seed bead soup of red, yellow, orange, and green (A)
36 size 6° seed beads (B)
17 chili pepper charms (C)
17 fruit and vegetable glass charms (D)
16 Czech pressed-glass leaf beads, drilled lengthwise (E)
Magnetic clasp
Beading thread

Tools

Size 12 beading needle

Setup

Mise en place (see page 8)

1 *Weave the daisy chain base.* Following Steps 1–3 on page 147 for weaving adjacent daisies that share side petals, make a chain of 6-petal daisies—2 petals for each side, 1 each for the top and bottom. Use 6A for the petals and 1A for the centers. Work for the desired length (the necklace shown measures 17" [43 cm] and contains 103 daisies).

2 *Embellish the necklace.* Lay out the design of the dangles before starting. This piece has two styles, chili dangles and fruit or vegetable dangles (see below). Pass the new thread through the first A (the bottom-edge or hanging-down bead). Make a chili dangle. Skip the next 2 bottom beads of the next 2 daisies and pass through the next one (Figure 1). Make a fruit or vegetable dangle. Skip the next two A beads of the next 2 daisies and pass through the next one.

Chili dangle
Pick up 10A, 1B, 2A, and 1C. Pass back through 2A, 1B. Pick up 10A (Figure 2).

Fruit or vegetable dangle
Pick up 10A, 1E, 1A, 1B, 1A, 1D. Pass back through 1A, 1B, 1A, 1E. Pick up 10A (Figure 3).

Alternate between the two styles of dangles, placing 17. Make another chili dangle at the midpoint of the chain and resume alternating until all 34 are placed. Remove any excess daisies that might remain on the chain.

3 *Finish the collar.* Sew one half of the clasp to positions 4 and 5 of the last daisy. Weave in the thread, making half hitches. Slide the tape from the tail. Thread the tail on a needle. Sew the other half of the clasp to positions 1 and 2 of the first daisy. Weave in the tail, making half hitches.

Independent Thread

Although not strictly necessary, it is advisable to start a new thread for embellishing. When you have finished embellishing, weave the tail into the embellishing beads, not into the original part work. This way, if the embellishment is broken or damaged, it is easy to replace or remove it without peril to the original work. (This is also sound advice for adding findings).

Figure 1

Figure 2

Figure 3

151

Did you notice . . .

Six-petaled daisy chain yields spiky edges if the sides are two beads tall. A six-petaled daisy chain could also be made with two beads at the top and bottom and only one per side. The sides can be shared by two adjacent daisies or belong to only one daisy (as in the Springtime Chain Bracelet on page 148). This recipe produces the spiky edge that is perfect for adding dangles. The sample shown, however, shows eight-petaled daisies. To make the pictured collar, the dangles were anchored by looping over the thread between beads 7 and 8 and passing back through the tenth A.

Try this. . .

The edge of any beadwork that has "hanging down beads" is a candidate for fringe and dangles. Many stitches produce such edges: netting, picot, peyote stitch, right-angle weave, cross-needle weave, and daisy chain. In addition to the beads themselves, the thread between the beads sometimes provides a place to embellish (Figure 4). (The Hot Chili Pepper necklace pictured on page 150 illustrates this, with embellishments placed between 2 petals of an 8-bead daisy.)

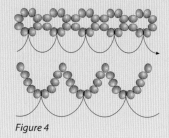

Figure 4

Nine

Ladder Stitch

|||||||||||||||||||||||||||||||||||||||||||||||||||||||||||||||||||||||||||||||||||||||||||||||||||||||||||||||||||||

The beadwork in most of the previous chapters starts by picking up a specified amount of beads for step/row/round one, with the beads aligning end to end. Conversely, some beadwork is built on a base row of beads situated side by side with their holes all pointing outwards, called a ladder. Often the thread connecting the bead-holes, rather than the bead-holes themselves, is employed in the weaving process. The projects in this section show a few ways to produce the ladder—sample each one to discover which way is your favorite.

For years it was very common to see brick stitch beadwork that was built from a ladder row of bugle beads. Their long sides made them easier to work up into a ladder than short or rounder beads, such as Czech seed beads. Some beaders produce ladders using 2 or 3-bead stacks to replicate the ease of working with bugle beads.

Start with longer ladders to create bracelets, necklaces, and lariats, without connecting the first and last rows.

Clockwise, Counterclockwise, Up and Down

The direction of the thread path alternates with each new addition. Adding an even-numbered unit to the ladder requires a clockwise thread path. An odd-numbered unit requires a counterclockwise thread path. (Recall that for the sake of clarity, the tail comes from the bottom, like a tail should, and be on the left when reading left to right.)

Odd numbers leave the thread exiting the top of the work. Even numbers leave the thread exiting the bottom of the work.

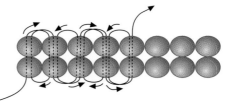

The direction of the thread path alternates.

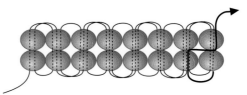

To reverse the direction of the thread, dip into the previous row.

Delicate Beaded Ladder Earrings

● ● ● ● ● ● ● ● ● ● ● ● ● ● ●

Enjoy this opportunity to sample two methods, single-needle and double-needle ladder stitch, while whipping up a pair of earrings that can be embellished in a multitude of ways. Alternate simple seed bead picot edges with more elaborate picots that feature fire-polished faceted beads for a little sparkle.

Ingredients
18 size 8° Japanese seed beads (A)
48 size 11° seed beads (B)
16 fire-polished 3mm faceted beads (C)
106 size 15° Japanese seed beads (D)
Beading thread
2 earring wires

Tools
3 size 12 beading needles

Setup
Mise en place (see page 8), allowing only half a
      wingspan per earring

1 *Use the single-needle method to build a ladder for the first earring.* Pick up 1A. Pick up 1A
and place it alongside the previous A. Pass through
the first A again, tying the new A to the previous
A (Figure 1). Pass through the new A, bringing the
needle to the far bead of the work so that another
bead can be added (Figure 2). *Mantra: Pick up a
bead, pass through the previous bead again, pass
through the new bead.*

Repeat until the ladder is 9 beads long.

2 *Use the double-needle method to build a
ladder for the second earring.* Thread a needle
at each end of a half wingspan of beading thread.
Center 1A on the thread, then pick up another A
with one needle. Cross through in the other direction with the second needle (Figure 3). *Mantra:
Pick up a bead with needle 1, cross through it with
needle 2.*

Repeat until the ladder is 9 beads long.

3 *Embellish the ladder.* Working each earring
separately, pick up 3B. Pass through the previous A. Repeat to the end of the ladder, leaving 8
picots (Figure 4).

Pick up 3D, 1C, 1D. Hold them close to the ladder. Pass back through 1C and 1D. Pick up 2D and
pass through the next A bead. Repeat to the end of
the ladder, leaving 8 faceted bead fringes (Figure 5).
Pass through the B beads again, skipping the center
one to pull it into a pointier picot and shore up the
earring (Figure 6).

4 *Attach the ladders to earring wires and finish.* Form a beaded loop at the top A of each
earring. Pick up 6D, then pass through 1A and 6D
again. Weave the thread and tail into the work,
making half hitches.

Try this . . .

The flatter and longer the beads' sides are, the easier it is to situate them in a ladder. If using plump or
shallow beads, make the ladder 2 beads tall. Follow
the same directions but use 2A in place of 1A, as
though they were stuck together hole to hole.

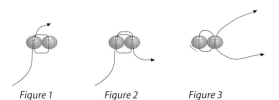

Figure 1   Figure 2   Figure 3

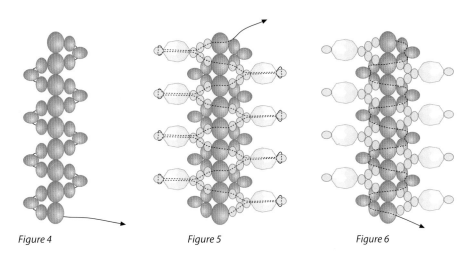

Figure 4   Figure 5   Figure 6

Tape-Your-Tail-to-the-Table Ring

Here is an alternate way to make a ladder. Even pesky donut-shaped or plump and rounded beads can be worked into a ladder using this technique. As you connect each new bead, you will rotate the ladder 90 degrees, to maintain the side-by-side alignment. As you work this stitch, remember that the first bead is the one nearest the tail. The last bead picked up is the bead nearest the needle. All too often with this technique, when instructed to pass through the second-to-last bead, the beader passes through the second (from the beginning) bead.

Ingredients
About 36 size 8° Hex or Japanese cylinder
    beads (A)
2 g size 15° Japanese seed beads (B)
About 30 faceted fire-polished 3mm beads (C)
Beading thread

Note: 36A produce a ring about size 7. Adjust the
    number for your desired size.

Tools
Size 12 beading needle
Ring mandrel (optional)
Tape

Setup
Mise en place (see page 8)

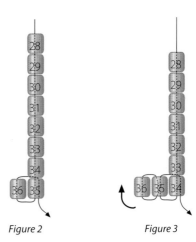

Figure 2   *Figure 3*

1 *Tape the tail to a table in front of you.*
Pulling the needle toward you and away from the table, pick up all 36A and allow them to fall down to the taped tail. Pull the thread taut toward you (Figure 1).

2 *Pass through the second-to-last bead again from the tail forward, entering the bead from behind (Figure 2).* This aligns the 2A nearest you (and the needle) to lie side by side in a ladder 2 beads long, which extends off the side of the taut thread.

3 *Pass through the third-to-the-last A bead (the next A back).* Pinch the short ladder between the thumb and index finger of your nondominant hand. While pulling the thread with your dominant hand, use your other hand to rotate the ladder one-half-turn under and toward yourself, allowing the ladder to arrange itself so the beads sit side by side (Figure 3).
 Repeat Step 3 until all 36 A beads are arranged side by side in a ladder.

Figure 1

157

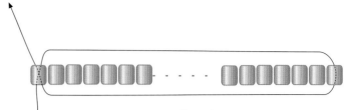

Figure 4

4 *Size the ring.* Wrap the ladder around your finger or a ring mandrel to check the size. To make the ring smaller, slide beads off the tail end. To make the ring larger, slide the tape off the tail of the thread and add the number of beads (use an even number) you estimate you'll need to correctly size the ring. Repeat Step 3 until all A beads are arranged in a ladder, side by side. Check the size again.

5 *Form the ring shape.* The tail extends from the bottom and the thread from the top of the first bead. Pass down through the top of the last bead. Pass up from the bottom of the first bead again (Figure 4).

6 *Embellish the band with loops.* Pick up 5B. Pass through the next A. Repeat around the ring, producing little loops of beads (Figure 5).

7 *Bridge the loops with beads.* Pass through the first 3 of the next 5B to make the step up (Figure 6). Pick up 1C and pass through the high bead of the next loop on this edge (Figure 7).

When all the loops are bridged, pass through 1A to begin bridging the loops on the other edge. Pass through the first 3 of the next 5B to make the step-up. Pick up 1C and pass through the high bead of the next loop on this edge. Repeat to bridge all the loops on this edge of the ring.

8 *Finish the ring.* Weave the thread and the tail into the work, making half hitches.

Figure 5

Figure 6

Figure 7

Try this . . .

Vary the size and content of the loops. Fringe the edges, or combine a loop with short fringe: pick up one half of the loop, a bead for the center high bead of the loop, and a turning bead (or 3 for a picot), then pass back through the center bead and pick up the other half of the loop. When bridging the loops, use fewer beads to draw the edges in or add a bead or two to ruffle the edges. Alternate between these every inch (2.5 cm) or so for a wavy ribbon of beadwork.

Edgy Eyeglass Leash

● ● ● ● ● ● ● ● ● ●

If none of the ladder methods hum at you, avoid them altogether and use this alternative technique. A strip of peyote stitch two beads wide provides a suitable edge and is a quick and easy alternative to the ladder-stitched base row. Maintain tension on the thread so the work doesn't become loose and thready. Because the row is turned with each new bead, the thread will want to slacken. (If you intend another pass through all the work, as when adding a picot edging, this is less critical.) When you've mastered the technique, read on for directions on a chevron stitch alternative (see page 160).

Ingredients
7 g Japanese cylinder beads (A)
7 g size 11° seed beads (B)
Glue (Duco, E-6000, or 527)
2 rounded end caps
2 jump rings
2 eyeglass holders (corrugated bead with ring and black elastic loop style)
Beading thread
Solder and flux

Tools
Jump ring tool
Needle-nose pliers
Soldering iron
Size 10 beading needle

Setup
Mise en place (see page 8)

1 *Build a peyote-stitched base*. Pick up 3A. Pass back through the first A bead (Figure 1). *Pick up 1A. Pass back through the last A bead (Figure 2). Repeat from * for your desired length.

Figure 1

Figure 2

2 *Add edging*. Because this is peyote stitch, the path across the row is not straight. To weave across the 2-bead row to the opposite edge: Pick up 3B. Skip 1A and pass through the next A bead (Figure 3).* Pick up a 3B. Skip the next bead and pass through the next 1A (Figure 4). Exit the opposite edge through the next near bead.
    Repeat from * to the end.

Figure 3

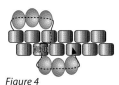

Figure 4

3 *Finish the leash*. Glue the end caps to the ends of the beadwork. Open a jump ring to attach an eyeglass holder to each end cap. Close the jump ring and solder (see page 20).

Chevron Stitch

Chevron stitch is the 2-bead wide peyote technique with extra beads between the A beads. Try 2B between each A bead or pick up 1A, 2B, 1A, 2B 1A, 2B. Ignore the B beads and, as above, pass back through the first A bead. Pick up 2B, 1A, 2B, and pass back through the newest A bead. In a nutshell, chevron stitch is the hybrid of 2-bead-wide peyote and short-row netting. Vary the number and bead type for B.

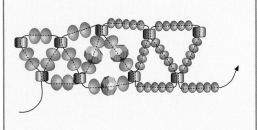

Try this . . .

To use this as a base for brick stitch (see page 189), use the thread between adjacent beads of one edge.

As the base for herringbone stitch (see page 161), after exiting the edge, pick up 2 beads and pass down the next bead and up through the following bead.

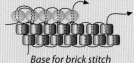

Base for brick stitch

Base for herringbone stitch

Ten

Herringbone Stitch

This weave, often credited to the Ndebele people of South Africa, produces columns of paired beads. The beads within the pair incline towards each other, yielding the herringbone pattern. Generally, each stitch involves adding 2 beads and passing through 2 beads. Many beaders, especially those who come to it from a background of peyote stitch, enjoy this two at a time pace, which is accelerated by the convenient angle that each new pair assumes.

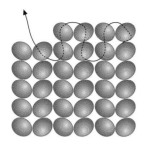

Pairs of beads incline toward each other.

Beginning of baseless herringbone stitch.

To make the basic stitch, pick up 2 beads, pass down through the bead you're inclined towards (the other bead of the pair) and right up through the bottom of the next bead (the first bead of the next pair) in one swoop. The first bead of the next pair is sitting at a jaunty angle that permits the needle easy access.

Some beaders who come to this stitch with years of other beadwork experience behind them sometimes have more difficulty picking it up. In their experience, it seems counterintuitive to place the 2 beads in a place where 2 beads wouldn't ordinarily fit. However, it's that very feature that gives the beads their distinctive tilt.

This stitch produces columns of beads whose tops tend to splay apart. This stitch lends itself to floral designs from simple to extravagant. Adding beads between the columns yields many interesting effects. Of course, that begs the addition of beads within the columns, which are not so easily accommodated, but result in wonderful structural and sculptural possibilities. I call these additional beads "inclusions." Explore their many manifestations in the recipes to follow.

Herringbone stitch is often woven off a base created by another stitch. The base can be a row woven just for this purpose, such as the ladders in Delicate Beaded Ladder Earrings on page 154 or Tape-Your-Tail-to-the-Table Ring on page 156, or it can be worked in place of a brick stitch row (as in You Are My Sunshine Beaded Pendant on page 203) or the edge of peyote stitch (Edgy Eyeglass Leash on page 159).

Baseless herringbone stitch

To start without a base, start with a strand of beads divisible by four. Weaving back across the row yields three rows of beadwork. (Because the thread shows on the exterior of a bead when turning the row, I prefer not to use this method.) Choose 3 colors of size 8° beads (A, B, C). Pick up 1A, 2B, 1A. Repeat this sequence for the desired width.

Pick up 1C. Pass back through the next 2A, skipping over the 2B between them. Pull the thread tight to bring the 2A close together.

*Pick up 2C. Pass through the next 2A, skipping over the 2B between them. Pull the thread tight to bring these 2A close together. Repeat from * across the row.

Each subsequent row starts by picking up only one bead and passing back through the last bead of the previous row. Continuing across the row, pick up 2 beads, pass down through the next bead and up through the following one of the previous row.

The ruffled collar shown on the cover is woven lengthwise using herringbone stitch. The ladder-stitched base of Japanese cylinder beads is long enough to meet around the throat. The following 4 rows are of size 11° Czech seed beads, followed by 2 rows of Japanese seed beads, 1 row size 10° seed beads, 4 rows of size 8°, and a final row of a single size 6° seed beads. Increasing the size of rows by increasing the bead size caused the work to curve. Exaggerating the curve in the final rows caused it to ruffle. The single size 6° seed beads are treated as high beads for a final row of embellishment using peyote stitch and an opaque druk, a lined 6°, and a clear druk alternately. A magnetic clasp at each end of the ladder row makes for easy-on, easy-off.

Stripy Bracelet

• • • • • • •

Explore the structure of this stitch by working with only two colors to achieve several striped and stippled patterns. Create a buttonhole within the beadwork by working the columns separately for several rows before returning to weaving across the entire row. Embellish the bracelet's other end with a bead or button, making a decorative closure.

Ingredients
20 g size 8° seed beads in each of 2 colors (A, B)
Coin-size and coin-shaped bead or button for
    closure
Beading thread

Tools
Size 10 beading needle

Setup
Mise en place (see page 8)

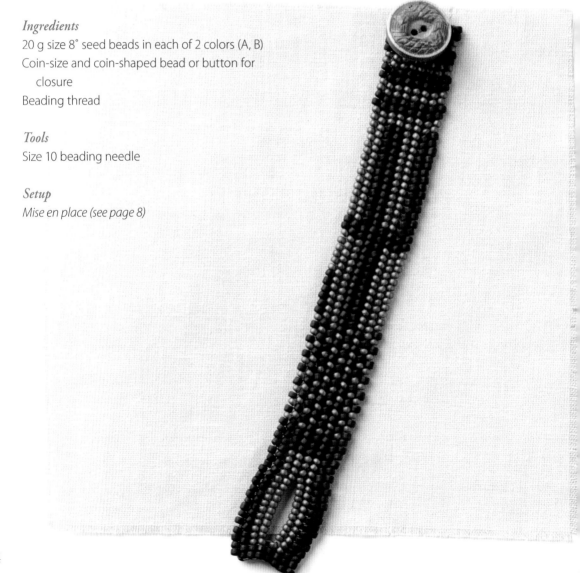

techniques
Flat herringbone stitch
2-bead tall ladder

1 *Build a 2-bead ladder-stitched (see page 153) base for Rows 1 and 2.* Pick up 4A. Pass through them again. Arrange them in 2 side-by-side stacks. Both the thread and tail come from the bottom of the work (Figure 1).

Ladder-stitch 8 pairs of A beads, weaving a 2-bead-tall and 8-stack-long ladder.

2 *At the end of the row, anchor the thread and come up to the top.* Because the work ends on an even number of stacks, the thread exits the bottom of the work. The thread must be brought up to the top of the work to continue. Let's identify the last 4 beads as lower left, upper left, upper right, and lower right. Pass up through the lower left and then upper right beads (Figure 2).

3 *Begin herringbone stitch by weaving off the ladder base.* There is no need to pass down through more than the previous row. Each row is woven onto the previous row. Pick up 2B. Pass down through the next bead on the base and up through the following (Figure 3).

Each stitch adds 2 beads woven into 2 beads—pick up 2B, pass down through the next A bead and up through the following A bead. Notice the angle of the new beads (Figure 4).

This is the distinctive look of herringbone stitch. It also allows the grace and speed to zip through 2 beads at a time.

Repeat Step 3 to the end of the row. Start by passing down through a bead to add a fourth pair of B beads, noticing that the stitch cannot be completed because there is no bead to pass up through.

4 *Turn the row.* Notice the bead that the thread is exiting and the one above it. Use these 2 beads plus the pair of beads beside them as the "last 4 beads" from Step 2. Hold the work so that the bead that the thread exits is the lower right bead. Repeat Step 2 to bring the needle to the top of the work and continue.

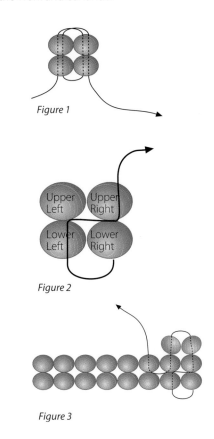

Figure 1

Figure 2

Figure 3

Figure 4

To produce the pattern as shown, weave every row following the directions above, using these combinations of beads:

Row 4: B.

Rows 5–16: Alternate weaving 2 rows of A and 2 rows of B.

Rows 17–30: Alternate between one row of 2A, 2B, 2A, 2B and a row of 2B, 2A, 2B, 2A.

Rows 31–32: 1A.

Rows 33–38: 2B, BA, AB, 2B.

Rows 39–44: Alternate between a row of AB, BA, AB, 2B, and a row of 2B, BA, AB, BA.

Rows 45–59: 1B and 1A

Rows 60–62: 1A.

Rows 63–66 (or more for additional length): 2A, 4B, 2A.

Repeat until the first row meets the last row around the wrist.

5 *Weave a buttonhole.* Weave short rows, turning after every 4 beads. Alternate between a row of 2A, 2B, and 2B, 2A. Weave until your stack of short rows is tall enough to make an opening to accommodate the button for the closing. The sample shown has 11 rows to accommodate a button that is 7/8" (2.2 cm) in diameter.

Weave the thread down through the stack of B beads and into the B bead of the last full row base (Figure 5). Pass up through the next B bead of the last full row base and repeat short rows as for first side. Weave across the remaining 4 beads of this last full row using 2B, 2A alternately with 2A and 2B.

Weave one last row of A beads to resemble the other end of the bracelet (square stitch). Pick up 2A. Pass down through the second bead of the previous row and, rather than passing up through the next one, pass up through the first bead of the previous row and both of the new beads (Figure 6).

Pass down through the second bead of the previous row and up through the third one. Pick up 1A. Pass down through the second A of this row and the previous row and up through the third bead of the previous row and this newest addition (Figure 7).

Square-stitch (see page 138) across the row, adding 1A at a time (Figure 8).

Weave the thread into the work, making half hitches.

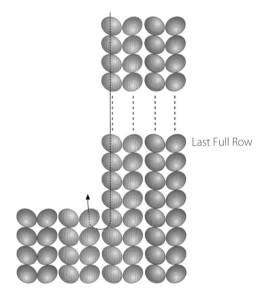

Last Full Row

Figure 5

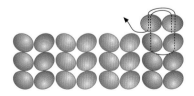

Figure 6

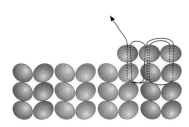

Figure 7

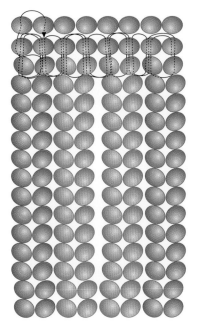

6 *Add a bead or button closure.*

Button
Slide the tape from the tail. Thread the tail on a needle. If the bead or button has no shank, pick up 2A. Sew a button to the center pair of B of Row 3. Weave the tail in when the button is secure.

Figure 8

Bead or Button
Slide the tape from the tail. Thread the tail on a needle. Travel through the beads to exit the center of the second row.

Pick up 1 size 8° seed bead as a shank, an M&M-size or larger bead or a coin-size button and 1 size 8° or 11° seed bead as a turning bead. Pass back through the big bead and the shank bead and into the bracelet. Make a half hitch and pass back up through all three beads again. Turn and pass back down through the big bead and shank and into the bracelet. Weave the thread in, making half hitches.

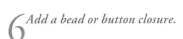

Seed-Stitch Look Bracelet

• • • • • • • • • • •

Achieve the look knitters call "seed stitch" by pairing two different bead sizes in each stitch and alternating their order in each row. Begin with a base of peyote two beads wide. A bead or button on the surface of one end becomes an adjustable closure with a series of beaded loops off the other end.

Ingredients
25 g size 8° seed beads (A)
5 g size 11° seed beads (B)
12–16mm bead for closure
Fireline 10# or Power Pro
    10# beading thread

Tools
Size 10 beading needle

Setup
Mise en place (see page 8), leaving a 12"
    (30 cm) tail

1 **Use peyote stitch to make a two-row base.**
Pick up 3A. Pass back through the first A.
Peyote-stitch 16A (total) into a row two beads wide
(see Edgy Eyeglass Leash on page 159) (Figure 1).
Because the weaving will continue from an edge
rather than a row, hold the work sideways so that
the tail comes from the bottom left and the thread
from the top right.

Figure 1

2 **Begin herringbone stitch by weaving off the base.** *Pick up 1A, 1B. Pass down through the
next bead of the previous row (the edge of the
peyote weave) and up through the following bead.
Notice the distinctive angle of the two new beads.
Repeat from * two more times. Pick up 1A, 1B. The
stitch cannot be completed because there is no
bead to pass up through.

3 *Turn the row.* Examine the last two beads of the previous row and locate the thread that connects them (Figure 2). Pass the needle under that thread before passing up through the last bead of the previous row and the last bead added to anchor the thread and prevent the last stitch from coming undone. (For another method of anchoring the thread, see the Stripy Bracelet on page 164).

4 *Work remaining rows.* Weave across the row, using 1A, 1B for each stitch. *Mantra: A B down and up, A B down and up, A B down and up, A B down, anchor and up . . .*) Anchor the thread by passing the needle under the horizontal thread between the last 2 beads of the previous row. Pass up through the last bead of the previous row and the last bead of this row (Figure 3).

Turn and continue to weave another row. Repeat until the piece meets around your wrist (about 6" [15 cm] in the example).

Weave across the next row using all A.

5 *Add the closure bead.* Remove the tape from the tail. Thread the tail on a needle. Travel through the beads to exit the center of the second row. Pick up a size 8° seed bead to serve as the shank, a 12–16mm bead (or larger), and a size 8° or size 11° seed bead as a turning bead. Pass back through the big bead and shank and into the bracelet. Make a half hitch and pass back up through the shank, bead, and turning bead again. Turn and pass back down through the big bead and shank and into the bracelet. Weave in the thread, making half hitches.

6 *Add adjustable closure loops.* Determine how many seed beads (B) are necessary to fit comfortably around the closure bead. Divide that number by 2 and add 1 more B—let's call this total number "Y." Travel through the beads to exit the last row between the fourth and fifth beads (Figure 4).

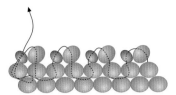

Figure 2

Figure 3

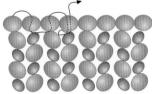

Figure 4

Pick up Y. Pick up 1A. Pick up Y. Pick up 1A. Pick up 2Y. Pass back through the last A bead, heading back toward the bracelet. Pick up Y and pass back through the next A. Pick up Y and pass back into the bracelet where the loops began (between the fourth and fifth beads). Travel through the beads as shown, making half hitches. Exit between the fourth and fifth beads and pass through the loops a second time, following the original thread path. Weave the thread in, making half hitches.

Try this . . .

Mix and match starts and finishes to the herringbone stitch projects: Use any of the ladder recipes (pages 153–160) or this peyote-style base. Try different methods for anchoring the thread at the end of each row so it can be brought up to the top of the work to resume weaving. Weave a beaded bead to use in place of the closure bead. Substitute another loop closure. Find your favorite techniques and explore your options!

Inclusions Between the Stitches Bracelet

● ● ● ● ● ● ● ● ● ● ● ● ● ● ● ● ●

Succumb to the temptation to fill those spaces between the splayed columns of beads that distinguish this stitch. Flat pieces yield fans and flowers; circular pieces produce triangles, squares, and other geometric shapes; tubular pieces can be short beaded beads, long ropes and any length in between. Sample a few styles to assemble in this bracelet, and learn to transition from herringbone stitch to peyote stitch.

Ingredients
10 g size 8° seed beads in each of 2 colors (A, B)
5 g size 11° seed beads (C)
5 g size 15° seed beads (D, E)
Beading thread

Tools
Size 10 beading needle

Setup
Mise en place (see page 8) for each shape

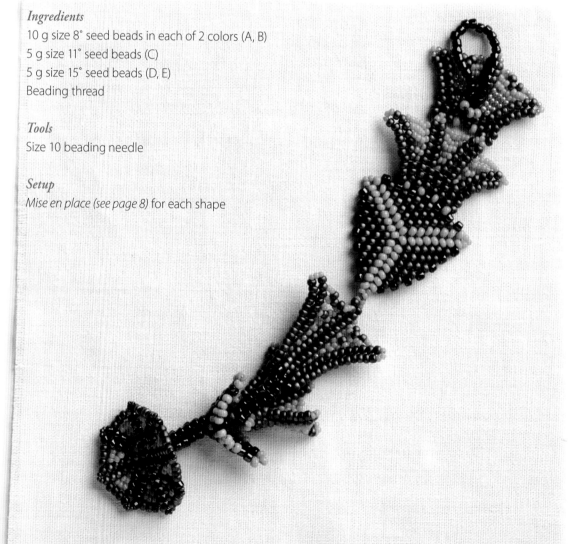

1 *Weave a tulip fan.* Use a bead to make a ladder-stitched strip 2 beads tall and 6 pairs wide (see page 153).

Rows 3–4: Weave 2 rows of herringbone stitch, following the basic directions on page 161 (Figure 1).

Rows 5–9: Weave 5 more rows, placing a C bead inclusion between the stitches as follows: Pick up 2A and go down through the next bead, but stop before coming up through the next (Figure 2). Pick up 1C and finish the stitch by passing up through the next A. Repeat this row 4 more times (Figure 3).

Row 10: Weave one row with 2C between the stitches.

Row 11: Weave one row with 3C between the stitches.

Row 12: Weave one row with C, A, C between the stitches (Figure 4).

Row 13: Weave one row with this inclusion: 2C, pass through the A of the previous row's inclusion; 2C (Figure 5).

Row 14: Weave one row with a 2C, 1A, 2C inclusion.

Row 15: Weave one row with 1A, 3C, 1A, pass down through 1A, and using this inclusion: 2C, 1A, pass through the A bead of the previous row's inclusion, and finish the stitch using 1A, 2C (Figure 6).

2 *Weave a circular square.* Repeat the *mise en place*.

Round 1: Pick up 4A. Pass through them again, then pass through the first 2 once more.

Round 2: Pick up 2A. Pass through the next A bead. Repeat 4 times around and step up through the first bead of this round.

Round 3: Pick up 2A. Pass down through the next A bead. Pick up 1C before finishing the stitch and going up through the next A bead (Figure 7). Repeat 4 times around and step up through the first bead of this round.

Round 4: Pick up 2A. Pass down through the next

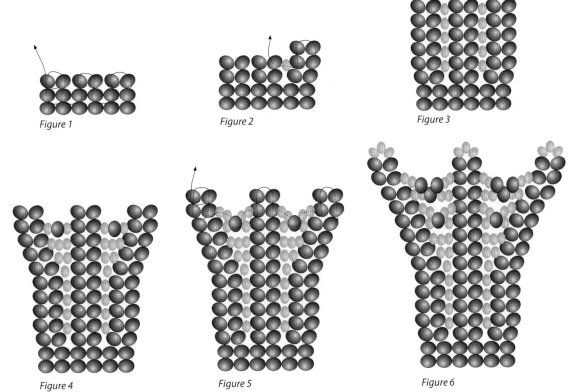

Figure 1

Figure 2

Figure 3

Figure 4

Figure 5

Figure 6

171

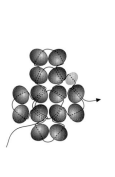

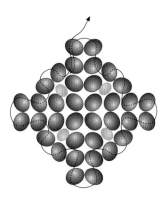

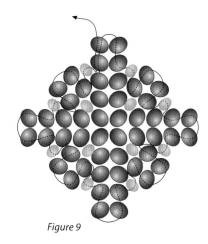

Figure 7	*Figure 8*	*Figure 9*

A bead. Pick up 2A and pass up through the next A bead. Repeat 4 times around and step up through the first bead of this round (Figure 8).

Round 5: Pick up 2A. Pass down through the next A bead. Pick up 1C and pass up through 1A. Pick up 2A and pass down through 1A. Pick up 1C and pass up through 1A. Repeat 4 times around and step up through the first bead of this round (Figure 9).

Round 6: Pick up 2A. Pass down through the next 1A. Pick up 2C. Pass up through 1A. Pick up 2A. Pass down through 1A. Pick up 2C. Pass up through 1A. Repeat 4 times around and step up through the first bead of this round.

Round 7: Pick up 2A and pass down through the next A. Pick up 3C and pass up through 1A. Pick up 2A and pass down through the next A bead. Pick up 3C and pass up through 1A. Repeat 4 times around and step up through the first bead of this round. (Notice that the inclusions have been used as an increase.)

Round 8: Pick up 3E and pass down through the next A. Pick up 3A and pass up through 1A. Pick up 3E and pass down through 1A. Pick up 3A and pass up through the next 1A. Repeat 4 times around and step up through the first bead of this round (Figure 10).

3 Weave a triangle. Repeat the *mise en place.*
Round 1: Pick up 3B. Pass through them again.
Round 2: Pick up 2B and pass into the next 1B. Repeat 2 times around and step up through the first bead of this round.

Round 3: Pick up 2B and pass down through the next B bead. Pick up 1A and pass up through the next B bead. Repeat 2 times and step up through the first bead of this round.

Round 4: Pick up 2B and pass down through the next B bead. Pick up 1A and pass straight through A. Pick up 1A and pass up through the next B bead. (Notice that the inclusions are being peyote stitched.) Repeat 2 times around and step up through the first bead of this round (Figure 11).

Round 5: Pick up 2B and pass down through the next B bead. Pick up 1A and pass straight through 1A. Pick up 1A and pass straight through the next A bead. Pick up 1A and pass up through the next B bead. Repeat 4 times around and step up through the first bead of this round. Repeat Round 5 for as many rounds as desired. As this is a triangle shape, increase the peyote stitch by 1 bead in each third of the round.

4 Weave a beaded bead.
Round 1: Make a ladder-stitched strip 2 beads high and 6 beads wide (see page 153). Pass up through the first 2 beads, down through the last 2 beads, and up through the first 2 beads again to make a foundation ring as in Bead Happy Bracelet on page 177.

Round 2: Pick up 2A and pass down through the next A. Pick up 1C and pass up through the next A. Repeat 2 times and step up by passing up through both the first bead of the previous round and the first bead of this round.

172

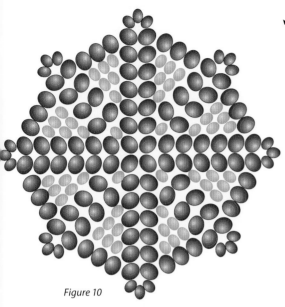

Figure 10

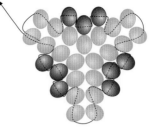

Figure 11

Figure 12

Round 3: Pick up 2A and pass down through the next A. Pick up 2C and pass up through the next A. Repeat 2 times and step up by passing up through both the first bead of the previous round and the first bead of this round (Figure 12).

Round 4: Pick up 2A and pass down through the next A. Pick up 3C and pass up through the next A. Repeat 2 times around and step up by passing up through the first bead of the previous round and the first bead of this round.

Round 5: Weave a round placing 4C between the stitches.

Round 6: Weave a round placing 5C between the stitches.

Round 7: Weave a round placing 4C between the stitches.

Round 8: Weave a round placing 3C between the stitches.

Round 9: Weave a round placing 2C between the stitches.

Round 10: Weave a round placing 1C between the stitches.

5 *Weave 3 more samplers.* In a spirit of experimentation and adventure, weave another 3 samplers of inclusions. This is the time to substitute different beads to see what effects result.

6 *Assemble the bracelet.* Arrange the 7 components end to end, starting with the circular square (which works well as a toggle closure when tucked into a loop added to the opposite end of the bracelet). Use the tail to tie a bead of one sampler to an adjacent bead of the next sampler; use the thread to tie a bead of one sampler to an adjacent bead of the next sampler. Finish by stringing a loop of beads long enough to accept the circular square. Weave in any remaining thread and tails, making half hitches.

Did you notice . . .

Inclusions are beautiful additions, offering color, texture, and dimension. In addition to increasing within herringbone stitch, they can also develop into peyote stitch.

When peyote stitch and herringbone stitch are used together, as in the triangle, they start to look like each other, like a long-married couple.

173

Jill's Reversible Herringbone Bracelet

In this bracelet, an extra bead floats between the pair that makes up the regular stitch. This extra bead is not part of the architecture of the stitch; it's simply picked up and carried along, and sits slightly above the surface of the beadwork. When the work is flipped over to start a new row, the new row's floating beads will sit above the surface, while the previous row's "floaters" will protrude through the back. If the alternate rows' floaters are two different colors, the piece is reversible. With tight tension, this produces a stiff and sculptural beadwork. For supple results, use a lighter tension.

Ingredients
15 g matte moss green size 8° seed beads (A)
5 g each yellow and purple size 8° seed beads
    (B, C)
Nickel-size button
Fireline 10# beading thread

Tools
Size 10 beading needle

Setup
Mise en place (see page 8)

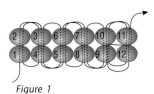

Figure 1

Figure 2

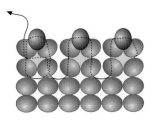

Figure 3

Figure 4

1 **Build the ladder base.** Make a ladder-stitched strip 2 beads tall and 6 beads wide using A beads. Bring the thread from the bottom to the top of the work by passing up through ninth and eleventh beads added (Figure 1).

2 **Weave herringbone stitch with floaters.** Pick up 1A, 1B, 1A, forming regular herringbone stitch with the addition of a floater bead within each stitch. Pass down through the next top-row bead (bead 10) and up through the next (bead 7). Pick up 1A, 1B, 1A, and pass down through the next top-row bead (bead 6) and up through the following (bead 3) (Figure 2). Note that the floater inclines towards the front or back. Bring it forward in the row being worked.

For the third (and final) stitch of the row, pick up 1A, 1B, 1A, and pass down through the next bead (bead 2), even though there is no bead to pass up through. Pass up through the adjacent bead and up through the last bead, the A just added (Figure 3). Repeat Step 2, using C in place of B (Figure 4).

3 **Weave for desired length.** Repeat Step 2, alternating B and C sides, until the piece is the desired length, (when the ends nearly meet around the wrist). Check frequently that the inclusion on the row being worked (B or C) is pushed forward and the inclusion on the previous row is pushed to the back, maintaining the reversible look.

4 **Add the closure and finish the bracelet.** If the closure button doesn't have a shank, pick up a few seed beads to use as a shank. Sew the button to the middle of the end of the bracelet (Figure 5). Weave in the thread, making half hitches.

At the opposite end, exit the corner. Pick up a sufficient number of beads to slide over the button. Instead of attaching to the opposite corner, attach it ½" (1.3 cm) in from the end. Weave in the tail, making half hitches.

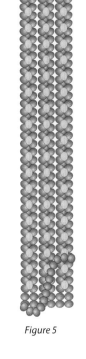

Figure 5

175

Try this . . .

The style and type of bead used affects how the
floating inclusion behaves. Drops really stick out,
even more than in peyote stitches. Triangles wedge
into place with a flat side raised up. Matte triangles
in size 10/11° are actually sharp. If the floaters are
smaller than the surrounding beads, they will recede
rather than bulge, diminishing their usefulness for
reversible work.

Bead Happy Bracelet

· · · · · · · · · · ·

Immerse yourself in color. Though it appears to be a strand of intricately beaded beads, this bracelet is one long tube of tubular herringbone stitch composed of fifty different bead types, with each round calling for a different bead. The bead sizes in each section graduate from small beads at the beginning, to larger beads in the middle, to small beads at the other end. Before beginning to weave, take a moment to decide what arrangement of colors you will weave in each segment. Finish with a distinctive self-closure: a two-headed end that tucks securely into a squared loop end.

Ingredients

3 g size 14/15° seed beads divided among seven colors

7 g size 11° seed beads divided among ten colors

12 g size 8° seed beads divided among twelve colors

5 g size 6° seed beads divided among five colors

4 g Japanese drops divided among four colors

1 g 4mm Japanese cube beads in a single color

1 g druks in a single color

1 g 4mm faceted fire-polished crystals in a single color

Fireline 6# beading thread

Tools

Size 12 beading needle

Setup

Mise en place (see page 8), allowing a 30" (76 cm) tail

Note: Before starting, measure your wrist and alter the number of rounds as necessary. The directions here are for a piece to fit a 6–7½" (15–19 cm) wrist. To accommodate smaller wrists, skip to Bead 2 after making the ladder. For a larger bracelet, work as given to the end, then repeat Bead 8 before proceeding to finishing.

Figure 1

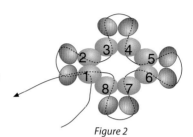

Figure 2

1 *Begin the first beaded bead section with a ladder base.* Using size 11° seed beads, make a ladder 8 beads long following the directions from any project in the ladder stitch chapter (page 153). Pull the ladder into a foundation ring by passing up through the first bead and down through the last bead again, then up the first bead again (Figure 1). Note that the tail is coming from the bottom of a bead and the thread comes from the top of the same bead. We will refer to the "top" and "bottom" of the ring this way.

2 *Weave beads and spacers, adding beads as specified.*

Bead 1

Round 2: Begin herringbone stitch off the ladder base. You will always add a pair of beads at a time, and each round is done entirely with one color and size bead.

Pick up 2 size 8° seed beads. Pass down through the next bead in the ring and up through the following; the added beads sit at an angle. Repeat twice more.

Pick up 2 beads and pass down through the next bead, then up through the next bead (below the first new bead added this round) and the bead above it. This brings the needle to the top of the work for another round—a step-up. You will step up at the end of each round (Figure 2).

Round 3: Repeat Round 2 using drops.

Round 4: Repeat Round 2 using 8°s the same color as Row 2.

Round 5: Repeat Round 2 using 11°s the same color as Row 1.

Spacer 1: Continuing with the same thread, work 4 rounds in 15°s, two rounds of one color and two rounds of another. Choose your colors to add contrast and interest with the beaded bead sections on both sides of the spacer.

Bead 2: Work 1 round 11°s, 1 round 8°s, 1 round 6°s, 1 round 8°s in the same color as the second round of this bead, and 1 round 11°s the same color as the first round of this bead.

Spacer 2: Repeat directions for Spacer 1, using a new color combination.

Bead 3: Work 1 round 11°s, 1 round 8°s, 1 round crystals, 1 round 8°s in the same color as the second row of this bead, and 1 round 11°s in the same color as the first row of this bead.

Spacer 3: Repeat directions for Spacer 1, using a new color combination.

Bead 4: Work 1 round 11°s, 2 rounds 8°s, 1 round drops, 2 rounds 8°s in the same color as the second and third rounds of this bead, and 1 round 11°s in the same color as the first round of this bead.

Spacer 4: Repeat directions for Spacer 1, using a new color combination.

Bead 5: Work 1 round 11°s, 1 round 8°s, 1 round cubes, 1 round 8°s in the same color as the second round of this bead, and 1 round 11°s in the same color as the first round of this bead.

Spacer 5: Repeat directions for Spacer 1, using a new color combination.

Bead 6: Work 1 round 11°s, 1 round 8°s. Work 1 round drops with one 8° between pairs: pick up two drops and pass down through the next bead, pick up an 8° and finish the stitch by passing up through the next bead (Figure 3). Work 1 round 8°s in the same color as the second round of this bead, and 1 round 11°s in the same color as the first round of this bead.

Spacer 6: Repeat directions for Spacer 1, using a new color combination.

Bead 7: Work 1 round 11°s, 2 rounds 8°s, 1 round druks, 2 rounds 8°s in the same color as the second and third rounds of this bead, and 1 round 11°s in the same color as the first round of this bead.

Spacer 7: Work 2 rounds 15°s.

Bead 8: Work 1 round 10°s, 1 rounds 8°s, 1 round 8°s in a different color, 1 round 8°s in the same color as the second round of this bead, 1 round 10°s in the same color as the first round of this bead.

Spacer 8: Repeat directions for Spacer 1, using a new color combination.

Bead 9: Work 1 round 11°s, 1 round 8°s, 1 round 6°s, 1 round 6°s in a different color, 1 round 6°s in the same color as the third round of this bead, 1 round 8°s the same color as the second round of this bead, 1 round 11°s the same color as the first round of this bead.

Spacer 9: Repeat directions for Spacer 1, using a new color combination.

Inclusions Between the Pairs of Beads

Ndebele herringbone is composed of stacks of pairs of beads inclined toward each other. Adding a bead to the work mid-stitch places it between the columns of bead-pairs. Compare and contrast it to inclusions within the pair of beads such as in Round 88.

Bead 10: All 8°s in this bead are the same color. Work 1 round 11°s, 1 round 8°s with one 11° between the pairs (as in Bead 6), 1 round 8°s with one 15° between the pairs (as in Bead 6), 2 rounds 8°s, 1 round 11°s in the same color as the first round of this bead.

Spacer 10: Work 2 rows 15°s.

Bead 11: Work 1 round 11°s, 1 round 8°s, 1 round 6°s,

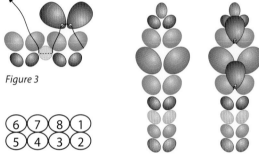

Figure 3

Figure 4

Figure 5

1 round drops, 1 round 6°s in the same color as the third round of this bead, 1 round 8°s the same color as the second round of this bead, 1 round 11°s the same color as the first round of this bead.

Spacer 11: Repeat directions for Spacer 10, but work 2 rounds 11°s.

3 *Weave the 2-headed closure.* Pinch the tube closed. You will make the next rounds on 1 pair of beads and the pair opposite, or beads 1 and 2 and 3 and 8 of the round (Figure 4). There will be only 4 beads in each round; step up after every other stitch.

*Weave each 4-bead (2-pair) round with 11°s for 8 rounds, changing colors each row.

Weave 1 round 8°s, 1 round 6°s, 1 round 8°s, and 1 round 11°s, changing colors each row.

Complete the head by using only one 11° for each stitch of these last 2 rounds: pick up 1 bead, pass down through the next bead, and pass up through the following. Repeat, stepping up. Weave the thread down through the beads to the round of 6°s. Sew on a drop bead between the 8°s on the round above and then on the round below the round of 6°s (Figure 5).

Weave down through the stack of beads to the base to the last full round of 11°s. Weaving from the remaining 4 beads of that round, repeat from * to complete the other head.

Weave down to the base round where the heads begin. Weave in the thread, making half hitches.

4 **Weave a square rope loop.** Remove the tape from the tail, thread the tail on a needle, and prepare to weave another column of 4 beads for the loop that will accept the "toggle" of the double-headed end.

Pinch the tube in half and weave off of beads 1, 2, 3, and 8 (Figure 4), stepping up after every other stitch. Weave 30 rounds of 11°s, changing color every 1–3 rounds.

Curve the end around to meet the 4 waiting beads of the ladder base, and match each bead of the ladder to a corresponding bead of the rope. Weave down through each bead in the ladder and up through the next one. Pass up through the corresponding bead of the loop and turn down through the next. Repeat for all 4 pairs, attaching each bead of the loop securely to the ladder.

Weave in tail, making half hitches.

Try this . . .

We step up upon completing a round of tubular weaving to connect the first and last beads in the round in a seamless and level way. After picking up the last pair of beads in the round, anchor them as usual by passing down through one bead and up through the next one of the previous round, then bring the needle to the top of the work by passing up into the first bead in this round to resume weaving.

Recall that peyote stitch starting with an even count requires a step-up at the end of each round. Being endless, odd-count peyote has no finite round and no opportunity to step up. By contrast, tubular herringbone stitch (which starts with an even number) offers the option to step up or not. To step up at the end of the round, pass up through the first bead of the previous round and the first bead of this round (a stack of 2 beads).

To avoid a step-up, after placing the last pair of beads, pass down through the last bead of the previous round, and instead of passing up through the 2-bead stack, simply pass up through the first bead of the new round. Hereafter all stitches will be placed this way, never stepping up through the 2-bead stack. The work will take on a subtle swirl (see below). Learn to exaggerate and manipulate the swirl in Fran's Swirling Ndebele Bracelet (page 185).

Silver and Pearls through Thick and Thin Bracelet

Weave silver seed beads with lustrous pearls to make a rope that guarantees no dull moments. Navigate the pitches and peaks created by varying the numbers of inclusions or bead sizes in each round of tubular herringbone stitch. Refer to page 16 before choosing metallic seed beads. Avoid beads with coating that will chip or peel. Choose plated beads for longer wear. Silver-lined beads will wear well when treated with the care that pearls deserve, removing them before bathing or applying perfume.

Ingredients
6 g Ceylon or pearly size 8° seed beads (A)
1 g Ceylon or pearly size 15° Japanese seed beads (B)
4 g silver-plated or silver-lined Japanese cylinder beads (C)
2 g Ceylon or other pearly Japanese cylinder beads (D)
11 round or potato 6mm pearls (PB)
12 round or potato 4mm pearls (PM)
24 round or potato 2mm pearls (PS)
Power Pro 10# beading thread

Tools
Size 12 beading needle
Skewer, needle, or stick for support (optional)

Setup
Mise en place (see page 8)

1 *Begin with a ladder-stitched (see page 153) base.* Weave a ladder 3C tall and 8 stacks long, form a ring by passing up through the first 3 beads, down through the last 3 beads, and up through the first 3 beads again. Notice that the tail and thread come out of opposite ends of the same stack. Each round will begin this way; the step-up will occur in the same stack.

2 *Weave a round of tubular herringbone stitch onto the ladder base.* *Pick up 2C. Pass down through the next C of the previous round. There is no need to drop down into deeper rounds; confine the work to the top round of the ladder. Pass up through the next C. Repeat from * 2 more times. Pick up a fourth pair of C, pass down through the next C, and step up through the topmost 2C in the next stack (which has the tail coming from its bottom). These 2C are the first one of the previous round and the first one of this round (Figure 1). This brings the thread to the top, ready for another new round.

3 *Alternate basic herringbone stitch with pearl and inclusion rounds about every ½" (1.3 cm) for 5" (12.5 cm).*
Basic herringbone stitch: Pick up 2C. Pass down through the next bead and up through the next bead. Do this 4 times per round, stepping up at the end of each round (Figure 2). *Mantra: Pick up 2 beads, go down a bead and up the next in one swoop.*

Inclusions: Pick up 2C. Pass down through the next bead, but pick up inclusions as specified below before passing up through the following bead. *Mantra: Pick up 2 beads and go down a bead. Pick up the inclusion and go up the next bead.* Step up at the end of each round.

Graduated inclusions: Weave 5 rounds using 2C for each stitch and the following inclusions between each of the 4 stitches (Figure 3):
Round 1: 1B.
Round 2: 2B.
Round 3: 3B.
Round 4: 2B.
Round 5: 1B.

Kinky corduroy: Weave 4 rounds basic herringbone stitch, placing 1A and 1C in each stitch. Then weave 4 more basic rounds, placing 1C and 1A in each stitch (Figure 4).

Pearly inclusion:
Round 1: Weave a basic round of 2C.
Round 2: Weave a round of 2C with a PS inclusion between each of the 4 stitches.
Round 3: Weave a basic round of 2C. Push each pearl forward to place the thread behind it.

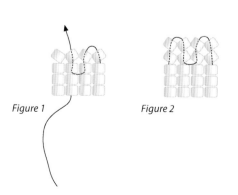

Figure 1   Figure 2

Figure 3

Figure 4

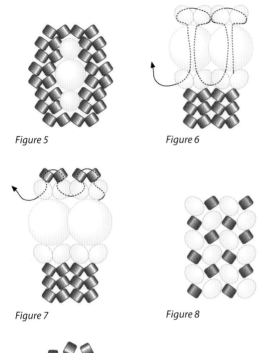

Figure 5

Figure 6

Figure 7

Figure 8

Figure 9

Round 4: Weave a round of 2C with a PM inclusion between each of the 4 stitches.

Round 5: Weave a basic round of 2C. Push each pearl forward to place the thread behind it.

Round 6: Repeat Round 2.

Round 7: Weave a basic round of 2C. Push each pearl forward to place the thread behind it (Figure 5).

Weave 7 basic rows.

The Big Pearl Trick:

Round 1: Weave a basic round of 2A.

Round 2: Pick up PB and 2A. Pass back down through the PB. Pass down through the next A bead and up through the following A bead, as in basic herring-bone stitch (Figure 6).

Repeat around, placing 3 more PB. Step up through the first 1PB and 1A.

Round 3: Weave a basic round of 2C onto the pairs of A beads placed in the previous round (Figure 7).

Weave with small pearls:

Round 1: Weave a basic round using 1PS, 2C, 1PS instead of 2 beads.

Round 2: Weave another basic round, using 2C and weaving into the Cs of the previous round.

Picot fringe woven off inclusions:

Rounds 1–3: Weave basic rounds with D beads.

Round 4: Weave a round using 2D with a 1C inclusion.

Round 5: Weave a round using 2D and a PS inclusion.

Round 6: Pick up 1C and 3B. Pass back through 1C,

Getting Around Pearls' Small Holes

There is the option to purchase a bead reamer and work on each pearl to enlarge the hole. In this piece, you will never need to pass through the pearl more than three times. Power Pro 10# beading thread fits through a size 12 needle, and this needle fits through the pearl hole even when there are already two passes of thread inside. It isn't necessary to pass through the small pearls more than twice if another round of beads is set on top of them.

making a picot of the 3B. Pass down through the next bead around and place an inclusion of 2C, passing up through the next C bead. Repeat 3 more times to complete this round. Do not step up here; pass through 2D and the first C bead of the inclusion.

Round 7: Weave a basic round, placing 2C within each pair of C bead inclusions.

The medium pearl trick:

Repeat Rounds 1–3 of the Big Pearl Trick, substituting 1PM and 2C for 1PB and 2A.

Seed Stitch

Round 1: Weave a basic round with 1A and 1C in each pair.

Round 2: Weave a basic round with 1C and 1A in each pair (Figure 8).

Repeat Rounds 1–2 four more times. There are 10 total rows in the sample.

4 *Weave a closure loop.* When the bracelet is ½" (1.3 cm) short of meeting around the wrist, weave 2 basic rows with C beads. Pinch to flatten the tube at the end. Weave basic herringbone stitch with 2C, using beads 1 and 2 and 7 and 8 as the ladder base (as in the Bead Happy Bracelet on page 177) and stepping up after every other stitch. Weave 36 rows with rows of C beads and rows of D beads.

Curve the end to meet the 4 unused beads at the base and weave the end of the loop into the base. Pass down through the corresponding bead of the base and up through the next. Pass into the corresponding bead of the loop and, changing direction, back through the next bead (Figure 9).

Repeat 3 more times to anchor the loop beads to the corresponding base beads. Weave the thread in, making half hitches.

5 *Weave the first head of the closure.* Slide the tape from the tail. Thread the tail on a needle. Pinch the tube closed as in Step 4 and weave 9 rounds using 2C, stepping up after every other stitch and placing 4 beads in each round. Weave 1 basic round with 2A. *Pick up 1B, 1PM, 1B. Pass back through 1PM, 1B, and 1A in the tube. Pass up through the next A bead. Pick up 1B, 1PB, 1B. Pass back through 1PB, 1B and 1A. Repeat from * once more.

6 *Weave the second head of the closure.* Travel down through the beads to exit one of the 4 remaining base beads. Pinch them and weave 11 basic rounds using 2C, stepping up every other stitch.

*Pick up 1A, 1PM, 1A, 1B, 1A. Pass back through 1PM, 1A, and down through the next C bead and up through the following. Repeat from * once more.

*Pick up 1PS and pass down through the next C bead and up through the following, situating 1PS between the A beads. Repeat from * once more.

Pick up 1A, 1PB, 1PS, 1B. Pass back through 1PS, 1PB, 1A, and into the beadwork. Weave the tail in, making half hitches.

Did you notice . . .

This exercise revealed how the diameter of the rope is influenced by inclusions. It provided different textural and pattern effects depending on the order that A and C beads were used. You can use this method of incorporating all types of larger beads into flat or tubular herringbone stitch.

Fran's Swirling Ndebele Bracelet

• • • • • • • • • • • • • • •

Have you noticed that deciding not to step up at the end of tubular herring-bone stitch lends a subtle twist to the rope? This is because the thread passes up through a higher bead in the next round. Instead of working off just the top round of the previous rounds, enhance that swirl by working down into three or so rounds of previous work.

Ingredients
5 g each in 3 colors size 8° seed beads (A, B, C)
16 size 6° seed beads (D)
12 size 3°, 4°, or 5° seed beads (E)
24 size 11° seed beads (F)
Fireline 10# beading thread

Tools
Size 10 beading needle

Setup
Mise en place (see page 8), with an 18" (46 cm) tail

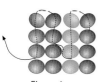

Figure 1

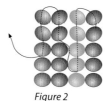

Figure 2

1 *Weave a ladder base.* Make a ladder of 3A, 3B, 3C, 3B (see page 153). Pass up through the stack of A beads, down through the last 3B, and up the stack of A beads again. The thread and tail exit the same stack of beads on the foundation ring.

2 *Weave herringbone stitch with a twist.* Pick up 1A and 1B. Pass down through 2B and up through the next 1C. Pick up 1C and 1B. Pass down through 2B and step up through the top first A of the next stack (Figure 1).

3 *Pick up 1A and 1B. Pass down through 3 beads in B stack and up through next C.* Pick up 1C and 1B. Pass down through 3 beads in the B stack, up through 1A, and step up through the first A bead of this round (Figure 2).

Repeat Step 3 until the piece measures 1" (2.5 cm) short of desired length to allow for beaded closure.

4 *Weave a fringed closure.* Weave 3 rounds using F beads. Weave 1 round each of A, B, and C beads. Weave 1 round of B beads with an inclusion of 1F between each stitch. (See page 170 for directions on making inclusions.) Weave 3 rounds of D beads with an inclusion of 1B between each stitch. Weave 3 rounds of E beads.

Weave in the thread, making half hitches. Pass up through 1E of the top round. *Pick up 2D and 1A (turning bead). Pass down through the 2D and 1E, making a fringe. Pass up through adjacent E bead. Repeat from * 3 more times.

Weave a pair of opposing fringes between the beads in the third round of D beads: exit one of the D beads in the third round. *Pick up 1C, 1B, and 2F. Skip the last F bead and pass back through 1F, 1B, 1C, and the D bead. Repeat from * to complete the opposing fringe. Weave in the thread, making half hitches.

5 *Weave a closure loop.* Slide the tape from the tail. Thread the tail on a needle, and string enough B beads to fit over the fringed ornament on the other end. Weave back down into the beadwork, making half hitches.

Tweak beaded closures to perfection

If the loop is too big to accommodate a beaded bead or toggle bar, weave a row of peyote stitch (see page 28) inside the loop, or bridge the loop with a bead or two by exiting a bead near one end of the loop, passing through the new bead or two, and entering a bead directly across the loop. You might decide to enlarge the beaded bead or toggle bar by stitching in the ditch (page 51) or fringing (page 39). Personally, I'd rather have the piece be a tad difficult to get on so it won't fall off!

Try this . . .

You can change the direction of the twist from Z to S by passing down through only 1 bead and passing up through 3. Try both ways, or even change direction within the piece, and see which way speaks to you.

Swirling Ndebele Toggle Bar

· · · · · · · · · · · · ·

One example of this beautiful toggle bar appears as a closure on the Luscious Leafy Pearl Bracelet on page 106. The dense, firm beadwork shown here produces a lovely toggle bar to any bracelet or necklace, but this segment of elegant swirl begs to be used as a beaded bead and worn proudly as a focal element.

Ingredients
2 g size 11° or Japanese cylinder beads (A)
2 g Czech tiny drop beads (B)
(An alternate, chunkier version of this toggle can be made with Miyuki 3.4 drops and size 8° seed beads.)
Fireline 10# beading thread

Tools
Size 10 beading needle

Setup
Mise en place (see page 8)

1 *Form the base for the stitch and establish the diameter of the tube.* Make a ladder of 8A. Pass through the first A, the last A, and the first A bead again, forming a foundation ring of 8 beads.

2 *Gently build the angle of swirl.* Pick up 1B and 1A. Pass down through the next 1A and up through the following one. Repeat 3 more times, placing 4 pairs of beads. Do not step up at the end of the row, but end by passing into the first bead of this round.

3 *Increase the angle of swirl.* Pick up 1B and 1A. Pass down through the next 1A and up through the stack of 2B. Repeat 3 more times, placing 4 pairs of beads. Do not step up.

4 *Place beads for the desired length, at desired angle of swirl.* Pick up 1B and 1A. Pass down through the next 1A and up through the top 3B of the stack. To make the toggle shown here, continue to add beads until the piece measures 1" (2.5 cm).

Expect an occasional drop to settle upside down. This is not only OK, but it is necessary to maintain the shape of the toggle.

5 *Finish the toggle.* Pick up 2A for each of the 4 stitches of the last row. Without adding beads, weave around this round again: with thread exiting the eighth A bead, pass down the first A bead and up the eighth A bead again. Pass down the first A bead and up the second A bead. Pass down the first A and up the second A bead again. Pass down the third A and up the second A bead again. (This maneuver of tying the adjacent beads together may remind you of square stitch.)

Try this . . .

Using plump little drop beads crowds the bead-work and yields a stiff toggle. Using regular seed beads yields a more flexible piece. Weave several inches for use as bracelet, necklace, lariat or belt.

Eleven

Brick Stitch

|||||||||||||||||||||||||||||||||||||||||||||||||||||||||||||||||||||||||||||||||||||||||||||||||||||||||||||||||||||||||||||||||||||||||||||||||

Sometimes called Comanche stitch, brick stitch has Native American origins. It looks like peyote stitch "turned on its ear." In fact, the two very different stitches can produce nearly identical results. Examined side by side, the difference might be visible only where a bead is broken: in a peyote-stitched piece, thread would cross the hole, while in the brick-stitched piece, thread would travel down to and around another thread and then back up. Each new bead in brick stitch is woven onto the thread that bridges the beads in the adjoining row rather than the beads of the work.

When I first studied brick stitch, I was confronted with two unacceptable obstacles: Every project I saw started with a ladder of bugle beads *and* had thread along the outside of the first bead or edge bead of each row. I'd spent years peyote-stitching with Japanese cylinder beads, producing supple, dense, smooth beadwork with thread visible only at the edges (known as selvedges). Any other appearance of thread is an anathema to "haute" beadwork, known in French and fashion circles as elegant, skillful and exclusive. Besides being an eyesore, thread along the outside of a bead is vulnerable to breakage.

If I was relieved to discover that bugle beads are not necessary, I was downright ecstatic when I learned to hide the thread along the outside of a bead within another bead.

Brick stitch is the perfect place to use those odd-size seed beads, where highly textured, dense, yet un-warped work is achieved by combining stack or bead heights properly. An oversize bead might occupy the next stitch perfectly, or two shorter beads used together might fit.

Bugle-free bases

Brick stitch requires a base, which is traditionally a row of ladder stitch (see page 153). Bugle beads are popular for the base because they are easy to ladder stitch. In order of ease, Japanese cylinder beads (the 3.3mm large one and the regular, smaller one), size 8° hex beads, and Japanese seed beads (size 8° and size 11°) can also be used. (Also, see Edgy Eyeglass Leash on page 159 for an alternate edge using peyote stitch.) You may skip the base altogether, replacing it with wire as in Marigold Fan Earrings and Kaja's Fan Bracelet on on page 197, thread as in the Winged Bead on page 198, or fabric as in the Backless Brick-Stitched Bezel on page 201.

Stacks vs. beads

Brick stitch provides the opportunity to make each row a different height, depending on how many beads are used at a time. To help you remember this, recipes will direct you to "pick up a *stack*" rather than "pick up a bead."

The Bountiful Garden Earrings on the next page illustrate the effect of stack size. One earring is made with one-bead stacks, yielding a nearly equilateral triangle. The second earring is an elongated version made of three-bead stacks. In theory, working with several beads at a time produces much faster results.

Basic brick stitch with a 2-stack start . . . or how to avoid, "Pardon me, but your thread is showing."

Pick up 2 stacks (which we'll call Stack 1 and Stack 2). Pass under the thread right where you want to place the 2 stacks. Pull the thread taut enough to cause them to sit side by side with their holes up, but do not permit them to slip through (Figure 1). Pass up through Stack 2, down through Stack 1, and back up through Stack 2 again (Figure 2).

For the rest of the round, simply pick up one stack and pass under the thread right where you want to situate the new stack. Pull the thread taut, but do not pull the stack through. Pass back up through the stack to bring the needle and thread up to the top, ready to place another stack (Figure 3).

Increases: To increase, simply place more than one stack in the same thread. Place them at regular intervals for uniformity. This applies to increasing within the work as well as on the edge.

Decreases: To decrease, simply skip over the thread and place the stack in the following thread. To decrease at the beginning of the row, place the first stack in the second thread. To decrease at the end of the row, stop one thread short. Place decreases at regular intervals for uniformity.

Brick stitch's versatility lends itself to sculptural beadwork. A piece can be made stiff and dense by crowding the beads onto the thread of the previous row; for supple results, situate each bead so they just barely meet.

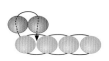

Figure 1

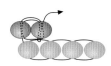

Figure 2

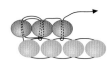

Figure 3

Bountiful Garden Earrings

• • • • • • • • • • • • •

Make a small amount of bead soup using every green and floral-colored seed bead in your stash. Weave the first earring one bead at a time, a one-bead-tall stack. Weave the second using a three-bead-tall stack. Compare their appearance, style, and time to produce. Finish them with fringes of different lengths and little flower fringe woven into place.

Ingredients
6 g assorted green size 11° seed beads (A)
3 g assorted floral-colored size 11° seed beads (B)
Beading thread
1 pair earring wires
Note: If you prefer, substitute size 8° seed beads for the size 11°s.

Tools
Beading needle
Pliers or jump ring tool (to open the earring loop)

Setup
Mise en place (see page 8), placing one needle at each end of the thread. Stir 20B into the A soup.

First Earring

1 *Weave a ladder-stitched base row.* Use the 2-needle method (see page 155) to weave an 8-stack ladder (each stack is 1A). Set aside one needle and thread for now; you will return to it for fringe.

2 *Weave across the row, decreasing by 1 bead.* This row will have one fewer bead than the previous row, and the beads of this row will sit between those of the previous row. Pick up 2A. To decrease, skip the first thread and instead pass under the next thread. Pass up through the second A, down through the first A, then up through the second A again (Figure 1). Weave across the row, using 1A in each stitch and following the general brick stitch instructions on page 189 (Figure 2).

Repeat Step 2 six times, decreasing 1 bead per row and ending with a 2A row.

3 *Make a loop.* Pick up 8A. Pass down through the other A in this row. Weave in the thread to the first row, but don't cut it until the fringe is completed.

4 *Create fringe off of each A of the ladder.* *First fringe:* With the abandoned needle and thread, pick up 7A, 3B, 7A, 5B. Pass back through 7A. Pick up 2B, skip 3B. Pass back through 7A and up

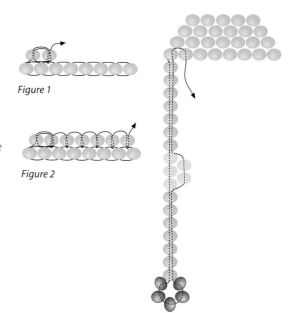

Figure 1

Figure 2

Figure 3

into the eighth bead of the ladder. Turn and pass back down through the seventh bead of the ladder (Figure 3).

Second fringe: Pick up 4A, 4B, and pass through the first of these B again, forming a loop (a flower) (Figure 4). Pick up 5A, 3B, 7A, 5B. Pass back through 7A, pick up 2B, skip 3B and pass through 5A, B, A, and up into the seventh bead of the ladder. Turn and pass back down through the sixth bead of the ladder (Figure 5).

Plaid People and Free-form People

I have a theory that people fall into two categories: plaid or free-form. Plaid people work best from a plan, with a pattern, order, and symmetry, where everything is plumb and square. Free-form people tend to work intuitively and spontaneously (though they are no less fastidious about construction and technique). They are comfortable with projects, like this one, that sometimes call for random selections, which can be painful for the plaid person. Listen up, plaid people: here is a remedy: Use a sorting triangle or ruler to arrange several beads from the soup in single file. When asked to pick up a bead randomly, simply pick up the next one in line. Don't judge it against others around it, just pick up that bead! The bead soup was made with care, from selected ingredients, so there can be no bad choice.

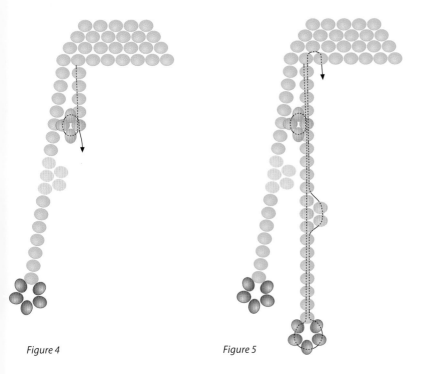

Figure 4 *Figure 5*

Third fringe: Pick up 6A, 3B, 6A, 5B. Pass through the first of the 5B again, forming a flower. Pick up 6A, 5B. Pass back through 6A, B, 6A. Pick up 3B, skip 3B, pass through 6A and up into the sixth bead of the ladder. Turn and pass back down through the fifth bead of the ladder.

Fourth fringe: Pick up 11A, 5B. Pass through the first of these B again, forming a flower. Pick up 7A, 5B. Pass through the first of these B again, forming a flower. Pick up 7A, 5B. Pass back through 7A, B, 7A, B, 11A, and up into the fifth bead of the ladder. Turn and pass back down through the fourth bead of the ladder.

Fifth fringe: Pick up 3A, 3B, 10A, 5B. Pass through the first of these B again, forming a flower. Pick up 6A, 5B. Pass through the first of these B again, forming a flower. Pick up 5A, 5B. Pass back through 5A, B, 6A, B, 10A. Pick up 2A, skip 3B, pass through 3A and up into the fourth bead of the ladder. Turn and pass back down through the third bead of the ladder.

Sixth fringe: Pick up 14A, 5B. Pass through the first of these B beads again, forming a flower. Pick up

6A, 5B. Pass back through 6A, B, 14A and up into the third bead of the ladder. Turn and pass back down through the second bead of the ladder.

Seventh fringe: Pick up 12A, 5B. Pass through the first of these B again, forming a flower. Pick up 4A, 5B. Pass through the first of these B beads again, forming a flower. Pick up 3A, 5B. Pass back through 3A, B, 4A, B, 12A, and up into the second bead of the ladder. Turn and pass back down through the first bead of the ladder.

Eighth fringe: Pick up 8A, 4B. Pass through the first of these B beads again, forming a smaller flower. Pick up 5A, 5B. Pass through the first of these B beads again, forming a flower. Pick up 1B. Pass back through the previous B, 5A, B, 8A, and up into the first bead of the ladder.

5 *Finish the earring and attach the ear wire.*
Weave the threads in, making several half hitches to secure. Open the loop on the ear wire and slip on the beaded loop. Close the ear wire loop.

Second Earring

1 **Weave a ladder-stitched base row.** Use the 2-needle method to weave an 8-stack ladder (each stack is 2A). Set aside one needle and thread for now; you will return to it for fringe.

2 **Weave across the row, decreasing by 1 stack.** This row will have 1 fewer stack than the previous row, and the stacks of this row will sit between those of the previous row. Pick up 2 stacks of 3A. To decrease, skip the first thread and pass under the next thread. Pass up through the second stack, down through the first stack, and back up through the second stack again (Figure 6).

Weave across the row, using 1 stack of 3A in each stitch and following the general brick stitch instructions

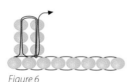

Figure 6

on page 189.

Repeat Step 2 six times, decreasing 1 stack per row and ending with a 2 stack-wide row.

3 **Make a loop.** Pick up 8A. Pass down through the other A in this row. Weave in thread, but do not cut it until the fringe is completed.

4 **Follow directions for Step 4 of first earring.**

5 **Finish the earring and attach the ear wire.** Weave the threads in, making several half hitches to secure. Open the loop on the ear wire and slip on the beaded loop. Close the ear wire loop.

Make a second earring.

Try this . . .

To achieve a diamond shape, repeat Steps 2 and 3 from the other edge of the ladder base. Make 5 diamonds, experimenting with stack sizes. Vary the stack size with each row. Assemble them in a circle to make a flower for embellishing a bracelet.

Marigold Fan Earrings

· · · · · · · · · · ·

A loop of beads is the foundation for colorful and textured rows of brick stitch finished with a picot edge. This is the perfect project to use your imperfect beads of different heights. Design a pair for earrings or make one to wear as a pendant.

Ingredients

90 colored, lined size 11° seed beads (A)

12 size 15° seed beads (B)

2 g size 11° seed beads in assorted colors and finishes (C)

2 g size 8° seed beads in assorted colors and finishes (D)

2 crimp beads

2 lengths 2" (5 cm) beading wire

Beading thread

1 pair earring posts or wires

Tools

Crimping pliers

Beading needle

Setup

Mise en place (see page 8)

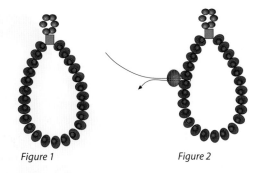

Figure 1   Figure 2

1 *String a foundation row.* Use 1 length of beading wire to string one crimp bead and 25A. Pass back through the crimp bead. Pick up 6B and pass back through the crimp bead again (the wire passes through crimp bead 3 times). Crimp the bead (see page 26) (Figure 1). Trim beading wire close to crimp bead.

2 *Begin brick stitch.* With needle and thread, pick up 1D, pass under the beading wire between fifth and sixth beads, and pass back through the D (Figure 2).

Weave off of the center 15A of the strung 25A as follows, using beads of varied sizes but similar heights. (If a C is as tall as a D bead, use either one, but if it takes 2 short Cs to equal the height of a D, use 2C or D interchangeably.) Pick up the 1C (or 1D or 2 short C) and push them close to the work. Pass under the beading wire between the pair of A beads. There is no hard and fast rule about securing a bead off the thread or wire between every pair in

the foundation; pass under the beading wire wherever it is necessary (Figure 3). Stop when 5A remain.

3 *Add 2 more rows of brick stitch.*
Row 2: Pick up 2 stacks. Count them off to yourself. Pass under the thread between the last 2 beads of the previous row. Pull the thread taut so that the beads lie side by side with holes up. Pass back up through the second, down through the first, and back up through the second again. Continue to weave across the row by picking up a stack, passing under the thread of the previous row directly beneath the new stack, and passing back up through the new stack. Use beads and stacks of similar height.
Row 3: Pick up 1C, 1A, 1C. Pass under the thread between the last pair of beads from the previous row. Pass up through the second C bead, down through the first C bead, and back up through the second C bead again. Continue to weave across the row, picking up 1A and 1C, passing under the thread between the next pair of beads from the previous row, and passing back up through 1C (Figure 4). (A is just along for the ride.)

4 *Finish the earring.* Weave the thread and tail into the beadwork. Open the loop on the earring post or wire, slip the small loop of B into the earring loop, and close the earring loop. Make a second coordinating or matching earring.

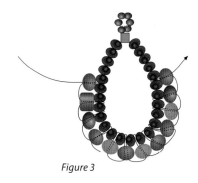

Figure 3

Figure 4

Single-bead Start

When the thread is already attached to the beadwork, avoid thread on the outside of a bead by starting every row with 2 stacks. When approaching the work with a new needle and thread, there are two options: tie it into the wire or thread that will serve as the foundation and work the 2-stack start, or pick up a bead, pass under the wire or thread, and pass back through the bead. This brings the thread out the top of a bead and ready to continue. Later, slide the tape from the tail. Weave the tail into the beadwork.

Try this . . .

Kaja's Bracelet

Kaja wove 10 fans to string with faceted rondelles in this stunning bracelet. To make your own, weave 10 fans in your choice of colors (Figure 5). On beading wire, string 1 faceted rondelle, then alternate stringing 1 fan with 4 rondelles until the piece is the desired length, ending with 1 rondelle (Figure 6). (When stringing the fans, tuck the small loop inside the larger loop.) There are 39 rondelles in the sample shown here, and it measures 7" (18 cm).

Attach a toggle bar, either purchased or beaded, to the ends using crimp beads. Push each fan down toward the right. Working from left to right, arrange them so that the last row of one fan rests on the small loop of the next fan. Tack them in place by square stitching a mid-bead of the picot edging of one fan to the mid-bead of the small loop of the next fan.

More ideas for working without a base row

This recipe used strung beading wire as the base, eliminating the base row. You could choose to replace the beading wire with a wire hoop earring or any other strand. It doesn't need to be strung as it is here—simply tie the thread onto the wire and commence the first round of brick stitch with the usual 2 stacks placed by passing under the wire and back up through the new beads. Consider simply stringing a ring of beads and brick-stitching around all or part of it.

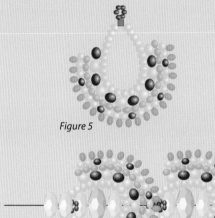

Figure 5

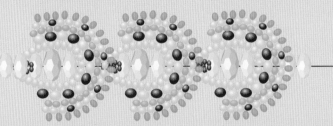

Figure 6

Winged Bead

• • • • • •

Choose a perfect round, a facetted briolette, or even a long tubular bead, and give it wings. A winged bead can be a distinctive closure for beadwork. Finish one end of a bracelet or necklace with a loop of beads (like the peyote-stitched loop from the Carpet of Beads Bracelet, page 36). Secure a winged bead to the opposite end by stringing it directly onto the work or weaving the wings into the work. Pinch the wings together and slip the bead through the loop like a toggle. This closure rivals any focal bead, so go ahead and wear it in the front.

Ingredients
6mm or larger bead to embellish
5 g assorted seed beads in different sizes and
    shapes (triangle beads are beautiful in this
    project)
Power Pro 10# beading thread

Tools
Beading needle

Setup
Mise en place (see page 8)

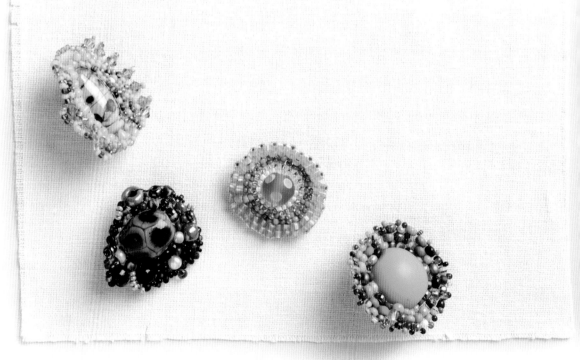

Figure 1

Figure 2

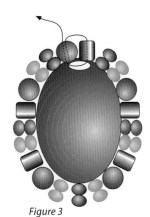

Figure 3

1 *Provide a baseless base.* Pass up through the large bead 5 times, resulting in 4 thread passes on its surface. Separate them into 2 pairs on opposite sides of the bead (Figure 1).

2 *Weave a round of brick stitch off the thread base.* Use a 2-stack start (see directions for Bountiful Garden Earrings on page 191). Use stacks of similar height within each row or round, combining beads if necessary. For the rest of the round, pick up 1 stack and pass under the thread where the new stack should sit (Figure 2). Pull the thread taut, but do not let the stack slip under the threads. Pass back up through the stack to bring the needle and thread to the top, ready to place another stack. When the last stack placed reaches the first one, pass down through the first one and up the last one again (Figure 3).

3 *Weave a round of brick stitch off of the previ-ous round, picking up 2 stacks at the start of each round or row.* This round can be a different height than the last. You will weave off the thread that connects the adjacent stacks of the previous round, but don't feel obliged to place one (or only one) bead for each section of thread. When the last stack placed reaches the first one, pass down though the first one and up the last one again.

Repeat Step 3 for as many rows as desired.

4 *Finish the bead.* Weave in the thread and tail, making half hitches.

Try this . . .

There are so many variations on this project; here are just a few:

Rather than weaving around the entire circumference of the base bead, weave from hole to hole: pick up 2 stacks, then turn and work back across the row to the opposing hole, following the directions for placing the stacks.

Feel free to make several passes of thread on the base bead and give it many wings, as in the red and amethyst piece.

Produce a fancier edge—add a bead in the final round by picking up an extra bead before the stack. Pass under the thread and back up through the stack, ignoring the extra bead.

To weave concentric circles—each round larger than the proceeding one—consider using a larger bead in each round.

Make one using one kind of bead for the entire round, followed by a round of another bead, and so on, like rings of a tree.

Use herringbone stitch for the last round or two (as in the You Are My Sunshine Beaded Pendant on page 203). Make two or more wings, separated by the hole that runs through the embellished bead or "jump over" the hole and weave one Saturnian ring around the entire bead.

Wear it singly as a pendant or dangle one from each ear. Join multiples for a stunning bracelet or necklace.

Backless Brick-Stitched Bezel

• • • • • • • • • • • • • • •

Weave a base to wrap around a cabochon (or a coin, mirror, or flat bead) and secure it with two rounds of brick stitch that are smaller in circumference than the base. Though the recipe that follows is specific to a ⅝" (1.5 cm) cabochon, it can apply to any size cabochon by altering the quantity of beads per round.

Ingredients
40 size 8° Japanese seed beads (A)
52 size 11° Japanese seed beads (B)
16 size 11° seed beads (C)
⅝" (1.5 cm) cabochon
Beading thread

Tools
Size 10 beading needle

Setup
Mise en place (see page 8)

Figure 1

Figure 2

1 *Weave a base row.* Make a base of peyote stitch 2A wide (see directions in Edgy Eyeglass Leash on page 159) that meets around the cabochon. Zip the ends together seamlessly (see page 40).

2 *Weave a round of brick stitch.* Pick up 1B, 1C, 1B. Remember that the first brick stitch of the round uses 2 stacks or beads. The C bead is just along for looks; ignore it once it's on the thread. Place 2 more regular brick stitches (using B and C beads) into the next available thread. When placing every fourth stitch, skip the next available thread, making a decrease. Continue to work around, placing 16B and 16C in this round (Figure 1).

3 *Weave a round of brick stitch on the opposite side to trap the cabochon in the bezel.* Weave down through 1C and 1B and diagonally through the 2 base rows created in Step 1. Place the cabochon in the opening and make a row of brick stitch around this side of the base: Pick up 2B for the start of the round, and thereafter 1B per stitch, placing 20B, or one per thread. Keep the tension firm and allow the beads to fall forward onto the face of the cabochon.

4 *Weave the last row.* Weave down through a B bead and diagonally through the 2 base rows, (B and C).

Pick up 1B and pass through the next C bead (as in peyote stitch), placing 16B (Figure 2).

Weave the thread and tail into the beadwork, making half hitches.

Did you notice . . .

This bezel is attractive from the front and back. You will notice that one side closes in more that the other. The shape of your cabochon will help determine which side of the bezel to use on the front or back.

Try this . . .

On the C-side, weaving additional rounds of decreasing peyote will give the cabochon a back. Because there are 16 high beads (divisible by 2 and 4), place the decreases of another round on every second or fourth bead. If there were 20 beads, you could decrease every second, fourth, or fifth bead.

And as always, herringbone stitch can be woven off brick stitch. An extra bead placed between the 2 regular beads of its stitch produces a picot-like point. Extending the "stack" concept to herringbone stitch lengthens the picot for a petal-like look.

You Are My Sunshine Beaded Pendant

Capture tiny images of your loved ones and surround them with herringbone-stitched rays of sunshine emanating from rounds of brick stitch.

Ingredients
2 photographs to cut and mount
2 g each in 3 colors size 11° Japanese seed beads (A, B, C)
1 g each in 2 colors size 15° Japanese seed beads (D, E)
Beading thread
2 Page Pebbles or round sticky glass tiles (find them in the scrapbooking aisle)
Lacy's Stiff Stuff (nonwoven backing), size of page pebbles
Glue (any type)
Leather or ultrasuede (optional)

Tools
Size 12 beading needle

Setup
Mise en place (see page 8)

1 ***Mount the photos.*** Remove the paper from the adhesive side of one Page Pebble and center it over the desired portion of the photograph. Trim it close. Repeat for the second photograph. Trace the outline of the Page Pebbles onto the backing. Cut ⅛" (3 mm) larger than the outline.

2 ***Bead Round 1 in ladder stitch.*** Make any kind of knot on the end of the thread and pass up through the backing in the traced area. Pick up 2A and pass down through the backing again, 2 bead's width away. Pass back up through so the needle exits the first A. Pass down through the second A and through the backing again. Position the beads so that they sit side by side with their holes up. Pass up through the backing 1 bead's width away. Pick up 1A and pass through down the second A and backing, then back up through the backing and through the 1A just added.

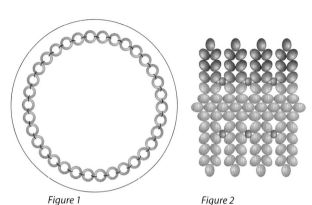

Figure 1   Figure 2

*Pick up 1A and pass down through the backing 1 bead's width away. Pass back up through the backing 1 bead's width away. Pick up 1A and pass down through the previous A and the backing, then back up through the A just added. Repeat from * to complete the round (Figure 1). You may need to finesse the final few beads so that you have an even number of beads in the round; for example, a ¾" (2 cm) Page Pebble will have 32 or 34 beads in this round.

3 *Brick-stitch around and mount the photo.* Brick-stitch (see page 189) 1 round of A beads, placing an 1A above and between each A bead of the base round, following directions on page 118 and referring to Figures 1 and 2. At the end of the round, pass down the first A bead and up the last A bead again, connecting the first and last A beads of this round. Turn back the edge of the backing so that you're working on the backside. Place a dab of glue on the backing and hold a mounted photo in place. Keep your tension firm as you weave another round of brick stitch.

4 *Weave herringbone stitch (see page 161) off the front and back of Round 1 simultaneously.* Pass through the beadwork to exit an A bead from Round 1. *Pick up 2A and pass down through the

next A bead of the original round. Pick up 2B and pass up through the next A bead of the original round. Repeat from * for entire round.

5 *Weave additional rounds.* Pass through the beads to exit the new row on the picture side of the round.
Next Round: Herringbone-stitch to make another round of C beads.
Next Round: Herringbone-stitch another round of C beads, but add a 1D inclusion mid-stitch: pick up 2C, pass down through the next C bead, and before finishing the stitch pick up 1D and pass up through the next C bead. Continue around.
Next Round: Weave another round of herringbone stitch, using 3C instead of 2C and passing down through the C bead of the previous round plus the 1B, 1D, 1B, and then up through the next C bead of the previous row, to produce a petal or ray effect (Figure 2).

6 *Finish the pendant.* Glue the second photo (and Page Pebble) to the back of the piece.
Create a loop of beads between the rays at the center top to slip the piece onto a chain or charm bracelet, using the method of your choice. (The loop shown here uses a column of square-stitched pairs of beads.) Weave in the thread and tail.

Twelve

African Polygon

This tubular stitch produces a rope with flat sides. Each stitch places a segment of beads, and the number of segments per round determines the number of sides, or faces. There are several ways to alter the look of this rope, including varying the number of beads per segment, and changing the position within each segment where you make the thread-to-thread attachment. The resulting beadwork can range from lacy to dense. The projects offered here produce dense beadwork, my personal preference. Try them once again, altering the number, type and combination of beads used. Experiment boldly!

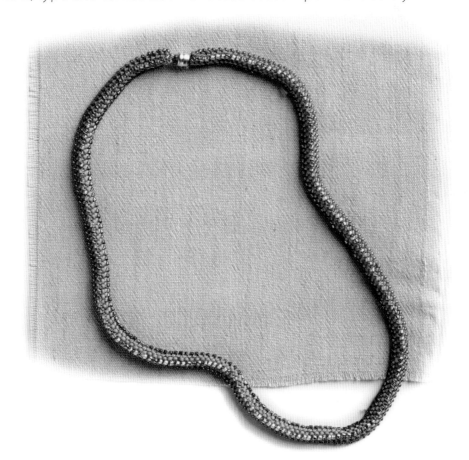

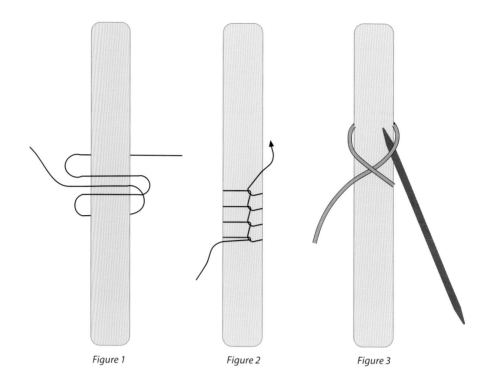

Figure 1   *Figure 2*   *Figure 3*

Like brick stitch, each stitch involves both passing under the thread *and* passing through a bead. Also like brick stitch, passing under the thread between two beads of the previous segment on this face anchors the new segment. But unlike brick stitch, where the bead passed back through is the one just placed, African polygon stitch requires passing through a bead in the next face. While in brick stitch passing through a bead is part of the anchoring process, in African polygon stitch passing through a bead positions the needle to pick up and add a segment on another face.

A stick is not just helpful for this tubular weave, it is imperative. Traditionally, the first step is to wrap the stick before even starting to weave.

Traditional Start

After the *mise en place*, fold the last 10" (25.5 cm) of the tail-end of the thread. Lay the stick on it and pass back through the loop it produces (Figure 1). Wrap with 3 more blanket stitches (Figure 2).

Cast-on Method

When first learning to knit, I was taught the simplest cast-on, wrapping the yarn around the index finger and slipping the loop produced it onto the knitting needle (Figure 3). This is a quick and easy method of producing the traditional start for African polygon stitch, too.

Basic Stitch

1 *Dress the stick as noted above, using traditional start.*

2 *Place the foundation round.* Pick up 3A (segment A). Pass under the top thread-wrap, but don't pull the beads through. Pick up 3B (segment B). Pass under the top thread-wrap, but don't pull the beads through. Pick up 3C (segment C). Pass under the top thread-wrap, but don't pull the beads through (Figure 4).

The segments should reach around the stick and may loop slightly.

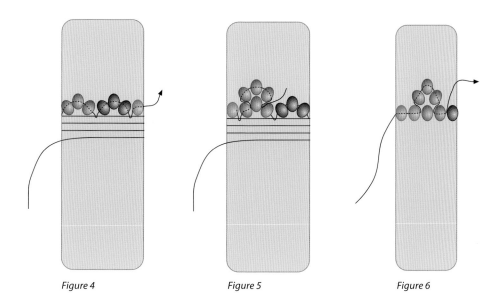

Figure 4   Figure 5   Figure 6

3 *Weave for the desired length.* Pass through the first A of segment A. Pick up a new segment A. Pass under the thread between the second and third A beads of the previous round. Push the new segment up while pulling the thread taut (Figure 5).

Repeat for segments B and C around.

To remove the work from the stick, undo the wraps from around the stick and slide the stick out. Secure the tail with more knots before cutting.

Wrap-less Start

When students ask, "What's with the thread-wrapping?" I can only reply, "That's the way it's done." It also results in thread showing. With all due respect to tradition, but in the spirit of innovation, I offer this alternate start that requires no wraps:

1 *Establish the diameter of the rope.* Pick up 2C, 2A, 2B. Tie a knot to make a ring and pass through the 2C. Put on a stick (skewer, knitting needle, etc).

2 *Build the foundation round.* Pick up 3A (segment A), skip a bead, pass under the thread, pass through a bead (Figure 6).

Repeat for segments B and C.

Follow Step 3 as for the traditional start above.

(The generic recipe in Step 1 is the number of beads per segment you'll use in Step 2, minus the number of beads on the end of the new segment.)

Triangular Rope Bracelet

· · · · · · · · · · ·

Seen from the end, this rope is triangular. The sides are flat, not curved as in other ropes. The first bead of a segment or stitch is diagonal, the second or middle one is horizontal, and the third or last is vertical. The effect baffles the uninitiated and intrigues the seasoned beader. A fun, fast and rewarding stitch, this places nine beads per round in just three stitches.

Ingredients
16 g each in three colors of size 8° seed beads
  (A, B, C)
3 charms (3 brass hands in sample)
Fireline 10# or size D beading thread to match
  the dominant color of the beads

Tools
Size 10 beading needle
Knitting needle, skewer, or dowel

Setup
Mise en place (see page 8)

1 *Prepare to weave the rope.* Use the traditional start (page 206) or wrap-less start (page 207).

2 *Place the first round.* Follow Step 2 of the basic stitch (if you started with the traditional start) or Step 2 of the wrap-less start (if you started with the wrap-less start).

3 *Follow Step 3 of the basic stitch (on page 207).* Continue to add beads until the bracelet reaches the desired length (the measurement of your wrist minus the length of the clasp).

4 *Finish the bracelet.* Place segments A, B and C. Pass down through the column of C beads, making half hitches. Continue weaving the thread through the column of C beads (Figure 1).

5 *Attach charms for the closure.* Weave back up to the last bead placed. Pick up 3A and a charm. Pass back through the A beads. Repeat 3 times, placing 3 charms on short fringes off the tip of the bracelet. Weave in the thread, making half hitches.

6 *Weave a loop for the closure.* Slide the tape from the tail. Thread the tail on the needle. Pick up 15A (enough to just fit over the largest single charm). Pass through the first bead of the bracelet again. Weave in the tail, making half hitches.

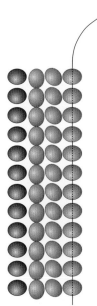

Figure 1

Try this . . .

Notice that one bead of a side carries over to show on the adjacent side, so no side is a solitary color. Explore other versions using a greater number of beads per segment, or using several colors or bead styles within a segment. For longer segments, rather than weaving into the first bead of each segment, weave through the second or third, and pass under the thread before the third-to-last or second-to-last beads, rather than before the last.

Octagonish Bracelet

• • • • • • • • • •

Weave a square rope by using four segments per round. Use a different bead at the edge to frame each face of the rope. Here, choose a triangle for the edge to flatten it, making it nearly an octagon. Navigate through the stitches to transition from polygon to peyote to herringbone to square stitch.

Ingredients
6 g each of 4 colors of size 8° seed beads (A, B, C, D)
5 g size 8° triangle beads (T)
Size D or F beading thread to match the dominant color of the beads

Tools
Size 10 beading needle
Knitting needle, skewer, or dowel

Setup
Mise en place (see page 8), leaving a 2' (61 cm) tail

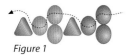

Figure 1

Figure 2 (tubular)

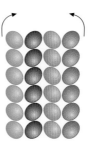

Figure 3 (tubular)

1 *Prepare the stick.* Use the traditional start (see page 206) to wrap the stick. For wrap-less method, pick up 1D, 1T, 1A, 1T, 1B, 1T, 1C, 1T. Tie into a knot. Pass through the D and T.

2 *Set up the foundation and begin weaving the rope.* Follow directions for the traditional method (page 206) or wrap-less method (page 207), but place four segments in each round—use 2A, 1T for segment A; 2B, 1T for segment B; 2C, 1T for segment C; and 2D, 1T for segment D.

3 *Weave the segments in order (A, B, C, D) to desired length.* For both methods, pass through the first A bead, pick up segment A, and pass under thread before the T bead. Repeat around, placing segments B, C, and D in the same way.

Repeat Step 3 until rope measures 1"(2.5 cm) short of the desired length.

4 *Complete the polygon section.* Taper the end by working one round, using only one A, B, C, or D in each segment, respectively. At the end of the last round, placing the D segment puts the needle and thread in front of an A bead.

5 *Transition from polygon weave to peyote stitch.* Use the bead that's oriented horizontally as the high bead. Pick up 1A and pass through the high A bead. Pick up 1B and pass through the high B bead (Figure 1). Pick up 1C and pass through the high C bead. Pick up 1D and pass through the high D bead. (Remember that we're ignoring the T beads in this round.)

6 *Weave rounds of herringbone stitch.* Pass through all 4 beads just added (A, B, C, D) again and pull them snug (Figure 2). Looking from above, you will see they are set up for weaving 4-bead rounds of herringbone stitch. Pass through 1A.

Pick up 1A, 1B, and pass down through B and up through 1C. Pick up 1C, 1D, and pass down through 1D and step up through up the next 2A. Weave 5 rounds in this manner (Figure 3).

211

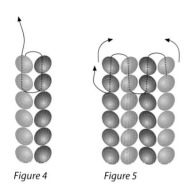

Figure 4   Figure 5

1 round, placing 2T within the stitch and weaving off the 2-bead increase, as follows: Pick up 1A, 2T, 1B, and pass down through 1B. Pick up 1B and pass up through 1B. Pick up 1B, 1T, 1C, and pass down through 1C. Pick up 1C and pass up through 1C. Pick up 1C, 2T, 1D, and pass down through 1D. Pick up 1D and pass up through 1D. Pick up 1D, 1T, 1A, and pass down through 1A. Pick up 1A and pass up through top 2A. Weave in the thread, making half hitches.

7 *Weave a buttonhole for one-half of a closure.* Pick up 1A, 1B. Pass down through B and back up through A and the new A (Figure 4).

Repeat 8 more times. Pass down through all 9B. Pass up through 1C. Pick up 1C, 1D. Pass down through 1D and back up through 1C and the new C bead. Repeat 8 more times.

8 *Return to weaving herringbone stitch.* Pass down through 1D and up through the last A bead placed. Weave 2 rounds of herringbone stitch as in Step 6.

9 *Add a flare.* Weave 1 round in herringbone stitch, placing a T within the stitch and 2 beads between the stitches, as follows: Pick up 1A, 1T, 1B, and pass down through 1B. Pick up 1B, 1C, and pass up through 1C. Pick up 1C, 1T, 1D, and pass down through 1D. Pick up 1D, 1A, and pass up through the top 2A. (See directions on page 171 for adding inclusions in herringbone stitch). Weave

10 *Add a tail-end closure.* Slide the tape from the tail. Thread the tail on a needle. Pass through 1A. To weave a square herringbone-stitched rope from the 4 beads here (1A, 1B, 1C, 1D), pick up 1A, 1B, and pass through 1B and 1C. Pick up 1,C, 1D, pass through 1D, and step up through the top 2A (the first A bead of the previous round and the A bead on top of it). Weave about 1" (2.5 cm) of tubular herringbone stitch (Figure 5).

Follow the directions in Step 9 to add a flare, or place inclusions of your choice to create a closure that will pass through the slit created in Step 7 and hold the bracelet securely.

Try this . . .

By identifying high beads on the end, you could opt for a round of peyote stitch, right angle weave, 6-bead daisy chain, triangle weave, etc. Test your beading legs and give those options a go.

Thirteen

African Helix

African Helix stitch produces a gently swirling rope of three or more panels separated by raised piping. It has more in common with bead crochet and stringing than with bead-weaving, because once the beads are picked up on the thread they are never passed through again. Unlike other off-loom bead-weaving techniques, the beads are incorporated into the beadwork solely by anchoring the thread that carries them to the thread between two previously placed beads. ("What about brick stitch?" you ask. Brick stitch does rely on anchoring thread to thread, but it also requires passing back through the new bead.)

A stitch in which the beads never have to accommodate more than one thread pass provides a great opportunity to use those beads with impossibly tiny holes. In general, Japanese seed beads have larger holes than their Czech counterparts, making them the top choice for beadwork that calls for multiple thread passes. But there are so many yummy Czech seed beads and reasons to love them. The shadows that their plumper profiles cast can give a subtle stippled effect to the beadwork. They provide texture to a piece that would be rendered sleek if composed of Japanese seed beads.

This stitch begs for those pesky beads with tiny holes. Use size 13°, charlottes, size 12° stripy,

and even marcasite Czech seed beads to your heart's content. Use pearls and even gemstones, but be wary of roughly drilled and abrasive holes.

If the piping is made of the same size bead as the sides, the beadwork is dense. If the piping beads are of a larger size, the work opens up slightly; if smaller, the beads may crowd too much, which can be remedied by adding another bead.

A three-sided rope swirls less, works up faster, and has a smaller circumference than a four-sided version of the same bead and panel size.

The size of the panels can also vary. Use 2 beads per panel for a narrower rope, or 4 or more beads per panel for a larger diameter rope.

Back in the Supple, Shiny, and Shapely Bracelet on page 62, we discussed the benefits of using a stick to hold tubular beadwork while weaving the first few inches. A stick is almost essential to weaving African helix, whose integrity is established by thread tension. Choose a knitting needle, straw, tube, or dowel that fits inside the initial ring of beads of your current project. Build each row on top of the previous one, pushing the stick up to extend from the top as you work

Basic African helix

To experiment with the basic African helix stitch, grab a needle and thread, panel beads (A) and piping beads (B).

1. *Determine the number of panels and diameter of the work.* Pick up 2B, 3A, once per panel (3 times for 3-panel rope, or 4 times for 4-panel).

2. *Tie the beads into a ring and slip the ring onto an appropriately sized stick.* Position the work so that the knot is to the left of 3A and right of 2B, flipping it over if necessary (Figure 1). (It may help to tape the tail to the stick.)

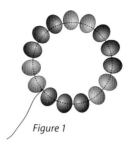

Figure 1

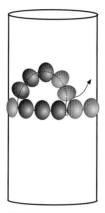

Figure 2

3. *Weave for the desired length.* Pick up 3A and 2B. Slide the needle up and under the thread between A and B of the next panel to the right (counterclockwise). Push the loop of 5 new beads up to arch above the work (Figure 2).

Pull the thread, being sure that the thread has settled between A and B.

Repeat until the work is the desired size.

4. *Finish the piece.* Finish by passing through the beads of the last row again, if possible, making half hitches. You could also finish by passing down into the next B, making a half hitch, and traveling through another B before making another half hitch. Repeat several times before cutting the thread.

When you slide the work from the stick, the panels will appear to recede slightly while the piping raises up.

Adding new thread

If it becomes necessary to add new thread, follow the line of piping from the last stitch. Enter the piping with the new thread at least an inch from the last bead. Travel through a few piping beads and make a half hitch. Pass through another piping bead and make another half hitch. Do not pull the thread when weaving through the piping; you don't want it to shorten. Place at least 4 knots before exiting the top bead of the piping, right where the abandoned thread was left.

You Say Your Piping Didn't Pop?

You've slid the work from the stick and in your hands is a beautiful piece of beadwork rope bereft of piping, panels, or any sign of relief.

If it's worked to the right (or counterclockwise) and each new addition is pushed up, piping will result. If it feels more natural to bead to the left, or clockwise, allow the work to develop below the previous rows by pushing each new addition *down*. The piping results from the particular combination of the thread passing down-and-over or up-and-under the connecting thread.

Harlequin Bracelet

• • • • • • • • •

You could grab two hanks of beads, a needle and thread, and a stick, and whip up a four-panel rope with contrasting piping of your own design. Or, in Harlequin style, weave this one of four brightly colored panels separated by black-and-white checkerboard piping. Embellish the midsection with festive fringe.

Ingredients

8 g each of 4 colors size 8° seed beads (A, B, C, D)
   (blue, burgundy, olive, saffron shown here)
4 g each white and black size 11° seed beads (E, F)
4 g each of 4 colors size 11° seed beads to match
   size 8° beads (aa, bb, cc, dd)
8 small lampworked or pressed-glass beads,
   6–10mm in coordinatng colors
Fireline 10# or Power Pro 10# beading thread

Tools

Size 10 beading needle
Knitting needle, straw, tubing, or dowel

Setup

Mise en place (see page 8), allowing a 24"
   (61 cm) tail

1 *Determine the number of panels and diam-eter of the work.* Pick up 1E, 1F, 3A, 1E, 1F, 3B, 1E, 1F, 3C, 1E, 1F, 3D. Tie the beads into a ring.

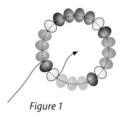

Figure 1

2 *Place the work on the stick.* Slip the ring of beads onto the stick. Pass through 1E and 1F, so that the thread is between 1F and 1A. The knot should be to the left of 3D, flipping it over if neces-sary (Figure 1). (It may help to tape the tail to the stick.)

3 *Weave rounds of basic African helix.* Pick up 3 panel beads (A, B, C, or D) and 2 piping beads (E and F). Slide the needle up under the thread between the panel and piping beads of the panel to the right, or counterclockwise (Figure 2). *Note:* To secure the position of the thread, slide the thumb-nail of the hand holding the stick up against the panel and piping beads that parted for the needle.

Push the loop up while pulling the thread. Repeat in order, placing 3A, 1E, 1F; 3B, 1E, 1F; 3C, 1E, 1F; 3D, 1E, 1F to complete each round.

Repeat Step 3 for approximately 8 rounds, or a little more than 1" (2.5 cm).

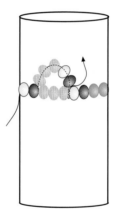

Figure 2

4 *Substitute the panel beads with smaller beads in the same colors.* Repeat Step 3, using aa for A, bb for B, cc for C and dd for D, for about an ad-ditional 2" (5 cm). *Note:* The bracelet shown here is nearly 7" (18 cm) long. For a smaller bracelet, weave less than 2" (5 cm) here.

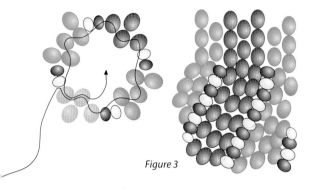

Figure 3

Figure 4

Figure 5

5 *Taper the end by reducing each round by 1 panel bead each round.* Weave 1 round of Step 3, placing only 2 of each panel bead.

Weave 2 rounds of Step 3, placing only 1 of each panel bead.

Weave the thread in, making half hitches.

6 *Weave the other half of the bracelet.* Repeat Steps 1–5 to weave the other end of the bracelet.

7 *Connect the halves with a tubular peyote-stitched midsection.* Slide the tape from the tail of one piece. Thread the tail on a needle. Ignore E and F. Using only 3A, 3B, 3C, and 3D (12 beads), weave a round of peyote stitch, picking a bead the same color as the bead being skipped. Pick up 1A, skip 1A, and pass through the next 1A. Pick up 1A, skip 1A and pass through 1B. Pick up 1B, skip 1B and pass through the next 1B (Figure 3). *Mantra: Pick up a bead, skip a bead, pass through a bead.* (See page 22 for more on peyote stitch.) Weave 6 rounds, stepping up at the end of each round.

Repeat with the other half of the bracelet, but weave only 2 peyote-stitched rounds. Connect the two halves of the bracelet by zipping the ends together seamlessly on the last peyote-stitched rounds, (Figure 4), as in the toggle directions on page 40.

8 *Weave a loop for one half of the closure with the thread from one half of the bracelet.* Using 2-bead-wide ladder stitch (see page 153) and smaller beads, weave a 1½" (3.8 cm) column off one side of the tube (Figure 5). Connect it to the opposite side of the tube, forming a loop. Weave in the thread, making half hitches.

9 *Weave a 2-drop peyote-stitched toggle bar and attach it.* Repeat the *mise en place* and make a 2-drop peyote-stitched toggle bar 8 beads wide and 6 beads long, using 1A, 1B, 1C, and 1D. Zip the ends together seamlessly (see page 40). With the thread from the other tapered end of the bracelet, pick up any 6 size 8° beads. Pass through the toggle bar perpendicularly. Pick up a turning bead (aa) and pass back down through the toggle and 6-bead stem and into the bracelet. Weave in the thread, making half hitches.

10 *Embellish the bracelet.* Fringe (see page 39) the tubular peyote-stitched midsection, avoiding a path 3–4 beads wide that will have contact with the wrist. Using sizes 11° and 8° seed beads, make fringes from 4 to 9 beads tall, some ending with an M&M sized hoo-hah and some with 1, 3, or 5 turning beads. Make loops in place of fringes in some areas.

Did you notice . . .

If the piping beads are the same size as the panel beads, and 2 piping beads are used per stitch, the weave is uniform and there is a slight space between the rows of panel beads. If the piping beads are smaller than the panel beads, the rows of panel beads lie close together. If the size difference is too great, the row of panel beads crowd and the work stiffens. For sculptural purposes, this can be an asset, but it can be a drawback for wearables. Increasing the number of piping beads per stitch produces open and lacy versions.

Only Once Through the Beads Bangle Bracelet

Typical of African helix, once the beads are on the thread, you never pass through them again—hence the name. Here's a great opportunity to use those tiny-holed size 12° stripy ones I adore, or those miniscule marcasite beauties. Attach findings as usual, or string it onto beading wire using secrets shared here to prevent slumping and sliding. Follow the directions below to hide the clasp within a tube of peyote stitch and add a safety chain of beads.

Ingredients
With smaller seed beads:
24 g size 11°/12° seed beads for
    panel (A)
8 g size 11°/12° seed beads for
    piping (B)
Fireline size 6# beading thread
With larger seed beads:
36 g size 8° seed beads for
    panel (A)
12 g size 8° seed beads for
    piping (B)
Fireline size 10# beading thread
With either size seed bead:
20 Japanese size 8° seed beads
    (or any that will fit within the
    beadwork rope and on the
    beading wire)
10" (25 cm) medium 0.018" or
    0.019" beading wire
4 crimp beads to accommodate
    2 beading wire passes
Strong magnetic closure

Tools
Size 10 beading needle
Crimping pliers

Setup
Mise en place (see page 8)

Figure 1

1 *Determine the number of panels and diameter of the work.* Pick up 1B, 3A, 1B, 3A, 1B, 3A. Tie into a ring.

2 *Place the work on the stick.* Slip the ring of beads onto a stick. The knot should be to the right of 3A.

3 *Weave rounds of basic African helix.* Pick up 3A, 2B. Pass the needle up under the thread between 1A and 1B of the next panel to the right (counterclockwise). Push the loop up while pulling the thread.

Repeat until the ends just meet around the wrist.

4 *Taper the end to match the beginning.* Weave one round using one fewer B bead in each stitch. Weave the thread into the piping beads, making half hitches, but don't cut the thread yet.

5 *Secure half the clasp to one end of 10" (25 cm) beading wire.* String 1 crimp bead, 4 seed beads that will accommodate two passes of beading wire, and half the clasp. Pass back through the seed beads and crimp bead (Figure 1). Crimp the bead (see page 26).

Slide the tape off the tail. Thread the tail on a needle. Thread the beading wire through the beadwork so that the 4 seed beads and crimp bead are hidden within and the magnet is outside the end. Secure the end of the bracelet to the beading wire by passing the thread around the beading wire between the 4 beads on it, avoiding the bead adjacent to the crimp bead because it may cut the thread. Weave the thread into the beads at the bracelet's end. Weave the thread into the beadwork, making half hitches.

6 *Size the bracelet.* Squash the bracelet to make it as short as possible without forcing it. Mark that spot on the beading wire by crimping a crimp bead here (on the single wire). Measure the desired length of the bracelet with a ruler or by wrapping it around your wrist. Mark that spot on the beading wire with a pen or marker. String as many seed beads as needed to cover the beading wire from the crimp bead (marking the shortened bracelet) to this mark (Figure 2).

7 *Attach the second half of the clasp.* Remove the last 4 seed beads, string a crimp bead, and replace the 4 seed beads. String the other half of the clasp. Pass back through the 4 seed beads, the crimp bead, and any additional beads you can reach. Slide the beadwork back to access the crimp bead, crimp, and trim the beading wire. Extend the beadwork to reach the magnet, sliding it back into its previous position. Anchor this end of the bracelet as for the other end.

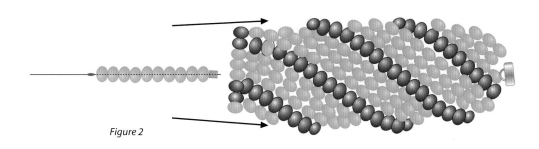

Figure 2

8 *Weave a peyote-stitched tube to hide the magnetic closure (optional).* Weave a peyote rectangle 8 beads wide, curl it into a tube, and zip shut, or whip up 1" (2.5 cm) of even-count tubular peyote stitch by following the directions on page 28. Weave just enough beads to fit around the circumference of the African helix rope. Use the thread or tail to weave one end of the peyote tube onto the helix, allowing the tube to cover the closure.

9 *Add a safety chain (optional).* Learn from Amy's mistake—when using a magnetic closure for a bracelet (and I highly recommend them) make a safety chain for it. Before cutting the thread from one end of the bracelet, string at least 1" (2.5 cm) of the remaining seed beads. Weave into the other end of the bracelet. Pass back through the seed beads and weave in the end of the thread. This allows the bracelet to slide over your hand, yet prevents it from falling off your wrist should the magnets be pulled apart. Amy's safety-chainless bracelet was flushed away before her very eyes!

Fourteen

South African Scallop

It starts with a strand of seed beads, which forms the foundation for a row of loops or swags of beads, attached in a way that recalls brick stitch, passing under the thread between beads and then back through one or more beads. Though graceful, even elegant, it is unremarkable. But wait—another pass of beadwork, one that drops behind one side of a previous scallop, only to emerge midway, interlocks the two passes, creating two layers.

The centermost beads of each swag provide a foundation for additional rows of scallop stitch. One or more rows can circle the neck as a collar. Several rows, each one shorter than the one before, make a bib.

Densely interlaced scallops of seed beads create textural beadwork. Substitute larger beads for those seed beads that anchor each stitch, and create textured but lacy results.

This stitch also makes a wonderful beaded edging on clothing, decorative fabrics and accessories, such as this silk scarf.

223

Saffron and Crimson Earrings

• • • • • • • • • • • • •

Whip up a pair of these earrings to warm up to the stitch and to match the elaborate layered Saffron and Crimson Necklace you'll make on page 226. Make additional pairs, substituting vintage beads, rice pearls, tulips, or any other 6mm bead for the bicones.

Ingredients

Size 11° seed beads, 120 in one color (A) and 160 in a second color (B)

12 crystal 6mm bicones (C)

Size 8° seed beads, 10 in color one color (D) and 40 in a second color color (F)

8 size 3° seed beads (E)

1 pair ⅞"–1" (2.2–2.5 cm) wire hoop earrings

Beading thread

Tools

Size 12 beading needle.

Setup

Cut 1 yd (91.5 cm) of thread.

1 Prepare the foundation. Tie the thread onto the wire near the eye. Leave an 8" (20.5 cm) tail, long enough to weave in later. String 20F onto the wire hoop (Figure 1).

2 Place the first swag. Pick up 1A, 1C, 12A, 1C, 1A. Pass under the wire hoop between the fourth and fifth F, come up over the wire, and pass back through the nearest 1A, 1C, 1A.

3 Place swags along the earring. Pick up 12A, 1C, 1A. Pass under the wire hoop between the eighth and ninth F, come up over the wire, and pass back through 1A, 1C, 1A (Figure 2). Repeat, coming

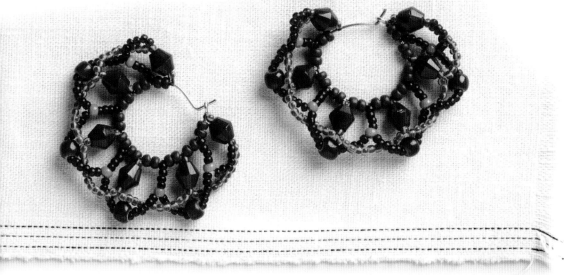

over the wire between F beads 12 and 13, then 16 and 17, and after 20, to finish the first layer of bead scallops.

4 *Begin a second layer, being careful to work consistently above or behind the beadwork and interlacing this layer with the first one.* Pick up 6B, 1D, 4B. Working from below, pass the needle under the wire, between beads 19 and 18 of the 20F on the wire. Pass back through the 4B and 1D, keeping the needle above the work.

5 *Complete the second layer.* Pick up 6B, E, 6B, 1D, 4B. Work behind and under the A-bead scallop while passing the needle under the wire between beads 15 and 14 of the 20F on the wire. Pass back through the 4B and 1D with needle above the scallop now (Figure 3).

Repeat, passing under the wire between beads 11 and 10, 7 and 6, 3 and 2.

6 *Join the first and second layers.* Pick up 6B. Back at the beginning now, pass through the first 1A, 1C, 1A (Figure 4).

7 *Finish the earrings.* Tie the thread to the tail and weave into the work before cutting, securing with several half hitches. Use flat-nose pliers to turn the last ⅛" (3 mm) of the earring wire.

Try this . . .

Make your own wire hoops. Use round-nose pliers to create an eye on one end of 3" (7.5 cm) 22-gauge wire. Repeat for a second piece. Coil the wire around a ring mandrel or roll of pennies to shape it round. After Step 1, use flat-nose pliers to turn up the opposite end at a 90-degree angle.

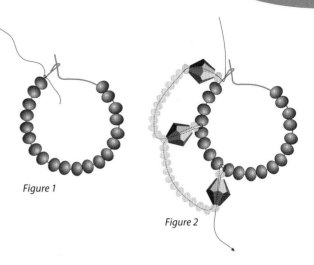

Figure 1

Figure 2

Figure 3

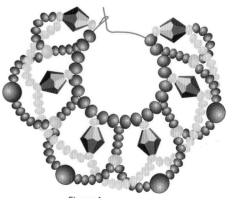

Figure 4

Saffron and Crimson Necklace

· · · · · · · · · · · · · · ·

Swags of crimson-colored vintage and striped seed beads alternate and intertwine with swags of saffron-colored vintage, seed, and white heart beads.

Ingredients

1 g size 15° hex beads divided between two
colors (A, B)

20⅝" × ½" × ³⁄₁₆" (1.5 × 1.3 × .5cm) beads (C)

25 g size 6° seed beads, divided among two
colors (D, E)

3 g size 11° seed beads (F)

38 size 5° white heart beads (G)

19⅜" × ⅛" × ³⁄₁₆" (1 × .3 × .5cm) beads (H)

Power Pro 10# beading thread

Magnetic closure (or
clasp of your choice)

Tools

Size 12 beading needle

Setup

Mise en place (see page 8)

1 **Establish the base.** On a separate 2' (61 cm)
length of Power Pro, pick up 36E, *6A, 6B;
repeat from * 18 more times, and pick up 36E. Fold
a piece of masking tape over the thread after the
last E, so that there is a piece of tape at each end
of the work.

2 **Begin the first swag.** With the wingspan of
beading thread, pick up 1D and 1C. Pass the
needle under the base between the thirty-sixth E
and the first A beads. Pass back through the C and
D (Figure 1).

226

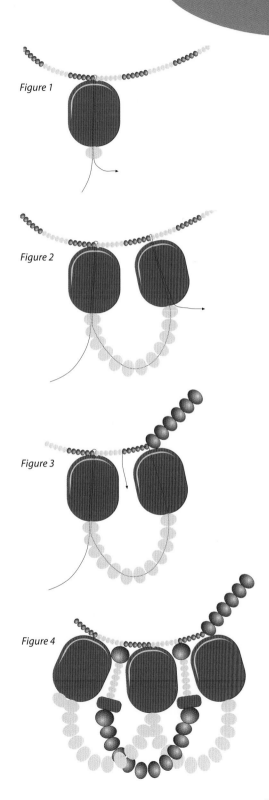

Figure 1

Figure 2

Figure 3

Figure 4

3 *Complete the first swag and add additional scallops.* Pick up 11D and 1C. Pass the needle under the base just before the next repeat of 6A. Pass back through 1C and 1D (Figure 2).

Repeat Step 3 until 19C have been placed. After picking up the twentieth C, pass the needle under the base and pass back through the last 6B (Figure 3).

4 *Begin the second row of swags.* Work back across the base, picking up 1G, 6F, 1H, 1G, 10E, 1G, 1H, 6F, 1G. *Pass the needle under the base just before the next repeat of 6A. Pass back through 1G, 6F, 1H, 1G with the needle above the previous swag. Pick up 10E, 1G, 1H, 6F, 1G, take the needle and thread under (behind) the next swag (Figure 4).

Repeat from *, placing 19 swags between the 20 of the previous pass.

5 *Finish the necklace.* Weave the thread and tails into the swags, making half hitches. Adjust the necklace to the desired length by removing or adding an equal number of E beads from each end of the base. Slide the tape off one end of the base. Thread the tail onto a needle. Pick up one half of the clasp. Weave the thread into the base, making half hitches between the E beads. Repeat for other end.

Try this . . .

Replace the C beads with ⅝" (1.5 cm) of seed beads. Reduce or increase the number of A and B to condense or spread the swags.

To create a bib-style instead of collar-style necklace, weave additional rows of swags that loop around the thread at the mid-point of each swag of the previous row, rather than the base row. Since each row starts and ends at the mid-point of the first and last swags, of the previous row, it will taper into a bib shape.

227

Fifteen

Bead Crochet

||||||||||||||||||||||||||||||||||||||||||||||||||||||||||||||||||||||||||||||||||||||||||||||||||||||||||||||||||||||||||||||||||||||||||||||||||||||||||||||||||

Bead crochet is a departure from the beadwork of the previous chapters. We've been adding one or more beads at a time using a needle and thread. But for this technique, we'll string all the beads onto the thread at the onset, and then use a hook to make stitches in the round, adding one or more beads within each stitch. The bead ropes produced are as supple as the thread they employ. Recall vintage photos of 1920's flappers wearing long faux pearl ropes, tied in large overhand knots? These were crocheted.

This is perfectly portable beadwork. Simply pull the project from your pocket or purse and work anywhere without a table, *mise en place*, or concern for bead spillage.

Crochet hooks vary widely in style, handle, and even size nomenclature. The easiest way to choose is to make sure yours is capable of hiding your thread "under the chin" (within the hook), so you can sneak the thread through the previous stitches, or loops. You'll develop a preference for whether you like a hook that's pointed or blunt, metal or plastic, chubby-handled or narrow. Crochet while standing in line, waiting for your entrée, sitting in the dentist's chair—anywhere and anytime your hands are idle. It's simply a slip stitch, repeated over and over. The results vary endlessly due to bead choice and order. The process is truly mindful meditation at its best.

That said, it is the bead technique that some beaders find most daunting. Some may not yet crochet; others might have taken a class and still don't "get it." Conquer bead crochet with the easy, successful, field-tested Bead Crochet Out Loud on page 230, then practice and bead crochet any-thing. Discover for yourself why we love it so.

What thread or yarn to use for bead crochet is a controversial topic. Cotton advocates will use nothing but cotton, which is supple and pleasing to handle. Though cotton has a reputation for stretching, this can be solved by blocking it, or wetting the finished bead crochet. However, cotton is easy to break and will deteriorate over time. Conso 18 and similar new nylon cords are virtually indestructible, do not stretch, and come in many colors. Jean Stitch is a popular choice that works well with small beads. Try them all and make your own decision.

To minimize the appearance of the thread, use thin thread on the smallest hook possible, and 5 or

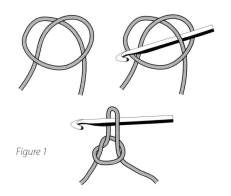

Figure 1

more beads per round. To play up the appearance of thread, use a thicker thread on a larger hook and use 5 or 4 beads per round.

1. Make a slipknot. After stringing all the beads to complete the project onto your yarn, make a slipknot near the end of the yarn and place it on the hook (Figure 1).

2. Create chain stitches. Hold the hook between your thumb and index finger, cradling the handle in your curled middle, ring and pinky fingers. Scoop the yarn with the hook and draw it through the slipknot, allowing the slipknot to fall off the end of the hook. Repeat this motion, drawing each new loop through the old and allowing the old to drop off the hook. (In crochet, this is called a *chain stitch*.)

3. Join the ring of chain stitches. Put the hook through the first chain stitch, scoop the yarn, and pull it through both loops on the hook to make a ring.

4. Make slip stitches. From this point on, you will make every stitch exactly the same way: by inserting the hook into a previous stitch, moving a bead into place, and drawing up a new loop of yarn onto the hook before dropping the old one off.

It is always the same little slip stitch. The variable is the order of the strung beads.

Crochet forces the beads outward, while the stitches remain inside the rope. If the hook falls out of the work, look in the center for the last loop. Dredge a small hook in the stitches there, or pull an additional stitch while watching where movement occurs.

To add thread, string the beads on it before making a slipknot in the new thread. Pull it through the loop currently on the hook. Continue to crochet around. Tie the old thread and the new tail in a single knot and weave each into the center of the bead crochet, using a tapestry needle.

Bead Crochet Out Loud Choker

Work with large beads that are easy to keep track of, on yarn that occupies the beads so much that they stay put. Without having to struggle with the beads, get comfy with how to capture them, one at a time, in a slip stitch.

Ingredients
1 ball of nylon ribbon yarn, such as "Jungle" by Plymouth (Any yarn that fills the bead hole enough that a bead doesn't slide along on it will work.)

Size E, 4, 3, or 2 beads that can be coaxed onto the ribbon yarn. (The exact quantity will depend on the bead size. 90 g of size E beads will produce a choker 16–17" (40.5–43 cm) long, 5 beads around).

Magnetic closure

Polyester sewing thread or Power Pro 10# beading thread

Tools
Crochet hook, size 3.5 to 5mm (The depth, angle and taper of hooks varies by brand. Choose one that easily accommodates the yarn.)

Beeswax, nail polish, or glue (to stiffen the yarn tip)

Sewing needle

Setup
Stiffen the yarn tip with bee's wax, nail polish, or glue, so that it will pass easily through the beads. String enough beads onto the yarn to measure five times the length of the desired finished piece.

230

1 *Chain stitches.* Make a slipknot near the end of the yarn and place it on the hook (see page 228). Make a chain of five stitches (see page 229).

2 *Form a ring.* Insert the hook into the first chain stitch, snag the yarn, and draw a new loop through both loops on the hook, making a ring of stitches (Figure 1).

3 *Place a ring of five beaded stitches.* In the directions that follow, right-handed beaders will work counterclockwise, while lefties will work clockwise. Insert your hook into the first stitch. Slide a bead down close to the work, then draw a new loop through both loops on your hook, leaving a bead captured in the stitch. Repeat four more times, leaving five evenly spaced beads around the ring of stitches (Figure 2). (If it's difficult to identify stitches in this round, simply insert the hook into the ring anywhere, to deposit 5 evenly spaced beads around the ring of chain stitches.)

4 *Work for the desired length.* For every subsequent stitch, insert the hook under the bead of the next stitch. Push the bead to the right, if you're right-handed (or to the left if you're left-handed). Place the working thread over the bead so it is under the working thread. Slide a new bead down the yarn to sit on top of this one

Snag the yarn and pull through both loops on the hook.

Failure to do each step will result in a bead askew. Repeat your mantra out loud with each movement:

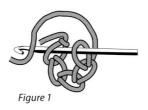

Figure 1

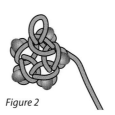

Figure 2

Did you notice . . .

All the beads of previous rows will be arranged with their holes vertical, because they were pushed over to the right (or left) and held down by the working thread and new bead.

The beads on the row being worked will always be arranged with holes horizontal.

Stop and identify your working round periodically to be sure you have not dropped or added stitches. (This is essential in the first three rounds to avoid making a doily instead of a rope.) Have fun. Get into your groove. You'll remember this day!

Mantra: Under the bead, push the bead to the right (left for lefties), under the working thread, slide a new bead down, snag the yarn, and pull through both loops.

After the last stitch, cut the thread 12" (30 cm) from the work. Pull it through the loop.

5 *Finish the choker and add a closure.* Use a needle and thread to sew the clasp to the ribbon-yarn center of the bead crochet ends. Following the directions on page 40, peyote stitch a rectangle to join seamlessly, concealing the magnetic clasp. Before cutting the thread, anchor the peyote tube to one end of the choker.

Stringing Beads to Crochet

For many projects in bead crochet, you will transfer the hanks of beads onto the crochet thread one strand at a time, instead of stringing the beads individually. Slide a thread from the hank by pulling it gently from the knot, or cut it close to the knot, being careful to keep the beads on the thread. Tie the hank thread onto the crochet thread with a single knot (Figure 1). (Don't make a second knot, as it will be too big and make transfer too difficult.)

Slide a few beads at a time onto the crochet thread. Resist the impulse to slide the entire hank at once, as the knot may come undone and the beads will scatter (Figure 2).

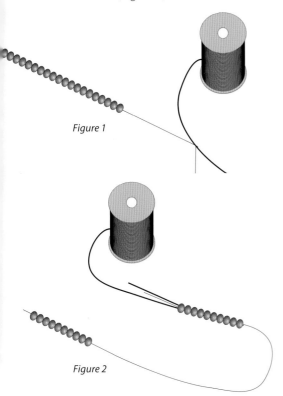

Figure 1

Figure 2

Bead Spinner

A bead spinner is a turned wooden bowl resembling a split-open and hollowed donut that spins on a ball-bearing assembly. This gadget and a long curve-tipped needle offer a quick way to load the crochet thread with beads. Thread the needle with several inches of thread. Pour the seed beads into the bowl. Arrange the curve of the needle so that when the bowl spins, the beads are forced onto the needle and onto the thread. Transfer the beads from the thread just as you would transfer beads from a hank.

When using an assortment of seed bead sizes, the spinner picks up the beads randomly. If you dredged a needle into a cereal bowl, all the tiniest beads would settle to the bottom. With the spinner, the tiniest of beads are picked up randomly with the others.

Bead spinner

Resources

||||||||||||||||||||||||||||||||||||||||||||||||||||||||||||||||||||||||||||||||||||||||||||||||||||||||||

Bibliography

Cook, Jeannette, and Vicki Star. *Beading with Peyote Stitch: A Beadwork How-To Book*. Loveland, Colorado: Interweave Press, 2000.

Davis, Jane. *The Complete Guide to Beading Techniques*. Iola, Wisconsin: Krause Publications, 2001.

Durant, Judith, and Jean Campbell. *The Beader's Companion*. Loveland, Colorado: Interweave Press, 1998, 2005.

Francis, Peter Jr. *Beads of the World*. Atglen, Pennsyvania: Schiffer Publishing Ltd; 1994.

Goodhue, Horace R. *Indian Bead-weaving Patterns*. St. Paul, Minnesota: Bead – Craft, 1984.

Hector, Valerie. *The Art of Beadwork*. New York: Watson-Guptill Publications, 2005.

Wells, Carol Wilcox. *Creative Bead Weaving*. Asheville, North Carolina: Lark Books, 1996.

———. *The Art & Elegance of Beadweaving*. Asheville, North Carolina: Lark Books, 2002.

Beading Magazines

Beadwork
Step-by-Step Beads
Step-by-Step Wire Jewelry
Stringing

Contributing Beaders

· · · · · · · · · · · ·

Amy Booth Raff, West Hurley, NY

Elaine M. Tate, Rhinecliff, NY

Elizabeth Buchtman
www.designsfromfenwood.com

Ellen Mahnken
Mountain House Design Studios
213 Mt. House Rd.
Palenville, NY 12463
(518) 678-9342

Fran X. Hancock
Woodstock, NY
SpecialFXCreations@yahoo.com

Irma Sherman, Saugerties, NY

Jane Booth, Shandaken, NY

Jill Van Etten, Rhinecliff, NY

Kaja Dedijer, c/o Beadzo, Tivoli, NY

Kitty Moynihan, Millerton, NY

Kristine Flones, Bearsville, NY

Louann Joyce
louann653@hotmail.com, Beacon, NY

Martha Arginsky, Ellenville, NY

Myrna Jargowsky, Ellenville, NY

Phyllis Dintenfass www.phylart.com
phylart@new.rr.com, Appleton WI

Seed beads and beading supplies

Amazing Threads
www.amazingthreads.com
(845) 336-5322

Beads by Blanche
www.beadsbyblanche.com
(201) 385-6225

Beadzo
(seed, ethnic, vintage, rare and collectible beads)
(845) 757-5306

Melek Karacan
(seed beads, lampworked beads)
(302) 644-3333

Osiris Beads
(seed beads and beading supplies)
www.orisirisbeads.com
(231) 933-4853

Sisters' Originals
(marcasite charlottes, seed beads, beaded items)
www.sistersoriginals.com
sis@sistersoriginals.com

Woodstock Bead Emporium
(seed beads, supplies, Joe Irvin lampworked beads,
vintage and Czech beads)
www.beademporium.com
(845) 679-0066, toll-free (888) 290-9663

Lampworked beads
Robert Michael Croft
croft@harbornet.com
(253) 383-2911

Harold Jargowsky
beadsinthebarn@aol.com

Joe Irwin
www.beademporium.com
(845) 679-0066, toll-free (888) 290-9663

Nancy Tobey
www.nancytobey.com
beads@nancytobey.com
(978) 772-3317

Bronwen Heilman (Ghostcow Glassworks)
www.bronwenheilman.com
(520) 622-7199

Dyed in the Fire Designs Inc., Patti Cahill
(828) 689-8934

Rockledge Glass, Linda LoPresti
lindad@ulster.net

Ovington Glass Studios, Karen Ovington
ovingtonglass@sbcglobal.net

Gail Felter Boo
gboo@hvc.rr.com

Wendy Vlahinic
WKVDesigns@verizon.net
(201) 394-5277

Lapidary
Gary B. Wilson (hand-cut cabochons and unique
focal point beads; specializing in rare agates, jaspers, petrified woods, and fossils)
sawsrocks@aol.com

Index

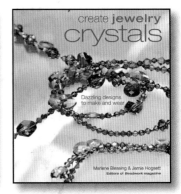